Fodor's 90

Madrid
& Barcelona

D1369857

Reprinted from *Fodor's Spain '90*

FODOR'S TRAVEL PUBLICATIONS
New York & London

ISBN 0–679–01790–9

Fodor's Madrid & Barcelona

Editors: Howell Llewellyn, Mark Potok
Area Editor: Hilary Bunce
Contributors: Hilary Bunce, Harry Eyres, Ailsa Hudson, Pamela Vandyke Price
Drawings: Beryl Sanders
Maps: Swanston Graphics
Cover Photograph: Owen Franken

Cover Design: Vignelli Associates

Special Sales

Fodor's Travel Publications are available at special discounts for bulk purchases
(100 copies or more) for sales promotions or premiums. Special editions,
including personalized covers, excerpts of existing guides, and corporate
imprints, can be created in large quantities for special needs. For more
information write to Special Marketing, Fodor's Travel Publications, 201 East
50th Street, New York, NY 10022. Inquiries from the United Kingdom should
be sent to Fodor's Travel Publications, 30–32 Bedford Square, London WC1B
3SG.

MANUFACTURED IN THE UNITED STATES OF AMERICA
10 9 8 7 6 5 4 3 2 1

CONTENTS

FOREWORD

Madrid is Spain's focal point in more ways than one. The center for political and social life, it also lies at the country's geographic heart. From it, roads and rail lines radiate out to every part of the peninsula, making excursions nearby or farther afield eminently easy. As an ancient capital, Madrid can offer riches to the visitor in search of historic or, especially, artistic interest. As a city that, in just a few short years, has welcomed the 20th century with open arms, it has a great deal to offer to anyone in search of the joys of modern metropolitan life.

Barcelona, however, refuses to forfeit its position as the most independent city in Spain. It stands as a port city located between two mountains, offering many visual contrasts. But diversity does not stop with the landscape. The people of Barcelona continue to speak their own language, to perfect their own personal style of food and drink, and to cultivate special talents in all areas of the fine arts. A visit to the "old capital" of Spain promises the traveler unique sights and sounds.

We offer this guide, abridged from our *Fodor's Spain 1990*, as a handy book for anyone whose visit to Spain is limited to Madrid, Barcelona, and/or their surroundings. For anyone needing a fuller treatment of the country, the larger guide is recommended.

While every care has been taken to assure the accuracy of the information in this guide, the passage of time will always bring change, and consequently the publisher cannot accept responsibility for errors that may occur.

All prices and opening times quoted in this guide are based on information available to us at press time. Hours and admission fees may change, however, and the prudent traveler will avoid inconvenience by calling ahead.

Fodor's wants to hear about your travel experiences, both pleasant and unpleasant. When a hotel or restaurant fails to live up to its billing, let us know and we will investigate the complaint and revise our entries where the facts warrant it.

Send your letters to the editors of Fodor's Travel Publications, 201 E. 50th Street, New York, NY 10022.

FACTS AT YOUR FINGERTIPS

WARNING. There has been a huge increase in street crime and in hotel room thefts all over Spain since the early 1980s. You would be well advised to check your valuables into the hotel safe and carry only a minimal amount of cash and one credit card with you. Keep your money in your pocket, not in a handbag or pocketbook. Additionally, women should avoid carrying bags, particularly shoulder bags which are easy to snatch. Make sure your jewelry is not visible, and keep purses as small and unobtrusive as you can. If you have a car, lock everything in the trunk, and in big cities drive with the doors locked.

Thefts are by no means confined to dark or dangerous streets. Many happen in broad daylight and on crowded main roads. Tour groups visiting monuments have been set on, and pickpockets are even known to have been at work in the Seville tourist office. Spanish onlookers who witness an assault are for the most part unlikely to come to your aid, and not all the police show the degree of concern, or take the positive action, you might expect.

We stress that it is your money and not your personal safety that is at risk. But to make sure that you do not help boost these sorry crime statistics, take extra care at *all* times and your vacation should not be marred.

SOURCES OF INFORMATION. The major source of information for anyone planning a vacation to Spain is the Spanish National Tourist Office.

Their addresses are:

In the U.S.: 665 Fifth Ave., New York, NY 10022 (tel. 212–759–8822); 845 N. Michigan Ave., Chicago, IL 60611 (tel. 312–644–1992); San Vicente Plaza Bldg., 8383 Wilshire Blvd., Suite 938, Beverly Hills, CA 90211 (tel. 213–658–7188).

In Canada: 102 Bloor St. West, Suite 1400, Toronto, Ontario M5S 1M8 (tel. 416–961–3131).

In the U.K.: 57 St. James's St., London SW1A 1LD (tel. 01–499 1169).

WHEN TO GO. The tourist season runs from the beginning of April to the end of October. If your primary aim is to sightsee, then undoubtedly the best months to visit are May, June and September, when the weather is usually sunny and pleasant without being overbearingly hot. At the height of summer, during July and August, Madrid can be rather unrewarding; not only is it hot and airless but, despite the tourist authorities' efforts to keep the city alive for visitors, you will find many places closed, especially restaurants.

Climate. The whole of the central tableland of Spain, the Castilian plateau with Madrid as its nucleus surrounded by cities such as Avila, Segovia, Toledo, Cuenca and Burgos, suffers (by European if not American standards) extremes of temperature from summer to winter. The key word to Madrid's climate, and to that of much of Spain, is unpredictability.

Average afternoon temperatures in Fahrenheit and centigrade for Madrid: (top) and Barcelona (below).

	Jan.	Feb.	Mar.	Apr.	May	June	July	Aug.	Sept.	Oct.	Nov.	Dec.
F°	47	51	57	64	71	80	87	86	77	66	54	48
C°	8	11	14	18	22	27	31	30	25	19	12	9
F°	56	57	61	64	71	77	81	82	78	71	62	57
C°	13	14	16	18	22	25	27	28	26	22	17	14

NATIONAL HOLIDAYS 1990. The following are national holidays when stores, businesses and many museums and monuments will be closed all over Spain. January 1 (New Year's Day); January 6 (Day of the Three Kings, Epiphany); March 19 (St. Joseph); April 12 (Holy Thursday—some cities only); April 13 (Good Friday); May 1 (May Day); June 25 (Corpus Christi, second Thursday after Whitsun); July 25 (Santiago); August 15 (Feast of the Assumption); October 12 (El Pilar); November 1 (All Saints); December 6 (Constitution); December 8 (Immaculate Conception); December 25 (Christmas Day). In addition to the above, every town and village has its own local fiesta when, with the exception of restaurants, everything will be closed—May 2 throughout Madrid province and October 9 throughout Valencia region.

GETTING TO SPAIN. By Air from the U.S. From North America there are direct flights from several major U.S. cities and from Montreal. Airlines include *Iberia* and *TWA,* and *Pan Am,* which reintroduced direct services from the U.S.A. to Spain in 1988. With airfares in a constant state of flux, the best advice for anyone planning to fly to Spain independently (rather than as part of a package tour, in which case your flight will have been arranged for you) is to check with a travel agent and let him or her make your reservations for you. Nonetheless, there are a number of points to bear in mind. The best bet is to buy an APEX ticket. First Class, Business and even the misleadingly named Economy, though giving maximum flexibility on flying dates and cancellations, as well as permitting stopovers, are extremely expensive. APEX, by contrast, are reasonably priced and offer the all-important security of fixed return dates (all APEX tickets are round-trip). In addition, you get exactly the same service as when flying Economy. However, there are a number of restrictions: you must book and pay for your ticket 14 days or more in advance, you can stay in Spain for no less than 7 days and no more than 6 months, and if you miss your flight, you forfeit the fare. But from the point of view of price and convenience, these tickets certainly represent the best value for your money. Charter fares are about the same as or slightly lower than APEX. In addition, there's a counter-terrorist security charge of around $35.

By Air from the U.K. London is linked with Spain by the national carriers, *Iberia* and *British Airways,* and there are also prolific charter flights.

By Train from the U.K. To reach Madrid and Barcelona from London it is best to travel via Paris. The distance from Paris to Madrid is some 1,450 km (900 miles) and from Paris to Barcelona 1,137 km (704 miles).There is only one daytime train to Madrid; this leaves Paris Osterlitz at 6:50 A.M. and you arrive in Madrid just before 10 in the evening. There are also two overnight services. The first of these is the *Madrid*

Talgo, with sleeping cars, dining car and bar car. It leaves Paris (Gare Austerlitz) at 8 P.M. and arrives in Madrid (Chamartin) at about 9 A.M. the next day. The other is the *Puerta del Sol* which leaves Paris around 6 P.M., reaching Madrid at 10 A.M.; it has couchettes and carries cars, thus forming part of the Motor Rail service.

Advance reservations for these long distance trains are essential, particularly for sleepers and couchettes.

There is one daily train to Barcelona that departs Paris Osterlitz and arrives at Station Sants in Barcelona.

By Bus from the U.K. *National Express-Eurolines* operates services from London's Victoria Station to Madrid and Barcelona four days a week. The fare to Madrid is around £120 return full fare, £108 for students. Students must prove eligibility by showing an I.S.I.C. or student union card. The fare to Barcelona is £99 return full fare. Buses depart at 10:30 A.M. Mon., Wed., Fri., Sat.

Details of services may be obtained from any National Express bus station, appointed travel agent or direct from *National Express-Eurolines,* The Coach Travel Centre, 13 Regent St., London SW1Y 4LR (tel. 01–730 0202).

By Car from the U.K. Direct to Santander from Plymouth by *Brittany Ferries,* a 24-hour voyage, or to St. Malo—also by Brittany Ferries—or to Le Havre by *P&O Ferries.*

VISAS. Neither American, British nor Canadian citizens need a visa to visit Spain. Americans are allowed a six-month stay after each entry. Britons are allowed a three-month stay instead. Australians and New Zealanders are advised to check current visa requirements before they travel.

HEALTH CERTIFICATES. Not required for entry to Spain.

CUSTOMS ON ARRIVAL. Each person (aged 15 and over) may bring into Spain 200 cigarettes or 50 cigars or 100 cigarillos or 250 grams of tobacco if arriving from European countries, double quantities if you are arriving from elsewhere. You are also allowed to bring in 1 liter of alcohol over 22° proof, or two liters under 22° proof and two liters of other wines; ¼ liter eau de cologne and 50 grams perfume; gifts to the value of 5,000 ptas. (2,000 ptas. for children under the age of 15).

TIME. During the summer Spain is six hours ahead of Eastern Standard Time, seven hours ahead of Central Time, eight hours ahead of Mountain Time and nine hours ahead of Pacific Time. During the winter, Spain puts her clocks back one hour, but as all America does likewise, the time difference remains the same. Spanish Daylight Saving Time begins at the end of March and ends at the end of September, so during April, Spain is seven hours ahead of EST, and five hours ahead in October.

Similarly, Spain is one hour ahead of British Summer Time and, during the winter, one hour ahead of Greenwich Mean Time. During October, Spain and Britain are in the same time zone.

MONEY. You can take an unlimited amount of pesetas into Spain, but it's wise to declare any quantity above 100,000 ptas. Any amount of foreign currency can be taken in but you can only take out the equivalent of 300,000 ptas. if on business; for tourists the amount is 120,000 ptas. It is generally better to change traveler's checks in banks than in hotels, restaurants or shops where the rate of exchange may not be quite as good; however, many Spanish banks take an enormous commission charge, so there may not be much difference. Always ask the bank what its commission is *before* you change money; if it exceeds 1½% take your business elsewhere.

The unit of currency in Spain is the peseta. There are bills of 200, 500, 1,000, 2,000, 5,000, amd 10,000 ptas. Coins are 1 pta., 5, 25, 50, 100, 200 and 500 ptas. At presstime (mid-1988) the exchange rate was around 121 ptas. to the U.S. dollar and 206 ptas. to the pound sterling. However, these rates will change both before and during 1989.

COSTS IN SPAIN. Prices have soared dramatically over the past decade. In January 1986 Spain joined the Common Market, which led to yet another increase in the cost of living. With Spain's E.E.C. membership came the inevitable levying of a sales or value-added tax known as the I.V.A., which has had a considerable impact on the average tourist's expenditure. I.V.A. has a complicated sliding scale structure, but is usually levied at 6% and this applies to restaurants and most hotels. Luxury, or 5-star, hotels are subject to 12% tax, however, as are car rental charges. The days when Spain was the bargain basement of Europe are now over, and the visitor will most probably find that the cost of living in Spain matches that of its northern European neighbors.

Hotels. Spanish hotels have raised their rates in leaps and bounds in the last few years, and since as from 1986 all hotels must now charge the I.V.A. sales tax, they are no longer the bargain they once were. Hotels are officially classified from 5-star to 1-star; hostels and pensions are classified from 3-star to 1-star. If an R appears on the hotel plaque, the hotel is classed a *residencia* and does not offer full dining services; breakfast and cafeteria meals may be available. The star-ratings equate roughly with our classifications of Deluxe (L), Expensive (E), Moderate (M), and Inexpensive (I). The number of stars a hotel has is usually—but not always—a guide to its price. Prices charged by each establishment are listed in the *Guía de Hoteles* (published annually and obtainable from bookstores) and should also be on display at the reception desk.

In many hotels rates change according to season and they are always quoted per room and not per person. Sometimes the rate includes breakfast but often this is charged extra. It is also worth checking to make sure you won't be charged for meals you don't take. If you stay more than two nights you have a right to full board terms, which should be the room price plus not more than 85% of the total cost of breakfast; lunch and dinner charged separately.

It is often advisable to inspect your room before you check in. Most hotels offer good standards but it is not unknown for an impressive lobby to camouflage shabby rooms upstairs.

Approximate prices for a double room are shown below. A single person in a double room will be charged 80% of the full price. Many of the larger new hotels have double rooms only. If you ask for an additional bed in your room, this should not cost more than 60% of the single room price or 35% of the double room price. Remember that the I.V.A. tax will be added on to your final bill; in the case of 1-star to 4-star hotels I.V.A. is charged at 6%, and in the case of luxury, or 5-star, hotels at the rate of 12%. Remember that if you are planning to pay your bill by credit card, check beforehand whether your hotel will accept your particular piece of plastic. Finally, should you have a complaint about your hotel, you can enter this in the hotel's complaint book kept for this purpose, report it to the local Tourist Office, or put it in writing to the Complaints Section of the General Directorate of Tourist Activities whose address is: Dirección General de Política Turística, Sección de Reclamaciones, María de Molina 50, 28006 Madrid.

Approximate prices (double room) excluding I.V.A.:

	ptas.
5-star: Deluxe (L)	16,000–30,000
4-star: Expensive (E)	10,000–15,950
3-star: Moderate (M)	6,000–9,950
2-star: Inexpensive (I)	3,750–5,950

These prices should be taken as indicators only and do not include breakfast. A very few hotels, such as the *Ritz* and *Villa Magna,* fall into a super-deluxe category which rates way above our Deluxe (L) rating.

Restaurants. Prices have increased considerably since Spain joined the Common Market in 1986, and, unless you stick to the set menus offered by many budget restaurants, dining out can run away with a large portion of your holiday budget. Finding a light *à la carte* lunch as you would at home is almost impossible, and there is always a charge for bread, whether you eat it or not, and mineral water. On the plus side, neither a cover nor service charge is ever added to your check.

Approximate prices per person (excluding drinks):

	ptas.
Deluxe	6,000 and up
Expensive	3,500–5,900
Moderate	1,500–3,450
Inexpensive	800–1,450

Note: Some restaurants include the 6% I.V.A. tax in their menu prices; others do not. It is always wise to check beforehand whether the menu says *IVA incluido* or *IVA no incluido.*

CREDIT CARDS. The four most commonly accepted credit cards in Spain are *American Express, Diner's Club, Visa* and *MasterCard* (incorporating *Access* and *Eurocard*). By far the most widely accepted card is *Visa.* Most hotels and restaurants, department stores and major shops will accept payment by credit card but in smaller stores and inexpensive restaurants this is unlikely to be the case. In all cases, if you are planning to pay by plastic, you should check first; it is not unknown for an establishment to display a credit card sign and then claim that it does not have the necessary charge forms. We have also had reports of some hotels limiting the amount you can charge to a credit card, so again if you are planning several nights' stay, check *first.* Some gas stations in Spain accept payment by credit card, but when you fill up your tank, be prepared to pay cash.

In the Practical Information sections of this book we have included credit card information for as many establishments as we have been able to verify. The initials we use for this information are AE, DC, MC, and V—which stand for American Express, Diner's Club, MasterCard (alias Access and Eurocard) and Visa.

TIPPING. Service charges are usually included in the price of hotel rooms, though some hotels may add on a tax of around 5% to your bill. But you should leave the chambermaid around 500 ptas. a week and tip the porters 50 ptas. a bag. If you call a bellboy give him 50 ptas. or more. Spanish restaurants rarely add a service charge to your tab, but you should always leave about 10%, even when it says "service and tax included." Waiters in nightclubs will expect more. Doormen and hat-check girls get 25 ptas.

Station porters operate on a fixed rate, usually 60 or 90 ptas. a bag. The taxi drivers get 10% if they use the meter, otherwise *nothing.* Theater and movie ushers get 10 ptas. Restroom attendants everywhere get 5 ptas. (perhaps 10 in a very smart establishment).

MAIL. Airmail rates are as follows: to the U.S., letters up to 15 grams cost 68 ptas., postcards 58 ptas.; to the U.K. and rest of Europe, letters up to 20 grams cost 48 ptas., postcards 40 ptas. Within Spain, letters cost 19 ptas., postcards 14 ptas. If you mail a letter in Madrid for Madrid, it costs 7 ptas. These rates usually change each year in mid-summer, so check first. Mail boxes *(buzones)* are yellow with red stripes and are plentiful. They usually have two or three slits, one marked *Capital* for Madrid city, one marked *Provincias* for the rest of Spain, and one marked *Extranjero* for abroad. The word for "post office" is *correos,* and for "stamps," *sellos.*

TELEPHONES. Public pay phones are silver gray in color and are located on city streets and at stations and airports. They are rarely found in hotel lobbies or in bars and cafes as in some countries. If you want to call from a bar or restaurant, ask the barman and he will usually let you use his phone and charge you afterwards. Pay phones work with 5, 25, 50 and 100 ptas. coins; 10 ptas. is the minimum for a short local call, long distance calls eat up many more coins. Place several coins in the groove at the top of the phone, lift the receiver and dial your number. Coins then fall into the machine as needed.

International calls to Europe can also be made from pay phones, but far and away the best method of making long distance calls abroad and within Spain (if you wish to talk for a long time) is to go to the *telefónica* (exchange). The telephonist dials your call for you and then indicates which cabin you should go to. In many telefónicas, once you have been told which cabin to use, you can dial the call yourself. You then pay the telephonist at the end and you will only be charged the regular rate; there are no supplements or service charges. If your call comes to more than 500 ptas. or more, you can pay with Visa or Mastercard.

Calls from your hotel room phone *always* cost much more than from a pay phone or the telefónica. Be warned that even if you make a collect call home, many Spanish hotels will make a service charge for this, of around 250 ptas. to Europe or 450 ptas. to the U.S.

ELECTRICITY. Most of Spain has now been converted to 220 volts AC, but some older hotels, hostels and private houses are still on 120 volts. Be sure to check *before* you plug in. British 240-V appliances work fine on 220-V sockets and 110- and 120-V appliances are also interchangeable. American visitors should bring voltage adaptors with them, as they are very hard to find in Spain, and even luxury hotels won't usually supply them. Bring plug adaptors along too—Spanish plugs are two-pin, round-pin. It's always best to take along a battery-operated razor.

OPENING AND CLOSING TIMES. Shops are open in the morning from 9 or 10 to 1.30 or 2. In the afternoon they open from approximately 4 to 7 in winter, and 5 to 8 in summer. The *Corte Inglés* and *Galerías Preciados* department stores mostly stay open throughout the siesta. Banks are open 9.30 to 2, Mon.–Fri., and 9.30 to 1 on Saturdays. A few banks open at 9 and some banks close at 12 on Saturdays in summer. Most churches and museums close for the siestas; some museums open mornings only. Post offices normally open 9 to 2, though there are exceptions. They often close early on Saturdays.

DRINKING WATER. Drinking water is perfectly safe all over Spain except perhaps in a very few out-of-the-way places. However, many Spaniards still tend to drink mineral water in preference to tap water, not least because it is actually much nicer. If you ask a waiter for water, he will bring mineral water unless you specify tap water. Mineral water comes in two types: still *(sin gas)* or fizzy *(con gas)*. It is usual to order mineral water by the half-liter *(media agua sin/con gas)*. If you really want tap water, ask for *agua natural*.

CONVENIENT CONVENIENCES. There are few public facilities in Spain, but restrooms are plentiful in hotels, restaurants, museums, cafes and bars. Department stores such as the *Corte Inglés* or *Galerías Preciados* always have restrooms, usually on the top floor. Ask for *los servicios* or *los aseos,* and then a picture of a man or a woman or the words *Senoras* (ladies) or *Caballeros* (men, literally knights!) will tell you which way to head.

BULLFIGHTS. The bullfighting season starts at Easter and continues till early October. The best bullfights usually take place at the biggest fiestas; for times and places see our chapter on bullfighting and the relevant section under *Sports*.

Try to buy your tickets from official ticket booths *(despacho oficial);* many other despachos sell tickets quite legally but if they are not "oficial" they will impose a surcharge of around 20% on the price of a ticket. If a ticket booth displays a sign *no quedan localidades* it means there are no seats left; and if it continues *ni entradas* there is no standing room either. Try another ticket office which may not have sold out yet.

Prices are determined by the proximity of the seat to the ring and by its position in the stand. Ringside seats are known as *barreras* and are naturally the most expensive; the cheapest seats are those known as *gradas* and are high up at the back of the ring. You will also have a choice of *sol* (sun), *sombra* (shade), or *sol y sombra* where you start off with the sun in your eyes, but as the fight progresses the sun will dip down behind the edge of the ring. *Sombra* are the most expensive but in high summer are well worth the extra pesetas to avoid sweltering or being blinded by the relentless sun.

Always ask the starting time when you buy your tickets. This varies between 4.30 and 7 P.M. depending on the place and month of the year. Be punctual—there is an old saying that the only things that start on time in Spain are bullfights and Mass—for once the corrida begins, you are not allowed in. Allow plenty of time to find your seat, which is not always easy in a large ring. Look closely at the numbers on your ticket; *tendido* is usually the gate through which you will enter the ring, and *fila* the row in which your seat is located. Cushions to sit on can be rented for a small fee and are a must unless you like sitting on hard stone benches with no back support. Most corridas last 2½–3 hours and there is usually a break between the third and fourth bulls which, if you have had enough, is the best time to leave.

CUSTOMS ON RETURNING HOME. If you propose to take on your vacation any *foreign-made* articles, such as cameras, binoculars, expensive time-pieces, and the like, it is wise to put with your travel documents the receipt from the retailer or some other evidence that the item was bought in your home country. If you bought the article on a previous vacation abroad and have already paid duty on it, carry with you the receipt for this. Otherwise, on returning, you may be charged duty (for British residents, VAT as well).

Leaving Spain. Tourists leaving Spain rarely have to go through a customs check, though it is possible that you will be asked how much Spanish currency you have on you. Officially, you are not allowed to leave Spain with more than 100,000 ptas. in cash.

U.S. residents. You may bring in $400 worth of foreign merchandise as gifts or for personal use without having to pay duty, provided you have been out of the country more than 48 hours and provided you have not claimed a similar exemption within the previous 30 days. Every member of a family is entitled to the same exemption, regardless of age, and the exemptions can be pooled. For the next $1,000 worth of goods a flat 10% rate is assessed.

Included in the $400 allowance for travelers over the age of 21 are one liter of alcohol, 100 non-Cuban cigars and 200 cigarettes. Only one bottle of perfume trademarked in the U.S. may be brought in. However, there is no duty on antiques or art over 100 years old. You may not bring home meats, fruits, plants, soil or other agricultural products.

Gifts valued at under $50 may be mailed to friends or relatives at home, but not more than one per day of receipt to any one addressee. These gifts must not include perfumes costing more than $5, tobacco or liquor.

If you are traveling with such foreign-made articles as cameras, watches or binoculars that were purchased at home or on a previous trip, either carry the receipt or register them with U.S. Customs prior to departure.

Canadian residents. In addition to personal effects and over and above the regular exemption of $300 per year, the following may be brought into Canada duty-free: a maximum of 50 cigars, 200 cigarettes, 2 pounds of tobacco and 40 ounces of liquor, provided these are declared in writing to customs on arrival. Canadian Customs regulations are strictly enforced; you are recommended to check what your allowances are and to make sure you have kept receipts for whatever you may have bought abroad. Small gifts can be mailed and should be marked "Unsolicited gift, (nature of gift), value under $40 in Canadian funds." For other details, ask for a Canadian Customs brochure, *I Declare.*

British residents. There are two levels of duty-free allowance for people entering the U.K.: for goods bought outside the E.E.C. or for goods bought in a duty-free shop within the E.E.C.; and for goods bought in an E.E.C. country but not in a duty-free shop.

In the first category you may import duty free: 200 cigarettes or 100 cigarillos or 50 cigars or 250 grammes of tobacco (*Note:* If you live outside Europe, these allowances are doubled); plus one liter of alcoholic drinks over 22% vol. (38.8% proof) or two liters of alcoholic drinks not over 22% vol. or fortified or sparkling wine; plus two liters of still table wine; plus 50 grammes of perfume; plus nine fluid ounces of toilet water; plus other goods to the value of £32.

In the second category you may import duty free: 300 cigarettes or 150 cigarillos or 75 cigars or 400 grammes of tobacco; plus 1½ liters of alcoholic drinks over 22% vol. (38.8% proof) or three liters of alcoholic drinks not over 22% vol. or fortified or sparkling wine; plus five liters of still table wine; plus 75 grammes of perfume; plus 13 fluid ounces of toilet water; plus other goods to the value of £250. (*Note:* Though it is not classified as an alcoholic drink by E.E.C. countries for Customs' purposes and is thus considered part of the "other goods" allowance, you may not import more than 50 liters of beer.)

In addition, no animals or pets of any kind may be brought into the U.K. without a license. The penalties for doing so are severe and are strictly enforced; there are *no* exceptions. Similarly, fresh meats, plants and vegetables, controlled drugs and firearms and ammunition may not be brought into the U.K. There are no restrictions on the import or export of British and foreign currencies.

Velasquez

MADRID

Hub of a Nation

Madrileños, as the citizens of Madrid are called, are fond of claiming that the only better place to be is Heaven. Certainly Madrid is unique, a Mediterranean city nearly 480 km. (300 miles) from the sea, graced most days of the year by a flawless intensely blue sky. Given this piercing light and lack of rain, it is little wonder that Madrid has developed into a city where work tends to be seen as the interlude between bouts of pleasure. Madrid and its inhabitants exude a warmth unique in Spain. The stranger feels irresistibly buoyed up by the vivacity of the people, their friendliness and quick humor. The streets are charged with energy. Madrid is a city that turns foreign visitors into residents.

By European standards Madrid is a relatively recent capital. It was only in 1561 that Philip II decided to fix the court in Madrid, then a small, inconsequential town of some 30,000, mainly very poor, inhabitants. His decision was governed by the fact that Madrid lies at the geographical center of the Iberian peninsula. Today its central position is often compared to the hub of a wheel from which all the main road and railroad lines radiate outwards like spokes to the farthest corners of Iberia.

Yet Madrid remains an odd place for a town, a plateau protruding 600 meters (2,000 feet) up out of the Castilian tableland and the highest capital in Europe. Although Philip II's court had been a byword for austerity, by the second half of the 18th century Madrid was famous among voluptuaries. Casanova came to Madrid for its renowned pre-Lent Carnival and returned to Italy with rapturous reports of its carnal delights. Franco closed down the brothels in 1956 but the enthusiasm with which Madrid has now embraced sexual freedom must cause the old dictator to twirl in his grave.

Madrid city center scores over Berlin, London and Paris by its size. Despite the fact that the city's population has doubled since 1960 and is now around four million, the central area is the same size as 50 years ago. Much of Madrid's charm resides in the fact that it is possible to walk about downtown, with no need to use transport. Turn off any main thoroughfare and you will most likely find yourself in a street of old bars and small artesans, plumbers or carpenters, old-fashioned grocers with shutters fighting the newer supermarkets, with perhaps a Chinese restaurant or a sex shop adding a contemporary flourish. Ambling around the center of Madrid is a pleasure that never cloys.

The rush hours in Madrid are as horrendous as those in any capital of an industrialized country. Madrid lacks the suburban rail and subway links of Barcelona, so many Madrileños insist on driving to work despite the hold-ups and parking problems involved.

The lack of rain in Madrid means that the city's pollution problem is one of the worst in the world, though of late the government has taken steps to counteract it. It is to be hoped that the cleaned-up Manzanares river is only the first in a series of such measures.

Life in Madrid is lived largely on its streets and in its bars and cafes, and there is no better way of sampling the flavor of this most vivacious of cities than by joining in the ritual of twice-daily visits to the city's packed taverns. The morning is interrupted by a coffee break, often a late breakfast. Twelve-thirty is too early for lunch but it is a popular time for the bars to fill with pre-lunch drinkers and those in search of a snack. Restaurants fill up quickly after 1 P.M., their opening time, with those who have only an hour for lunch.

Madrid is not only a Mediterranean city because of the light and the atmosphere but because it also has some of the best seafood in Spain. Every day the pick of the catch is flown to the capital. Some of the most delightful summertime restaurants are a few kilometers out of the city on the roads to Guadalajara, Burgos and La Coruña, where you can eat out of doors: shellfish followed by steak or charcoal-grilled baby-lamb chops, their taste unique in the world.

Instead of sitting down to dinner many Madrileños prefer to go *tasca*-crawling. *Tascas* are small taverns serving tantalizing *tapas*, perhaps black pudding or squid fried in batter, pigs' ears or *mollejas*, bulls' testicles sliced wafer-thin and fried with garlic, a dish for the gods. All bars have tapas, but the tascas concentrate on them and so have a wider range. The tascas are located around the Puerta del Sol, on the Calle de la Victoria and Calle de la Cruz, in Echegaray and on the narrow side streets around the Plaza Santa Ana, home of the *Cervecería Alemana* that Hemingway used to patronize, and on the streets around the Plaza Mayor. In the latter you may chance upon the *tuna*, students playing guitars and clad in the gear of the Inquisition. The tradition is 400 years old and it is worth tipping generously to help keep it alive; as well as their traditional songs they will also play requests.

Madrid's Holy Week processions are not as spectacular as those of more religious cities like Valladolid, Avila or Zamora, but the *Procesión del Silencio* on Good Friday night is nevertheless impressive.

In May the flowers are in bloom and the *económicos* are serving fresh asparagus and strawberries. May 15 is the fiesta of San Isidro, the patron saint of Madrid, an excuse for two weeks of bullfights, fireworks, street festivals and open-air dances. On May 15 it is traditional to drink from the spring at the saint's hermitage just across the Manzanares, where there is an attendant funfair and stalls. This is the authentic San Isidro celebration as portrayed by Goya.

Most Madrileños take their vacation in July or August, and escape to the mountains or the coast. Ten years ago Madrid was deserted in August but gradually as more and more of its citizens have awoken to the charm of scant traffic, cinemas and shops open, and a full program of open-air evening events including opera, operetta, drama and variety performances is organized by the City Council.

Discovering Madrid

To do Madrid ample justice, you need to stay a minimum of three days, after which at least another couple of days or so can be dedicated to excursions to Toledo, Aranjuez, Segovia, Avila, the Escorial and the Valley of the Fallen.

With the exception of the northern reaches of the city around the upper part of the Castellana, Madrid is still a fairly compact capital and you can usually walk from one tourist attraction to another and be assured that enough sights will line your way to reward your efforts. If you get tired, simply take a bus or one of the numerous cabs, still quite cheap, back to your hotel. Or you can relax in one of the many sidewalk cafes and renew your strength for further sightseeing.

The Prado as a Starting Point

Since the attraction most tourists head for first upon arrival in Madrid is the Prado Museum, we will start our tour of the city from this world-famous art gallery, one of the great storehouses not only of Spanish art, but of Flemish and Italian masterpieces.

Located on the main north–south axis, the Castellana (here called the Paseo del Prado), the Prado is best entered through its main entrance on its northern side opposite the Hotel Ritz. Here there is a statue of the artist Francisco Goya. The Prado's other door facing onto the Paseo del Prado, behind a statue of the painter Diego Velázquez, is used mainly as an exit.

The Prado was originally opened in 1823 and has since been superbly stocked with the works of Velázquez, Murillo, Zurbarán, Ribera, Valdés Leal, Alonso Cano, El Greco, Berruguete and Goya as well as with a fine collection of Titian, Rubens, Raphael, Botticelli, Correggio, Mantegna and Bosch which were transferred from the Escorial Monastery outside Madrid where King Philip II had originally housed them. Both he and his father, Emperor Charles V, were avid collectors and brought many art treasures from southern Italy and the Netherlands, both at that time part of the Spanish empire.

To view the Prado's vast collection of paintings and treasures properly would take weeks. But the highpoints most popular with tourists are usually the El Greco, Velázquez, Goya, and Bosch galleries. Explanatory notes on the major artists are available in the relevant galleries at a small charge.

The greatest treasures are on the upper floor and a visit is best begun at the Goya (north) entrance end. The main gallery and adjoining rooms contain El Grecos, Riberas, Titians, Murillos, and, of course, the works of Diego Velázquez. Be sure to see the *Surrender of Breda,* one of his most impressive paintings, *The Drunkards,* and his series of four dwarfs. *Las Meninas,* perhaps his best known canvas, has been placed in a room by itself, with a strategic mirror to help you appreciate its extraordinary complexities.

The Prado provides a unique opportunity to see the full diversity of Goya's styles in several adjacent rooms at the far end of the upper gallery. Among highlights are portraits of the royal family, including the superb *Family of Carlos IV,* and the beautiful *Marquesa de Santa Cruz* purchased from Britain in 1986 amid much controversy. In a nearby room hang the *Naked Maja* and the *Clothed Maja,* and next door two of the artist's most celebrated works, the *2nd of May,* showing the uprising of the Spaniards in 1808 against the French Mamelukes in the Puerta del Sol, and the *Fusillade of Moncloa,* or *3rd of May,* which depicts the execution of patriots by a French firing squad with the same intensity of reaction to its subject as the later *Guernica* by Picasso.

Downstairs on the ground floor are the paintings of Goya's "Black Period," when he was already deaf and living outside the city. The most startling are *The Pilgrimage to San Isidro, Meeting of Witches,* and *Saturn.* Most of the ground floor is given over to the Flemish school, notably to Rubens, Van Dyck, and Brueghel, and to a sizable collection of late medieval religious paintings, mostly by Spanish artists including Luis de Morales. But before you leave, be sure not to miss the astounding collection of Hieronymus Bosch paintings displayed to the side of the Goya entrance, which includes his *Garden of Earthly Delights,* and the triptych *The Hay Wagon.*

In the fall of 1981 Picasso's *Guernica* was brought to Spain after its years of exile in New York. Its arrival in Madrid was the highlight of that year's celebrations of the centenary of the artist's birth. It is now housed permanently in the Casón del Buen Retiro, an annex to the Prado Museum which stands nearby at the end of the Calle de Felipe IV. The Casón del Buen Retiro is also the home of 19th-century Spanish painting and can be visited on the same ticket as the Prado. On one side of the small square in front of it rises the Royal Academy of the Spanish Language, the learned body charged with safeguarding the Castilian language. It re-edits its monumental dictionary every ten years or so.

In the vicinity of the Prado are three other museums of lesser interest to the tourist on a short stay but nonetheless worthwhile for those with more time to spare. Adjacent to the Post Office on the Calle Montalban is the Navy Museum, small but well-furnished, with ship models, nautical instruments, and Juan de la Cosa's famous map of the New World. At the end of the same street heading towards the Retiro Park is the Decorative Arts Museum, and close to the Cason del Buen Retiro is the Army Museum, fronted by a terrace covered with vintage cannons and mortars. The museum has a good collection of weapons, armor, flags, maps and paintings.

MADRID

0 Miles   ¼
0 Kilometers   ¼

Points of Interest

1   Atheneum
2   Biblioteca Nacional
3   Casa Cisneros
4   Casa de Lope de Vega
5   Casa de la Villa (City Hall)
6   Casón del Buen Retiró
7   Centro de Arte Reina Sofía
     (Queen Sofia Arts Center)
8   Fuente de la Cibeles
     (Cibeles Fountain)
9   Monasterio de la Descalzas Reales
10   Monasterio de la Encarnación
11   Municipal Museum
12   Museo Arqueológico
13   Museo de Artes Decorativas
14   Museo de Carruajes (Coach Museum)
15   Museo de Cera (Wax Museum)
16   Museo Cerralbo
17   Museo del Ejército (Army Museum)
18   Museo Etnológico
19   Museo Lázaro Galdiano
20   Museo Naval
21   Museo del Prado
22   Museo Romántico
23   Museo Sorolla
24   Palacio de Liria
25   Palacio Real
26   Puerta de Alcalá
27   Puerta del Sol
28   Real Academia de Bellas Artes de
     San Fernando
29   Real Fábrica de Tapices (Royal
     Tapestry Workshops)
30   San Antonio de la Florida
31   San Francisco el Grande
32   San Ginés
33   San Jerónimo el Real
34   San José
35   Teatro Español
36   Teatro Real
37   Teatro Zarzuela
38   Templo de Debod
39   Torre de Lujanes
40   Torre de Madrid

i   Information
✉   Post Office
Ⓜ   Metro Station

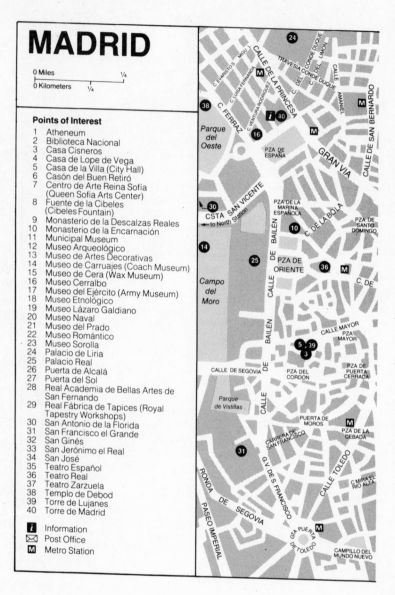

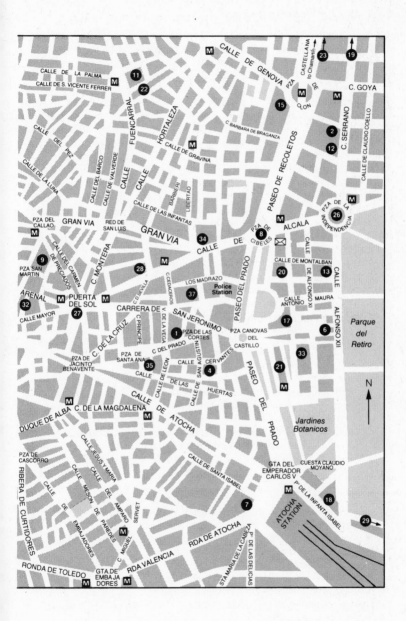

From the Prado to Atocha

After visiting the Prado you could take a stroll through the adjacent Botanical Gardens, opened in 1774 in the reign of Charles III, and come out upon the Cuesta Claudio Moyano, the site of a fascinating second-hand-book market whose stalls offer hours of splendid browsing. A little further on at the corner of Alfonso XII and the Paseo de la Infanta Isabel you come to the Ethnological Museum, of minor interest except to the most dedicated of museum goers. The Plaza Atocha, or to give it its full name, the Glorieta del Emperador Carlos V, has recently undergone a huge transformation. In 1986 an ugly overpass was demolished and an underground tunnel constructed to alleviate the considerable traffic problems of this southern end of the Castellana. The demolition of the overpass has revealed the imposing 19th-century glass-and-steel structure of the old Atocha Railroad Station, designed by Eiffel of Eiffel Tower fame. Though sadly dilapidated at the moment, this old building should shortly undergo a facelift when it is incorporated into the new adjacent station, currently under construction. The large building opposite is the Centro de Arte Reina Sofia which opened in 1986 in a former hospital and now houses some of Madrid's most exciting art exhibitions. If from here you proceed up the Calle de Atocha, you will enter an old working-class area, well worth a stroll for those seeking offbeat neighborhoods and local color.

From the Retiro to Cibeles

By far the best plan after a bout in the ever-crowded Prado is to take a stroll in the Retiro Park just a couple of streets away. Madrid's prettiest and most popular park, the Retiro dates back to the 15th century, though it was not opened to the public until 1876. Among the park's attractions are several outdoor cafes, Florida Park, a leading nightclub, a lake for rowing, playgrounds for children and shady lanes, often decorated with statues and monuments and fountains, ideal for strolling. In spring and summer, band concerts are held on Sunday mornings, and members of the Catalan colony in Madrid meet and solemnly dance the sardana. The Retiro plays host annually to a dog show, art exhibitions in the 19th-century glass-and-iron Crystal Palace and in summer, puppet shows and outdoor theatrical performances.

In addition to the large lake with its huge monument to Alfonso XII, there are two smaller ones, stocked with ducks and swans and surrounded by weeping willows. Fountains, statues and busts, beautiful flower arrangements and a delightful rose garden all help to make the Retiro a welcome haven from the city's bustle.

Leaving the Retiro at its main exit, the Plaza de la Independencia, you'll see a large arch, the Puerta de Alcalá, built in 1778 by Sabatini in Charles III's reign. The arch was formerly one of the gates to the city, with an adjoining customs' station; beside it stood the old bullring, which was later moved to its present location on the Calle de Alcalá at Ventas.

If at the Plaza de la Independencia you turn down the Calle de Alcalá, you will come to the Plaza de Cibeles, named after the Greek goddess Cybele (daughter of Uranus) who sits mounted on a chariot. The fountain has become the unofficial emblem of the city. Cibeles, as the square is known to Madrileños, is the great crossroads of the city, the intersection of the Calle de Alcalá and the Castellana. The cafes in the central promenade on the southern side are perennial favorites and here also a small playground, trees and benches make the area between Cibeles and the Neptune fountain an especially inviting place to rest after sightseeing.

The Salamanca Neighborhood and Beyond

The area northeast of Cibeles, the Salamanca neighborhood, is named after the financier José Salamanca who started building this then-new residential area in the 1870s. The *barrio* or neighborhood is bounded on the south by the Calle de Alcalá and the Calle Goya, the latter a busy shopping street lined with shops and branches of the two leading department stores, the Corte Inglés and Galerías Preciados.

You can now proceed north along either the Castellana or the Calle Serrano, the latter being the most elegant and expensive shopping street in the city. The surrounding streets parallel and perpendicular to Serrano are the domain of elegant shops and boutiques as well.

Going up Serrano from the Plaza de la Independencia (Puerta de Alcalá) you come first on the left to the Archeological Museum, a large, sprawling building with sections dedicated to Greek, Roman, prehistoric and Christian and Moorish cultures. Here you can see a reproduction of the Altamira prehistoric caves in Santander, a worthwhile visit since visits to the caves themselves are limited. Beside the museum once stood the old Mint, which has now been torn down to make room for a huge esplanade decorated with olive trees, sculptures by Vaqueros Turcios, allegorical of the Discovery of America, and the statue of Columbus high up on a pillar, which formerly stood in the center of the Plaza de Colón (Columbus Square). Underneath is the airport bus depot, as well as arcades, shops, and the Villa de Madrid theater, a leading cultural center and experimental theater.

Crossing the Calle Goya, you come on the right to the Celso García department store and then on the left to another branch of the Galerías Preciados department store. After passing many sidewalk cafes and art galleries, as well as the American Embassy and the British ambassadorial residence and dozens of boutiques, you finally reach the Lázaro Galdiano Museum on the corner of María de Molina.

Housed in what was formerly the luxurious private villa of José Lázaro Galdiano, writer, journalist and antique collector of the early 20th century, the museum contains a magnificent collection of *objets d'art*, all tastefully displayed, which ranges over clocks, paintings from Spanish and foreign masters, armor, furniture, tapestries, enamels and jewels—in all a really splendid array which is well worth a visit.

If you have walked as far as the Lázaro Galdiano Museum, you may well opt for a bus or cab ride back down the Castellana to Cibeles. If, on the other hand, you decide to brave the streams of fast-flowing traffic and the accompanying exhaust fumes, there are many sights to reward your efforts on this impressive modern avenue. Few of the noble palaces of old remain, but just every now and again, tucked away between glass and concrete structures, you will catch a glimpse of these splendors of yesteryear. Heading south down the Castellana from the Glorieta de Emilio Castelar, you will come to the overpass linking the Paseo de Eduardo Dato to the

Calle Juan Bravo. Underneath this is a pleasant garden adorned with several sculptures forming the outdoor sculpture museum, an agreeable place to sit for a while. The Castellana at this point is lined with the embassies of several countries, Finland, Germany and Belgium among them, before reaching the Plaza de Colón. Here in the northwest corner on your right are two large office buildings, the Torres de Jerez, much criticized for their graceless obtrusiveness and architectural non-style. Curiously enough, they were built from the top downwards, using a narrow central tower as a support. Inside one of them is the famous Chicote's bottle museum with its 10,500 bottles formerly housed in the basement of Chicote's bar on the Gran Vía. Across the street in the Centro Colón office complex is the Museo de Cera, one of Europe's more worthwhile wax museums. On the other side of the square are the Gardens of the Discovery of America and the monument to Columbus which you will have already seen on your walk up the Calle Serrano.

Continuing on down the Paseo de Recoletos, the first building on the left is the impressive National Library which often features exhibits and art shows in its salons. Next, also on the left-hand side, comes the sumptuous Banco Hipotecario, formerly the home of the Marquis of Salamanca. Then on the right comes the famous old Cafe Gijón, full of nostalgic atmosphere for the time when it hosted some of the greatest *tertulias* (political, literary or artistic discussions) of the capital. It is still worth a visit for those in search of shades of a more romantic past, and in summer tables and chairs are set outside on the avenue's sidewalk in front of the cafe.

Arriving back at the Plaza Cibeles, the building on the northwest corner is the Palacio de Buenavista, built originally for the Duke of Alba in 1769. Today, surrounded by lush gardens and guarded by soldiers, it serves as the Ministry of the Army. Opposite, on the northeast corner, is a palace built at the turn of the century for the Marquis of Linares. During the Franco era it was slated to be torn down, like so many other palaces lining the Castellana, but, in 1976, a reprieve came from the new government, which recognized the palace's historical worth. The City Hall is currently negotiating to purchase it and convert it into a museum.

Cibeles to Gran Vía

On the southeast corner of Cibeles rises the huge, cathedral-like Palacio de Comunicaciones which the people of Madrid often jokingly refer to as Nuestra Señora de Comunicaciones—Our Lady of Communications. It is, in fact, the Main Post Office, built in 1918, and one of the landmarks of the city.

On the southwest corner of Cibeles is the Banco de España (1891), analogous to the Federal Reserve Bank in the U.S. In the bank's underground vaults are stored the gold reserves of Spain.

Progressing along the Calle de Alcalá, on the right is the Church of San José, completed in 1742. Just past the church, branch right onto the Gran Vía, lined with shops, cafes, newsstands and numerous movie theaters. On the left side you will see the elegant Grassy jewelry store, and on the right Loewe, Spain's leading leather store, and then the Museo de Chicote, now a restaurant but formerly Chicote's bar, a favorite meeting place during pre-war days and much frequented by Hemingway and other writers.

The small traffic circle you come to next is the Red de San Luis. You can here branch left down the Calle Montera which will take you to the Puerta del Sol, or go toward the right up the rather dismal Calle Hortaleza or the Calle Fuencarral. The latter is lined with inexpensive shoe shops, and ultimately links up with the "boulevards," a network of avenues skirting the center, which start at Colón and end at the Parque del Oeste. On the way notice the impressive Churrigueresque façade sculpted by Pedro de Ribera in 1722 on what was formerly a hospital. Today the building houses the city's Municipal Museum and close by is the 19th-century Romantic Museum. Off to the left in the streets around the Plaza Dos de Mayo is the area known as Malasaña, whose narrow streets are packed with music bars very popular at night with the young of Madrid. However, it is an area best avoided by the visitor as it has become the center of Madrid's drug scene, and violence and unpleasant incidents are not infrequent. If you continue as far as the Glorieta de Bilbao, the crowded Café Comercial, another of the famous cafes of old, is well worth a visit.

Back on the corner of Fuencarral and Gran Vía stands the old Telephone Building (La Telefónica), at one time the highest structure in the city. During the Civil War of 1936–39, when Madrid remained loyal to the Republic, the Telefónica was the main observation point for Republicans surveying the battleground around the university campus and the Casa del Campo Park, when it was piled stories-high with sandbags. Walking on past the movie theaters with their large canopies, you come on the left to the Plaza del Callao. The main building of the Galerías Preciados department store, together with its annex, takes up most of the square. Two pleasant shopping streets, which are closed to traffic and where benches and flowers have been installed, the Calle de Preciados and the Calle del Carmen, both lead down to the Puerta del Sol. At the lower end of Preciados is the original Corte Inglés department store, which now has branches all over Madrid. If instead you branch right, down the Calle Preciados toward the Plaza de Santo Domingo, you come to several excellent restaurants.

The Plaza de España to the Victory Arch

Continuing down the Gran Vía past Callao, you pass on the right the Sepu budget store as well as numerous cafeterias, movie theaters, airline offices, hotels, travel agencies and shops. Cross the Calle de San Bernardo (which toward the right takes you to the old university building, the Music Conservatory and then links up with the boulevards) and a few streets on you come to the large, spacious Plaza de España, flanked by two highrise towers, the Torre de Madrid, with 37 floors and the highest building in Madrid, and the Torre de España, the second-highest building with 25 floors. On the ground floor of the former is the Tourist Office, which supplies handy maps and other useful information; the latter houses the elegant Hotel Plaza, long a favorite with American visitors.

A large, three-story garage was built under most of the Plaza de España, but the square, as all others where similar facilities were built, was then tastefully redone. Now the Plaza is a delightful place for reading, relaxing or refreshment. Around the fountain, tourists sun themselves and hippies strum guitars. In the middle of the park stands a monument to Cervantes surrounded by his best loved characters, Don Quixote and Sancho Panza.

From this square, should you proceed straight ahead up the Calle Princesa, you'll first see on the left a conglomerate of shops and restaurants huddling in the large courtyard of an office building, which has become a popular meeting place for young Madrileños.

On the right of the Calle Princesa stands the Palacio de Liria, privately owned by the Duchess of Alba and open to the public by arrangement only. It is one of the few palaces which still belong to an aristocratic family, and is actually lived in by the much-titled Duchess. Work on it began in 1770. After being badly damaged during the Civil War, it was subsequently rebuilt. A pleasant cafe and a mesón-restaurant in the small park in front make ideal stopping-off places.

Continuing up the street on the left is the Hotel Meliá Madrid. Further up you come first on the right to the Hotel Princesa Plaza, then on the corner of the boulevards another Corte Inglés department store; there are shopping arcades on either side of the street. Beyond, as far as the Triumphal Arch, is an area known as Argüelles, popular with students from the university of Madrid who come here to drink *cañas* (small draft beers) and eat plates of squid. At the top of Princesa on the left is the Airforce Ministry building, a copy of Juan de Herrera's Escorial, and in front the Victory Arch built by Franco in 1956 to commemorate his triumphal entry into Madrid at the end of the Civil War.

The University City and Moncloa

Beyond the Victory Arch lies the University City, an area with several points of interest but too spread-out to visit on foot. However, it can be reached on city bus routes or by a short cab ride, and its main places of interest can be glimpsed from tour buses on excursions to the Escorial.

The University City was begun in 1927 but was mostly destroyed during the Civil War when it was the battleground for the Nationalist troops besieging Madrid. However, it was rebuilt, though generally in undistinguished style, and is today one of Spain's most prestigious universities, with over 100,000 students, many of whom come from Latin America.

Just off to the right of the Avenida de la Victoria is the Museum of the Americas and, further on, on the left, at the beginning of the Avenida Puerta de Hierro, you will come to the Museum of Contemporary Spanish Art. The word "contemporary" may seem to be something of a misnomer, but it is nevertheless a worthwhile museum. Beyond lies the Moncloa Palace, home of Spain's Prime Minister. At the end of this avenue, Madrid's western limit is marked by the Puerta de Hierro, an iron gateway built in 1753 by the Bourbon monarchs who used to come hunting around El Pardo. The road which branches off to the right here leads to the Zarzuela Palace, home of King Juan Carlos, and eventually to Franco's former home, the palace of El Pardo, now a museum.

From the Plaza de España to the Casa de Campo

At the Plaza de España you can take an alternative route. Walk to the other side of the square, cross the Calle Ferraz, and enter the Parque del Oeste (West Park), formerly the Cuartel de la Montaña (a barracks), and you'll come to the Temple of Debod, an authentic Egyptian temple which formerly stood in the Aswan area of the Nile. It was transported stone by stone to Madrid from Egypt when the Aswan area was flooded. The temple and its pleasant surroundings and palm-tree landscaping are well worth a visit.

Crossing over Ferraz, you come to the Cerralbo Museum, formerly the private mansion of the Marquis of Cerralbo. The building is crammed full of paintings, furniture and personal mementos, and is rather less museum-like than the Lázaro Galdiano Museum. Visiting it is akin to paying a call on a nobleman's private quarters at the turn of the century. The mansion was built by the traditional-minded marquis in 1876.

Returning to the Parque del Oeste across the street, you continue up the Paseo de Rosales (named after a 19th-century bohemian painter from Madrid). Lining the paseo are countless outdoor cafes, delightful in fine weather. The park is well cared for. Especially beautiful is a large rose garden, with bowers, a fountain and benches.

At the corner of Rosales and Marqués de Urquijo (the end of the boulevards) is an excellent ice-cream parlor with dozens of exotic flavors. Across, at the corner beside the children's playground, is the end station of the cablecar *(teleférico)* which takes you over the Manzanares river to the Casa de Campo Park, popular with Madrileño families. It is a trip well worth making, for it affords some breathtaking views of the city and the Royal Palace. At either end of the cablecar are restaurants—the one on the Casa de Campo side with outdoor self-service facilities. Buses run regularly from the cablecar station to the zoo and the amusement park.

From near the cablecar entrance in the Parque del Oeste, it is possible to make your way down to the Hermitage of San Antonio de la Florida where the church is decorated with Goya frescos revealing the artist's somewhat sarcastic attitude to the Church. Beneath the crypt of the church lies Goya's headless body, brought back to Spain from France in 1888.

Old Madrid

A tour of Old Madrid can best be started from the Plaza Mayor, a few streets down from the Puerta del Sol. This, the oldest section of the city, was built during the rule of the Habsburg dynasty prior to the mid-18th century. Old Madrid is a warren of narrow streets, silent churches and small squares, a welcome respite from the hectic pace and fumes of the city, an area ideal for the cursory wanderer who will let whim dictate his steps and so encounter charming vistas, streets and buildings at each turn. Getting lost here is part of the fun, for you are sure to come out eventually at some imposing monument or church which will act as a landmark. Much of the area around Calle Segovia is now coming back into fashion with many old buildings being restored and several good restaurants flourishing in hidden nooks and corners.

The Plaza Mayor

The Plaza Mayor measures approximately 110 by 90 meters (360 by 300 feet) in length and width and is one of the most beautiful and also one of the most representative squares in the city. Work on it was begun by Juan Gómez de Mora in 1617 in Philip III's reign and when it was completed in 1620 eight days of merrymaking followed. Fires gutted parts

of the structure in 1631, 1672 and 1790; complete restoration was not undertaken till 1853.

In the 17th century the square was used for bullfights and also once
for an *auto da fé*, the burning of a heretic, with the king watching from
the section called the Panadería (Bakery) in the center of the northern side,
while the 476 balconies were full of nobles and dignitaries enjoying the
fun. The square was also used for the canonization of San Isidro, San Ignacio de Loyola, San Francisco Xavier, Santa Teresa de Jesús and San Felipe
Neri. In it were held masked balls, firework displays and plays, among
them those of Lope de Vega.

In 1629 the square was lavishly decorated for 42 days to celebrate the
marriage of the Infanta María and the King of Hungary. Here also was
celebrated the arrival in 1623 of the Prince of Wales, the future Charles
I of England. During his reign, King Philip V turned the square into a
market; and in 1810 triumphal arches were raised to receive the Duke of
Wellington; later, in 1812 the square's name was changed to the Plaza de
la Constitución. And in 1847 the last bullfights were held here to commemorate the marriage of Queen Isabel II.

Until the late '60s the Plaza Mayor was a bustling, commercial square,
with buses and trolley cars and traffic noisily clanking through it. But with
the crush of tourists invading Madrid, the city decided to close it to traffic.
Around 1970 a large parking lot was built under the square, but the cobblestones and the equestrian statue of Philip III by Juan de Bolonia, made
in 1616, were dutifully replaced.

Though the day-to-day vitality of the Plaza Mayor is gone, it is still lined
with old shops and taverns; the most famous of the former are the hat
and uniform shops where an extraordinary selection of head-gear can be
bought—anything from a pith helmet to a cabby's tweed cap. Three good
restaurants with tables and chairs placed outdoors provide a pleasant opportunity for outdoor lunching or dining. In summer, theatrical performances and the Festivales de España are sometimes held here; before
Christmas the square fills with stands selling decorations, noisemakers and
Nativity scenes, while all around fir and pine trees are placed on sale. On
Sunday mornings the square fills with stamp and coin collectors who cluster on the sidewalks and cobblestones as they buy, sell and swap parts of
their collections. Though the plaza is always bustling in summer, you
should take care here if you're visiting in winter, especially at night, when
it's often deserted except for groups of dropouts and drug addicts.

Researching the Mesones

Walking down the time-worn steps under the Arco de Cuchilleros, in
the southwest corner of the square, you come to one of the most picturesque tourist areas in the city. The two streets leading from the Calle
Mayor down to the Plaza de Puerta Cerrada (marked by a stone cross),
the Cava de San Miguel and the Calle Cuchilleros, are lined with taverns
and mesones which at night are a-bustle with a merry crowd spearing
tapas and drinking beer and wine. To make the taverns still more enticing,
many owners hire guitarists and accordion-players to liven things up. Especially on Saturday nights, the area has a touch of carnival about it as
tourists and locals spill out onto the streets and the noise reaches a boister-
ous pitch.

The Cuevas de Luis Candelas, one of the oldest of the mesones, has an old barrel-organ to provide the music. The Cuevas is named after a famous bandit (1806–37) whose exploits passed into the realm of folklore over the years. In an effort to prove its authenticity, the tavern has hired a doorman and dressed him up in a bandit's costume. Some wags feel that it is the tourists instead of the coach travelers who are now being fleeced; but apocryphal or not, the Cuevas is always a fun spot for roving visitors.

From Luis Candelas' you can proceed to the Mesón del Toro, the Mesón de la Tortilla, or a half-dozen other mesones, each specializing in local foods, which are usually recognizable in their windows where you may see mushrooms frying in oil or omelets being flipped into the air. Most of the taverns are more suited for a drink or a tapa than a full-course Spanish meal. For that, you can go to El Cuchi, a fun-packed restaurant at the foot of the Cuchilleros steps, or to Botin's, one of the quaintest old restaurants in town which makes a determined effort at being picturesque on its three stories crammed with wooden furniture and Castilian knickknacks. The prices are moderate, the rooms oozing with charm, and the crowd of tourists usually impenetrable.

Around the corner at the Puerta Cerrada lurks another oldtime haunt, Casa Paco, unbeatable for its thick, juicy steaks served on sizzling plates. This atmospheric and always crowded restaurant began life as a tavern over 50 years ago. If you haven't reserved a table, you will most likely have to wait a while in the bar up front, a not altogether unpleasant fate.

The Royal Palace

Bearing right, the narrow, curvy Calle de San Justo takes you to the Plaza del Cordón and the Casa de Cisneros, originally built in 1537 and restored in 1915. The house once belonged to the nephew of Cardinal Gonzalo Ximenez de Cisneros, Primate of Spain and Inquisitor General, much maligned abroad for his role in the Inquisition.

A sharp right takes you up the Calle del Cordón to the Plaza de la Villa, the site of Madrid's City Hall (Ayuntamiento) and the Torre de los Lujanes, where King Charles V supposedly kept his main European rival, François I of France, prisoner for a while after winning the Battle of Pavia.

Continuing down the Calle Mayor, past the Consejo de Estado y Capitanía (Council of State and Captaincy), you come to the Calle de Bailén where, on turning right, you come across the Royal Palace, second only to the Prado as one of Madrid's greatest sights. Beside it stands the stark Cathedral of La Almudena, a modern afterthought which has been ignominiously shrugged off by the Madrileños, who consider it an intrusive pastiche. Construction remains incomplete though work is once again in progress.

The Royal Palace, a magnificent Bourbon structure, stands on the site of the former Alcázar, or fortress, which burned down in 1734. The first stone of the palace was laid in 1737 in Philip V's reign using plans drawn up by Juan Bautista Sacchetti, but it wasn't completed until 1764, under Charles III's rule. The palace provided a stylish abode for Spanish monarchs for almost 200 years. Even Napoleon's brother, Joseph, was sumptuously housed in it in the early 19th century. After the French were ousted, King Ferdinand VII moved into the palace. The building remained a royal residence until the coming of the Second Republic in 1931 when King Alfonso XIII left it for exile in Italy.

Though General Franco sometimes used the palace for official state receptions and audiences, he lived in the El Pardo Palace just outside the city, leaving most of the Royal Palace as a museum. King Juan Carlos presently lives in the less ostentatious Zarzuela Palace, also outside the city.

A tour of the Royal Palace could easily take several hours, especially if you really want to appreciate the sumptuous salons with their precious carpets, porcelain, clocks, and chandeliers, and include visits to the Pharmaceutical Museum, the Royal Armory, and the Library. But guided tours are now obligatory and most of the guides will whisk you round the main highlights of the Royal Apartments in about 1½ hours. The Coach Museum is at the other end of the gardens and must be entered from that side, a five-block walk away.

Outside the palace is the spacious Plaza de Oriente, enhanced by large stone statues of pre-unification kings and warriors. Originally 108 of them were intended to adorn the roof, but their weight was so great it was considered more prudent to place them in this park and in the Retiro. The Plaza de Oriente has traditionally been used for demonstrations for and against the regimes in power. Across from the palace stands the old Opera House, which now serves as Madrid's main concert venue, though a new concert hall is due to open shortly in the northern reaches of the Castellana.

San Francisco el Grande

If, on reaching the bottom of the Calle Mayor, you turn left onto the Calle Bailen and walk southward over the viaduct bridge, you pass the pleasant Vistillas Park on the right, and the nearby Plaza de Gabriel Miró commanding some good views, and the studio of the painter Ignacio Zuloaga, before coming to the most important church in Madrid, the basilica of San Francisco el Grande, begun in 1761 by Fray Francisco de las Cabezas and completed in 1784 by Francisco de Sabatini.

The inside decorations date from 1881. Outstanding is the large dome which can be seen from many points in the city. It measures 29 meters (96 feet) in diameter, larger than St. Paul's in London. Paintings in the chapels include works by Goya, Claudio Coello and Lucas Jordán. The 50 splendidly-carved choir stalls originally stood in El Paular Monastery outside Madrid. The fine English organ dates from 1882.

A few streets ahead along a rather bleak section takes you to the Puerta de Toledo, an arch built in 1827 under Ferdinand VII's rule by Antonio Aguado.

Double back up the Calle Bailén and then right to the Carrera de San Francisco, formerly the scene of lively summer verbenas or street festivals during the celebrations in honor of La Paloma, which takes you to the Puerta de Moros square, opposite the Cebada market. The present "barley market" is a relatively new structure and replaced the steel-and-glass one long a landmark of the city. Beyond the Plaza de la Cebada and crossing the Calle de Toledo, go down the Calle de Maldonadas and you come out at the Plaza de Cascorro, the threshold of the Rastro.

The Flea Market

The Rastro, or Flea Market, has long been one of Madrid's main tourist sights, especially on Sunday mornings, but beware, for it is also a haven for pickpockets who fare well among the jostling crowds. It is a sprawling indoor and outdoor emporium that attracts gypsies and art connoisseurs, tourists and dropouts, where you can find anything from a rusty flintlock rifle to a new puppy dog. Despite the fact that decades of bargain-hunters and professional antique dealers have raided the Rastro, new objects turn up constantly, and bargains are still occasionally found if you know what you're after. Some of the wares are wildly overpriced, so watch your step. It really takes repeated visits before you get the hang of it and know which sections to hunt in. Though the most active time is Sunday mornings, the better antique shops are open every day of the week, but not the street stands.

The main thoroughfare of the Rastro is the steep hill of the Ribera de Curtidores, which on Sundays is jammed full with pushcarts, stands and hawkers and gypsies selling trinkets, plastic toys, records, camping equipment, new furniture and foam rubber mattresses. The better wares are usually kept inside the stores on either side of the street.

Those seeking antiques, though hardly at bargain prices, might enter the two sections off the Ribera de Curtidores, about halfway down the length of the street. On the left, the Galerías Piquer is renowned for its choice art pieces, and on the right another Galería is equally reputable. The Galerías each consist of a large courtyard surrounded by a dozen or so antique stores on two levels. To pick through the Galerías carefully takes hours.

Also leading off from the Ribera de Curtidores on the left are two narrow streets, one specializing in the sale of modern paintings and the other selling birds, fish, puppies and other pets.

At the bottom of the Ribera, where the iron junk market starts, you turn right down the Calle Mira el Sol one block and come out on the Campillo del Mundo Nuevo, a square with a park in its center, where among other stands and items spread on tables and blankets, you'll find a book and record fair where bargains can occasionally be found. The Rastro sprawls across the Ronda de Toledo, to the other side of the road, but that section of it is mostly reserved for electrical appliances, old bicycles and spare machinery parts.

Instead walk back up one of the steep narrow streets such as the Calle Carlos Arniches or the Calle Mira el Rio Baja, lined with junk shops and stands, a good bargain-hunting area. Wind up at the Plaza General Vara del Rey, another recommended area surrounded by antique shops and jammed on Sundays with stands of every description.

Vendors start putting away their wares and locking their shops around 2 P.M. at which time you can dip into some tapas at one of the taverns on the Plaza del Cascorro.

Another Stroll from the Prado

Back at the starting point at the Prado Museum, another itinerary takes you across the Paseo del Prado, up past the Palace Hotel to the Carrera de San Jerónimo; on the right stands the Congreso de los Diputados or the Palacio del Congreso, the Spanish Parliament, opened in 1850 and in front of which crouch two lions cast from the molten metal of cannons captured in the war with the Moroccans in 1860. At the back of the Parliament building is the delightful and superbly restored Teatro de la Zarzuela where operas and colorful musicals, known as *zarzuelas*, are staged.

Crossing over the street in front of the parliament, and going down the Calle de San Agustín, you come to the Calle Cervantes, on which, at no. 15, stands the house where Spain's famous playwright, Lope de Vega, lived from 1610 until his death in 1635. Close by, on the corner of Cervantes and the Calle León, stood the house in which Cervantes died in 1616. Turn right on León and walk to the Calle del Prado, where in front of you stands the Atheneum, an influential club and cultural center.

Turning left up the Calle del Prado, you'll come out on the Plaza Santa Ana, where on one side of the square you'll see the Teatro Español, one of Madrid's leading theaters, which specializes in Spanish classical drama. Across the square is the old-world Hotel Victoria, much favored by bullfighters in the days when Hemingway was in Madrid. The wood-paneled Cervecería Alemana on one side of the square used to be a popular rendezvous for literati, and in recent years became for a while a bohemian haunt. Today it is a favorite with tourists.

A short walk down the Calle Príncipe, or the Calle de la Cruz, past Seseña, the store specializing in capes, takes you to the Carrera de San Jerónimo, where some refreshment at the Museo del Jamón or the old-world Lhardys delicatessen may now be in order. Not far away up Calle Sevilla on Alcalá is the recently refurbished Real Academia de Bellas Artes, whose fine display of Spanish masters—Velázquez, El Greco, Murillo, and Goya among them—is second only to the Prado's magnificent collection.

The Puerta del Sol

A few more steps lead you into the Puerta del Sol (Gate of the Sun), among the major crossroads of Madrid and, indeed, of all of Spain. Kilometer distances in the country are still measured from this zero point. In 1986 the Puerta del Sol underwent an impressive remodelling to improve traffic flow and accommodate the revamped metro station beneath. The facades of its old houses were cleaned and repainted an attractive buff-pink, La Mariblanca, a copy of the statue which 250 years ago adorned a fountain in the square, is now back on an island in the center, and the much loved bear and *madroño* (strawberry tree) statue, symbol of the city, moved to the bottom of Calle Carmen. Formerly, the Puerta del Sol was famous for its bustling, all-night cafes and hectic traffic. Around it on the Calle de Alcalá and the Calle Arenal a generation of artists and intellectuals thrashed out the problems and theories of an as-yet non-industrial Spain in endless *tertulias* and talk-sessions. Unfortunately none of the cafes remain, and much of the action has moved on to other parts of town. However, the square is still a very lively intersection, as can be seen any evening around 8 o'clock, when the citizens of Madrid begin their ritual evening stroll, the *paseo*. On December 31 it fills with people cheering in the New Year as they watch the golden ball on top of the Dirección General de Seguridad building descending at midnight. Most still follow the old custom of trying to swallow one grape at each stroke of the clock. The large ministry building is now police headquarters. On one corner, the old Hotel París overlooking the square still keeps its vigil. On another is the perennially popular La Mallorquina bakery to which Madrileños with a sweet tooth have been flocking for pastries and sweets for decades. The tearoom upstairs commands a good view of the square.

The Puerta del Sol has been the scene of many stirring events and its history is closely linked to that of the country. The most famous incident that occurred here was the uprising in 1808 against the French, depicted in Goya's painting, *El Dos de Mayo*.

Arenal to the Opera and Calle Mayor

Proceeding on the Calle Arenal, you come on the left to the old Teatro Eslava, now one of the city's leading discos, and next to it the Church of San Ginés. Branching to the right off the Calle Arenal, along the Calle San Martin, you come to the Convent of the Descalzas Reales, founded in the 16th century by Princess Joan of Austria, daughter of Charles V and the Queen of Portugal. In 1559, the Franciscan sisters of Santa Clara moved into the building. Since then it has been lived in by many famous scions of royalty and to this day contains cloistered nuns in one part of the convent. Tours through other sections of the building are provided so that tourists can now admire the superb tapestries and assorted paintings by El Greco, Velázquez, Titian and Breughel the Elder that decorate its historical walls.

The building across the refurbished square (again with an underground garage) houses the Montepío, or Government Pawnbrokers Office; on another side of the Plaza de las Descalzas is a Portuguese fado restaurant and an excellent antiquarian bookshop, Luis Bardón.

Leaving the square at another exit, along the Calle de Trujillos, you come out eventually on the Plaza de Santo Domingo. Turn left down the Calle de la Bola at the far side, then right at the third street and you will emerge at the Plaza de la Marina Española, where you'll see a large building which was the Spanish Parliament in 1820. Originally it housed the Colegio de Doña María de Aragón, one of the earliest university-type institutions in Madrid. Under Franco it was the headquarters of the Falangist Movement, and today the building houses the Palace of the Senate.

You can then continue on to the Plaza de España, or down to the Plaza de Oriente facing the Royal Palace and back around the Opera into the Calle Arenal. Finally, you might like to cut up through one of the old narrow streets linking Arenal with the Calle Mayor, the "Main Street" of old Madrid. As you wander down this historic street, lined with old-fashioned shops selling books, curios and religious objects, look out for no. 50 where Lope de Vega was born in 1562, no. 75 the home of the the 17th-century playwright Calderón de la Barca, and no. 53 glorying in the name of *El Palacio de los Quesos* (Cheese Palace), a shop selling cheeses from all over Spain. Leaving the past behind you, this route brings you out once more in the bustling hub of Madrid, the Puerta del Sol.

Excursions from Madrid

Madrid is ideally situated for side trips as there are several towns and cities of outstanding interest lying within easy reach of the capital. Should you decide to keep your hotel base in Madrid, such places as Toledo, Aranjuez, Chinchón and Alcalá de Henares in New Castile, Avila and Segovia in Old Castile, and the nearby Monastery of El Escorial and the Valley of the Fallen in Madrid province, all lie within 100 km. (60 miles) of Madrid and are easily reached on day trips by private car, on public transport or, in the case of the larger cities, on tour buses which make regular excursions from the capital.

PRACTICAL INFORMATION FOR MADRID

GETTING TO TOWN FROM THE AIRPORT. The least expensive way to travel from the airport to the city center is to take the yellow airport bus to the Plaza Colon terminal on the Castellana. The journey takes around 20–30 mins. These buses leave the national and international termini at Barajas airport about every quarter hour from 5.15 A.M. to 12.45 A.M., and the fare, including baggage, is around 200 ptas. The Colon terminal is underground, taxis meet the buses, and it is only a short ride then to most of Madrid's hotels. Left luggage lockers are available at the terminal.

Taxi fares into central Madrid are not prohibitive. The average ride will cost what is on the meter (800–1,200 ptas.) plus surcharges (see *Getting Around* below). If your hotel is in northeast Madrid, on the airport side of town, best take a cab straight away; it will cost only a little more than the combined airport bus and cab ride.

TOURIST OFFICES. The main *Madrid Tourist Office* is on the ground floor of the Torre de Madrid on Plaza de España, near the beginning of Calle Princesa. It is open Mon. to Fri. 9–7, Sat. 10–2, closed Sun. There is another branch in the arrivals hall of the international terminal at Barajas airport, open Mon. to Fri. 8–8, Sat. 8–1, closed Sun. The *Municipal Tourist Office* is at Pza. Mayor 3 and is open 10–1.30 and 4–7; closed Sat. P.M. and Sun.

TELEPHONE CODE. The area code for the city of Madrid and for anywhere within Madrid province is (91). This should only be used when calling from outside Madrid province.

GETTING AROUND. By Metro. The subway is the easiest and quickest way of traveling around Madrid. There are ten lines and over 100 stations. The metro runs from 6 A.M. to about 1.30 A.M. Fares are 60 ptas., whatever distance you travel. Subway maps are available from ticket offices, hotel receptions, and the tourist offices at Barajas airport and on Pza. España. Plans of the metro are displayed in every station and in the trains themselves. Many ticket windows close at 10 P.M., so you will need change for the automatic machines at night or to be in possession of a *taco*.

Savings can be made by buying a *taco* of ten tickets with costs 410 ptas., or by buying a tourist card called *Metrotour* which allows you unlimited metro travel for 3 days at 675 ptas., or 5 consecutive days at 975 ptas.

By Bus. City buses are red and run between 6 A.M. and midnight. The fare is 60 ptas., or 85 ptas. for a transfer. The yellow microbuses, which are airconditioned, cost 70 ptas. Plans of the route followed are displayed at bus stops, and a map of all city bus routes is available free from EMT kiosks on Pza. Cibeles or Puerta del Sol. A *bono-bus,* good for ten rides, costs 370 ptas. and can be bought from an EMT (Empresa Municipal de Transportes) kiosk or any branch of the *Caja de Ahorros de Madrid.* Books of 20 tickets valid for microbuses are available from the kiosk on Plaza Cibeles, cost approximately 1,325 ptas. *Note:* These fares may well increase before 1989.

A good way to get acquainted with the city is to ride the *Circular* bus, marked with a red C. Its route passes several monuments and a number of the main streets, and a ride will cost you only one ticket. Another good ride is on bus 27 along Paseo del Prado, Paseo Recoletos and the Castellana.

By Taxi. Taxi meters start at 90 ptas., and the rate is 40 ptas. per kilometer. Supplements are 50 ptas. Sun. and holidays, 50 ptas. between 11 P.M. and 6 A.M., 50 ptas. when leaving bus or railroad stations, 50 ptas. to or from a bullring or soccer stadium on days when there is a fight or match, 75 ptas. to sporting facilities on the edge of Madrid, 150 ptas. to or from the airport, and 25 ptas. per suitcase. Taxis available for hire display a *Libre* sign during the day and a green light at night. Taxi stands are numerous or you can flag them down in the street. Taxis hold three or four passengers. Always check the driver puts his meter on when you start your ride. Tip 10% of the fare. To call a radio cab, call 247 8200/8500/8600.

RAILROAD STATIONS. There are three main stations. Chamartín in the north of the city is the departure point of most trains to the northwest, north and northeast (including Barcelona), and more and more trains to Valencia, Alicante, and Andalusia now leave from here too. Atocha at the far end of Paseo del Prado is the departure point for some trains to the Valencia region and Andalusia, and for most to Extremadura and Lisbon. Always be sure to check which station your train leaves from. An underground line connects Atocha with Chamartín. Trains to local destinations such as El Escorial, Avila, Segovia, Guadalajara, and Alcalá de Henares, can be boarded at either Atocha Apeadero or Chamartín Cercanías.

The other main station is Estacíon del Norte (North station, or Príncipe Pío), just off Cuesta de San Vicente. There you can get trains to Salamanca, Fuentes de Oñoro, Santiago de Compostela and La Coruña—and all other destinations in Galicia.

For train information and tickets in advance, go to the RENFE office at Alcalá 44, any of the main stations (Norte is the least crowded), or call 733 3000. The RENFE office is open Mon. to Fri. 8.30–2.30 and 4–5, and Sat. 8.30–1.30. The advance ticket offices at Chamartín and Atocha stations are open daily 9–9, and at Norte daily 9–7. There is also a RENFE office in the international arrivals hall at Barajas airport, open Mon. to Sat. 8–8, Sun. and fiestas 8–2. Travel agents displaying the blue and yellow RENFE sign also sell rail tickets, at no extra charge, and are a good bet in the crowded summer months.

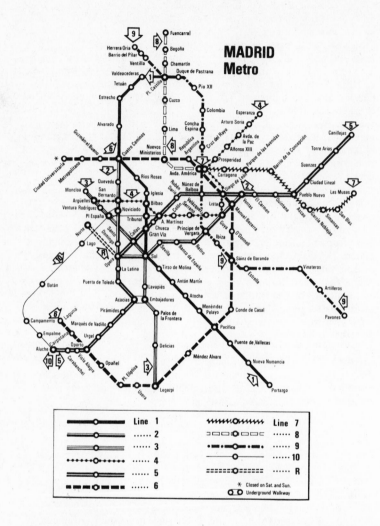

BUS STATIONS. Madrid has no central bus depot. There are two main bus stations, the Estación del Sur, Canarias 17 (tel. 468 4200), and Auto-Res, Pza. Conde de Casal 6 (tel. 251 6644). Buses to Aranjuez and Toledo, Alicante and many destinations in the south leave from the Estación del Sur; to Cuenca, Valencia, Extremadura and Salamanca from Auto-Res. Auto-Res has a central ticket and reservations office at Salud 19 just off Gran Vía. To other destinations, they leave from all over the city and it is best to enquire at the Tourist Offices.

As a guide to some of the more popular destinations, buses to Avila, Segovia, and La Granja are run by *La Sepulvedana* (tel. 247 5261) and leave from Paseo de la Florida 1; to Escorial and Valle de los Caidos by *Empresa Herranz* (tel. 243 8167) leaving from Isaac Peral 10; to Chinchón by *La Veloz* (tel. 227 2018) from Sánchez Bustillo 7.

HOTELS. Madrid offers a wide range of hotels, all the way from the millionaire *Ritz* to modest little pensions where you can get a room for around 2,000 ptas. a day. Many hotels are fully booked at Easter and around July and August. There are hotel accommodations services at Chamartín and Atocha stations, and at both the national and international airport termini. Or you can contact *La Brùjula* hotel agency (tel. 248 9705) at Torre de Madrid, 6th floor, in the Pza. de España; open 9 A.M.–9 P.M. All hotels have all rooms with bath unless stated otherwise. For a guide to prices, see *Hotels* in *Facts at Your Fingertips.*

Super Deluxe

Ritz, Plaza de la Lealtad 5 (tel. 521 2857). 156 rooms. Elegant and aristocratic with beautiful rooms, large suites and a justly famous dining room; Spain's most exclusive hotel. AE, DC, MC, V.

Villa Magna, Paseo de la Castellana 22 (tel. 261 4900). 194 rooms. The most luxurious of hotels and Madrid's international rendezvous. With restaurant, bars, banquet rooms and garage. Decor is elegant and tasteful; pleasant garden. AE, DC.

Deluxe

Barajas, Avda. de Logroño 305 (tel. 747 7700). 230 rooms. Luxurious airport hotel with pool; 24-hour courtesy bus service from airport. AE, DC, MC, V.

Castellana Intercontinental, Castellana 49 (tel. 410 0200). 311 rooms. Elegant hotel right on the Castellana, just above Plaza Emilio Castelar. AE, DC, MC, V.

Eurobuilding, Padre Damían 23 (tel. 457 7800). 520 rooms. An enormous hotel with two entrances, one on Padre Damían and one on Juan Ramón Jiménez. With a pool, gardens, several bars, nightclub; *Balthasar* restaurant and *Le Relais* coffeeshop. Popular with Americans and businessmen. AE, DC, MC, V.

Fenix, Hermosilla 2 (tel. 431 6700). 229 rooms. A new 4-star hotel located near Plaza Colón between the Castellana and Serrano. Has new bar and Louis XV–style lounge.

Holiday Inn, in the Azca Center off Calle Orense (tel. 456 7014). 313 rooms. Part of the big shopping and entertainment complex close to the Castellana in the north of the city; decor is luxurious, and there is a pool, sauna and gymnasium, executive suites, banqueting salons, conference rooms, underground garage, an Italian-style cafeteria, and a steak house. AE, DC, MC, V.

Meliá Castilla, Capitán Haya 43 (tel. 571 2211). 936 rooms. Madrid's largest hotel in the increasingly fashionable and gourmet area in the north of the city. It has a pool, and also boasts the *Scala* nightclub, one of Madrid's leading nightspots. AE, DC, MC, V.

Meliá Madrid, Princesa 27 (tel. 241 8200). 266 rooms on 25 floors. Well-appointed hotel just up from Plaza España. AE, DC, MC, V.

Miguel Angel, Miguel Angel 31 (tel. 442 8199). 305 rooms. Luxurious hotel with elegantly appointed public and private rooms. Conveniently located in smart area, it has fast become a favorite. Pool. AE, DC, MC, V.

Mindanao, San Francisco de Sales 15 (tel. 449 5500). 289 rooms. In residential area close to the University City in the northwest of the city. With pools and sauna. *Domayo* restaurant offers regional Spanish dishes and French cuisine, while the *Keynes* bar is a favorite spot for Spanish society. AE, DC, MC, V.

Monte Real, Arroyo Fresno 17 (tel. 216 2140). 77 rooms. In the Puerta de Hierro section out of town, and the last word in ritzy elegance, quiet and dignified. With pool and large gardens, and just 1 km. from Puerta de Hierro golf club. AE, DC, MC, V.

Palace, Plaza de las Cortes 7 (tel. 429 7551). 518 rooms. Dignified turn-of-the-century hotel, a slightly down-market step-sister of the nearby *Ritz* and long a favorite of politicians and journalists. Its *belle époque* decor—especially the glass dome over the lounge—is superb, if now somewhat faded in parts—some of the rooms are in need of refurbishing. Very central, opposite parliament and close to the Prado Museum. AE, V.

Princesa Plaza, Serrano Jover 3 (tel. 242 3500). 406 rooms. Modern hotel on corner of Princesa, a focal point for Madrid businessmen. AE, DC, MC, V.

Tryp Palacio, Paseo de la Castellana 57 (tel. 442 5100). 182 rooms. Totally renovated in 1988 to high standards of luxury and comfort; now the flagship of the big Tryp chain. AE, DC, V.

Villa Real, Plaza de las Cortes 10 (tel. 420 3767). 115 rooms. Recently opened (Apr. '89) luxury hotel in a renovated 19th-century building opposite the Palace and facing the Cortes Parliament building. AE, DC, MC, V.

Wellington, Velázquez 8 (tel. 275 4400). 257 rooms. An old favorite in the Salamanca district close to Retiro Park, attracting a solid, conservative clientele. It has long been a focal point of the bull-fighting world, and in the May San Isidro festivals plays host to famous toreros, breeders and bullring critics. AE, DC, MC, V.

Expensive

Aitana, Castellana 152 (tel. 250 7107). 111 rooms. A comfortable, modern hotel much favored by businessmen, on the northern reaches of the Castellana close to the Azca Center and the Bernabeu soccer stadium. AE, DC, V.

Alcalá, Alcalá 66 (tel. 435 1060). 153 rooms. Convenient for Retiro Park and Goya shopping area. Good value. AE, DC, MC, V.

Arosa, Calle de la Salud 21 (tel. 232 1600). 126 rooms. Elegant older hotel between the Gran Vía and Plaza del Carmen. Helpful, friendly service. AE, DC, MC, V.

Calatrava, Tutor 1 (tel. 241 9880). 99 rooms With disco, private garage. Close to Plaza de España. AE, DC, MC, V.

Chamartín, above Chamartín station (tel. 733 7011). 378 rooms. Large, modern hotel, part of the huge government-financed Chamartín complex. Its size makes it rather impersonal, and it is a long way from the center, though convenient for the station. AE, DC, MC, V.

El Coloso, Leganitos 13 (tel. 248 7600). 84 rooms. Modern, well-appointed hotel, centrally located just off Gran Vía and Plaza España. AE, DC, MC, V.

Convención, O'Donnell 53 (tel. 274 6800). 790 rooms. A huge hotel, opened in 1978 near Goya shopping area. Caters largely for business travelers and international conventions. AE, DC, MC, V.

Cuzco, Castellana 133 (tel. 456 0600). 330 rooms. Modern and pleasant, close to the Bernabeu stadium. AE, DC, MC, V.

Emperador, Gran Vía 53 (tel. 247 2800). 231 rooms. Popular, comfortable, older hotel on corner of San Bernardo. Rooftop pool and terrace with good views. AE, DC, MC, V.

Emperatriz, Lopez de Hoyos 4 (tel. 413 6511). 170 rooms. Attractive, stylish hotel just off the Castellana. Good service; recommended. AE, DC, MC, V.

Florida Norte, Paseo de la Florida 5 (tel. 542 8300). 399 rooms. Pleasant modern hotel in west of town close to North Station; a little geared to tour groups. AE, DC, MC, V.

Los Galgos Sol, Claudio Coello 139 (tel. 262 4227). 359 rooms. Comfortable; rooms well-appointed and most with balcony. Near Serrano shopping area. One of the most expensive in this category. AE, DC, MC, V.

Gran Atlanta, Comandante Zorita 34 (tel. 253 5900). 180 rooms. Recent, functional hotel close to the Azca Center on Orense. Decor is dark and gloomy in typically Spanish style, but the hotel is comfortable and the service friendly. AE, DC, MC, V.

Gran Hotel Versalles, Covarrubias 4 (tel. 447 5700). 145 rooms. Functional but pleasant hotel with regular clientele, located in the Alonso Martínez area. AE, DC, V.

Mayorazgo, Flor Baja 3 (tel. 247 2600). 200 rooms. Pleasant hotel tucked away in a side street off Gran Vía. AE, DC, MC, V.

Plaza, Plaza de España (tel. 247 1200). 306 rooms. Elegant, central hotel very popular with Americans. Rooftop pool, with superb views. One of the most expensive in this category. AE, DC, MC, V.

El Prado, Calle del Prado 11 (tel. 429 3568). 45 rooms. Modern comfortable hotel in an old part of town close to Plaza Santa Ana. AE, DC, V.

Sanvy, Goya 3 (tel. 276 0800). 141 rooms. Recently renovated hotel just off Castellana. AE, DC, MC, V.

Suecia, Marqués de Casa Riera 4 (tel. 531 6900). 128 rooms. Once patronized by Hemingway, this hotel boasts a good Scandinavian restaurant. Close to Cibeles and next to the Teatro Bellas Artes just off Alcalá. AE, DC, MC, V.

Tryp Velázquez, Velázquez 62 (tel. 275 2800). 130 rooms. Oldish, but comfortable and spacious with some style, though it has begun to take tour groups. It is a regular venue for Madrileños, who favor its banqueting rooms for their weddings, while its bar frequently hosts one of the few remaining teatime *tertulias.* AE, DC, MC, V.

Moderate

Anaco, Tres Cruces 3 (tel. 522 4604). 37 rooms. Small, modern and comfortable hotel just off Plaza del Carmen. Very central. AE, DC, MC, V.

Carlos V, Maestro Vitoria 5 (tel. 531 4100). 67 rooms. Pleasant old hotel, centrally located just off main shopping street. AE, DC, MC, V.

Colón, Dr. Esquerdo 117 (tel. 273 5900). 389 rooms. Large 4-star hotel with good rates, though a little out of the center. AE, DC, MC, V.

Liabeny, Salud 3 (tel. 532 5306). 209 rooms. Comfortable, functional 4-star hotel, centrally located near Pza. del Carmen and main shopping area. AE, MC, V.

Opera, Cuesta Santo Domingo 2 (tel. 241 2800). 81 rooms. Modern and very comfortable, centrally located in the old part of the city close to the Opera and only a short walk from the Royal Palace.

Príncipe Pío, Cuesta San Vicente 14 (tel. 247 8000). 157 rooms. Pleasant hotel near the Royal Palace and North station. Good service. AE, MC, V.

Regina, Alcalá .19 (tel. 521 4725). 142 rooms. Elegant, older hotel, recently renovated. Overlooks Calle Sevilla and close to Puerta del Sol.

Serrano, Marqués de Villamejor 8 (tel. 435 5200). 34 rooms. Small hotel in smart area between Calle Serrano and the Castellana.

Tryp Rex, Gran Vía 43 (tel. 247 4800). 146 rooms. Good, smallish hotel on corner of Silva, just down from Callao. AE, DC, V.

Tryp Victoria, Plaza del Angel 7 (tel. 531 4500). 110 rooms. Stylish old hotel with stained-glass windows and decorative cupola, pleasantly located between Plaza Santa Ana and Plaza del Angel. Long a favorite of bullfighters and aficionados. It will appeal more to those who are seeking old world charm rather than modern comforts. AE, DC, MC, V.

Zurbano, Zurbano 81 (tel. 441 5500). 262 rooms. Modern, elegant hotel in a fashionable area. High standards. AE, MC, V.

Inexpensive

Clíper, Chinchilla 6 (tel. 531 1700). 52 rooms. Good-value hotel on a narrow street off the central part of Gran Vía, between Callao and Red de San Luis. AE, MC, V.

Francisco I, Arenal 15 (tel. 248 0204). 58 rooms. Old hotel with modernized decor, halfway between Puerta del Sol and the Opera. Top-floor restaurant is recommended.

Inglés, Echegaray 10 (tel. 429 6551). 58 rooms. An old budget favorite. Location is somewhat shabby but convenient, close to (I) restaurants and Puerta del Sol. AE, DC, MC, V.

Metropol, Montera 47 (tel. 521 2935). 72 rooms. Well renovated hostel with high standards on corner of Gran Vía.

Moderno, Arenal 2 (tel. 531 0900). 98 rooms. Renovated old hotel in a very central position just off Puerta del Sol. Traffic can be noisy. AE, V.

Mora, Paseo del Prado 32 (tel. 239 7407). 42 rooms. Convenient to Prado and not far from Atocha Station.

París, Alcalá 2 (tel. 521 6496). 114 rooms. A delightful hotel full of stylish, old-fashioned appeal; currently being renovated. Right on Puerta del Sol. DC, V.

Regente, Mesonero Romanos 9 (tel. 521 2941). 124 rooms. Simple, old-fashioned hotel close to Gran Vía and the pedestrian shopping streets of Callao. Low rates and reasonable value for the price. AE, MC, V.

Tryp Asturias, Sevilla 2 (tel. 429 6676). 175 rooms. Old-world charm, but on a rather busy intersection overlooking Plaza Canalejas, just up from Puerta del Sol. Much-needed renovations are underway—check your room is one of those already refurbished before booking. AE, DC, V.

Motels

Los Angeles (M), on the N-IV to Andalusia (tel. 696 3815). 46 rooms. 14 km. from town. With pool and tennis.

Avion (M), Avda. Aragón 345 (tel. 747 6222). 64 rooms, pool. 14 km. out on N-II. Convenient for those driving in from Barcelona.

Los Olivos (I), on the N-IV to Andalusia (tel. 695 6700). 100 rooms. 12 km. out of town. With pool.

Youth Hostels. There are two youth hostels in Madrid: the biggest is **Richard Schirrmann,** in Casa del Campo park (tel. 463 5699), with 120 beds; the other, more central, one is **Santa Cruz de Marcenado,** at No. 28 on the street of the same name (tel. 247 4532), with 78 beds. The nearest metro to the former is Lago, to the latter it's Argüelles, San Bernardo or Ventura Rodriguez.

RESTAURANTS. If Madrid is your first stop in Spain, you may feel ravenous before you see any signs of food on the way. Normal meal hours in the capital are even later than in the rest of Spain—where they are already later than elsewhere in Europe! Few people think of eating lunch in the capital before 2 P.M., 3 P.M. is quite normal, and 3.30 not at all unusual; and while most Spanish diners begin to eat at 9.30 or 10, 10.30 is more usual for Madrileños. However, if you just can't wait, a few restaurants and most hotels open their dining rooms earlier for the benefit of foreigners, or you can get a snack in any of the numerous cafeterias around town.

Madrid is plentifully provided with restaurants of all classes and of all types. The truly cosmopolitan mix includes French, German, Italian, Chinese, Mexican, Latin American, Japanese, Moroccan, Polish, Russian and American cuisine—not to mention Asturian, Basque, Galician, Valencian, Catalan, as well, of course, as Castilian.

All restaurants, except those in the top 4– and 5–fork classifications, are theoretically required to offer a *menu del día* (although not all of them do, and the practice is becoming less and less common), comprising a 3-course, fixed-price set meal, including bread, wine and dessert. Though there is often a choice, unless the fixed meal happens to be exactly what you want, you may well prefer to compound your own *menu*—though this is almost certain to prove more expensive.

A word of warning: many of the best-known restaurants close for a month in summer, and some are also closed in Easter week. Many close on Sundays, and some also on one other day during the week; be sure to check.

For an approximate guide to prices, see *Restaurants* in *Facts at Your Fingertips.*

Deluxe

El Amparo, Puigcerdá 8 (entrance Jorge Juan 10) (tel. 431 6456). Elegant restaurant with the emphasis on Basque traditional and *nouvelle cuisine.* Imaginative dishes and pleasing decor. Closed Sat. lunch, Sun., Easter week and Aug. AE, V.

Club 31, Alcalá 58 (tel. 531 0092). International cuisine and Spanish regional dishes. Under same management as *Jockey* and with same high standards. Ideal for late diners as orders are taken uptil midnight. Closed Aug. AE, DC, MC, V.

Horcher, Alfonso XII 6 (tel. 522 0731). One of Madrid's most famous—and expensive—restaurants. Service is excellent, ladies are even brought a cushion to rest their feet on! Specialties are Central European dishes and game. Closed Sun. AE, DC.

Jockey, Amador de los Ríos 6 (tel. 419 1003). A long-standing favorite and one of the best. Closed Sun. and Aug. AE, DC, MC, V.

La Paella Real, Arrieta 2 (tel. 542 0945) Recently acquired by the owners of Valencia's famous *Los Viveros,* it now claims to be Madrid's top paella and Valencian food spot. Closed Mon. AE, DC, V.

Ritz Hotel, Plaza de la Lealtad 5 (tel. 521 2857). A considerable part of the six million dollars recently spent on renovating the Ritz went on refurbishing the dining room, which is now resplendent with silk curtains and marble columns. The hotel garden is probably the most attractive place to dine in summer. AE, DC, MC, V.

Zalacaín, Alvarez de Baena 4 (tel. 261 4840). Considered Spain's best restaurant by gourmets. In a private villa with elegant decor and topnotch food; highest recommendations. Closed Sat. lunch, Sun., Easter week and Aug. AE.

Expensive

Al-Mounia, Recoletos 5 (tel. 435 0828). Outstanding Moroccan restaurant specializing in North African cuisine, Moroccan pastries and mint tea. Closed Sun., Mon. and in Aug. AE, DC, MC, V.

Annapurna, Zurbano 5 (tel. 410 7727). One of Madrid's top Indian restaurants. Superb cuisine and atmosphere. Closed Sun. AE, DC, MC, V.

Bajamar, Gran Vía 78 (tel. 248 5903). Offers some of the best seafood in town in its downstairs dining room. AE, DC, MC, V.

El Bodegón, Pinar 15 (tel. 262 8844). Small restaurant with outstanding food and a regular, faithful clientele. Closed Sun. and in Aug. AE, DC, MC, V.

Cabo Mayor, Juan Hurtado de Mendoza 11 (tel. 250 8776). Imaginative cuisine. Closed Sun., and last 2 weeks of Aug. AE, DC, V.

Café de Oriente, Plaza de Oriente 2 (tel. 241 3974). Stylish restaurant. In summer, you can dine on a terrace overlooking the Teatro Real and the Royal Palace. Closed Sat. lunch, Sun. and Aug. AE, DC, V.

El Cenador del Prado, Calle del Prado 4 (tel. 429 1561). Imaginative cuisine and beautiful decor. Closed Sat. lunch, Sun. and Aug. AE, DC, MC, V.

Combarro, Reina Mercedes 12 (tel. 254 7784). Outstanding Galician restaurant with superb fish and seafood though meat dishes are also excellent. Closed Sun. and Aug. AE, MC, V.

Las Cuatro Estaciones, General Ibáñez Ibero 5 (tel. 253 6305). Decor and menu to match the four seasons. A novel and attractive restaurant but the prices are high. Closed Sat. and Sun., and in Aug. AE, DC, V.

La Dorada, Orense 64 (tel. 270 2004). Outstanding seafood restaurant serving fish flown in daily from Costa del Sol. Closed Sun. and Aug. AE, DC, V.

Gure Etxea, Plaza de la Paja 12 (tel. 265 6149). An excellent Basque restaurant, much praised by readers. Closed Sun. and Aug. AE, DC, V.

Irízar, Jovellanos 3 (tel. 531 4569). A renowned and luxurious restaurant serving Basque cuisine with some French and Navarre nouvelle influence; a good place to go for a treat. Closed Sat. lunch and Sun. dinner. AE, DC, V.

Itxaso, Capitán Haya 58 (tel. 572 0247). Basque restaurant with elegant, somber decor, close to Hotel Meliá Castilla. Its fish and seafood dishes are outstanding. Closed Sun. and Aug. AE, DC, MC, V.

Korynto, Preciados 36 (tel. 521 5965). A long-established seafood restaurant in the heart of Madrid. Prices are high but the freshness and quality are tops. AE, DC, MC, V.

Lhardy, San Jerónimo 8 (tel. 522 2207). A veritable old Madrid institution. Worth a visit as much for its old-world decor as for its long-famed cuisine. Closed Sun. and in Aug. AE, DC, V.

El Mentidero de la Villa, Sto Tomé 7 (tel. 308 1285). Stylish restaurant whose cuisine shows Japanese and French influences. Well recommended. Closed Sat. lunch, Sun., and 2 weeks in Aug. V.

Nicolasa, Velázquez 150 (tel. 261 9985). Top Basque dishes served by owners of its namesake in San Sebastián. The decor is most attractive and the waitresses wear Basque costume. Closed Sun. and Aug. AE, DC, MC, V.

O'Pazo, Reina Mercedes 20 (tel. 253 2333). An elegant Galician restaurant with a reputation for some of the best seafood in Madrid. Closed Sun. and Aug. AE, DC, MC, V.

El Pescador, José Ortega y Gasset 75 (tel. 402 1290). Prime-quality fish dishes and good service. Closed Sun. and mid-Aug. through mid-Sept.

Platerías, Plaza Santa Ana 11 (tel. 429 7048). Good menu based on fresh market produce. Daily specials are recommended. Closed Sun. and Aug. AE, DC, MC, V.

Príncipe de Viana, Manuel de Falla 5 (tel. 259 1448). Fashionable restaurant with Basque, Navarre and international dishes. Closed Sat. lunch, Sun., Easter week and Aug. AE, DC, MC, V.

Sacha, Juan Hurtado de Mendoza 11 (tel. 457 5952). Cozy, with exquisite decor; outdoor dining in summer. Closed Sun., Easter week and Aug. AE, DC, MC, V.

Señorío de Bértiz, Comandante Zorita 6 (tel. 233 2757). Managed by former members of *Zalacaín* team, it offers outstanding cuisine, service and decor. Closed Sat. lunch, Sun. and Aug. AE, DC, V.

Solchaga, Plaza de Alonso Martínez 2 (tel. 447 1496). Several charming diningrooms of distinctive character resembling an old-fashioned private house rather than a restaurant. Closed Sat. lunch and Sun. AE, DC, MC, V.

La Trainera, Lagasca 60 (tel. 276 8035). A good, reliable fish and seafood restaurant with a regular clientele. Closed Sun. and Aug. V.

Moderate

Alkalde, Jorge Juan 10 (tel. 276 3359). Cave-like rooms, pleasant atmosphere, excellent food and service. One of Madrid's most consistently good restaurants. Closed Sat. night, and Sun. in July and Aug. AE, DC, V.

Apriori, Argensola 7 (tel. 410 3671). Inventive dishes in relaxed informal setting; pleasant decor, English spoken. Closed Sat. lunch and Sun.

Armstrong's, Jovellanos 5 (tel. 522 4230). Charming English-owned restaurant opposite Teatro Zarzuela. Imaginative cuisine includes good choice of salads, brunch on weekends and teatime. Opens for dinner at 6 P.M. Closed Sun. evening and Mon. AE, DC, MC, V.

Balzac, Moreto 7 (tel. 248 0177). Serves its own original style of Basque cuisine, and is especially well-known for its desserts. Closed Sat. lunch and Sun. AE, DC, V.

La Barraca, Reina 29 (tel. 232 7154). A cheerful Valencian restaurant just behind the Loewe leather store on Gran Vía; it's *the* place for *paella* other than Valencia itself. AE, DC, MC, V.

El Callejón, Ternera 6 (tel. 522 5401). An old Hemingway favorite just off Preciados. Closed Sat. AE, DC, MC, V.

Carmencita, Libertad 16 (tel. 531 6612). Charming old Madrid favorite serving mixture of nouvelle and traditional dishes. Well worth a visit. Closed Sun. V.

Casablanca, Barquillo 29 (tel. 521 1568). Popular and original restaurant; well recommended. Closed Sun. and Aug. AE, DC, MC, V.

Casa Botín, Cuchilleros 17 (tel. 266 4217). Just off Plaza Mayor, this is Madrid's oldest restaurant, having been catering to diners since 1725. It was a great favorite with Hemingway, and though popular with Spaniards, too, it is definitely aimed at tourists. Service is pleasant and efficient, the food reasonably good—and, though it has become a tourist mecca, it is still worth a visit. Two sittings for dinner, at 8 and at 10.30; booking essential. AE, DC, MC, V.

Casa Lucio, Cava Baja 35 (tel. 265 3252). Characterful restaurant near Plaza Mayor, serving topnotch Spanish fare (steaks, lamb, eel, etc.) in mesón setting in a maze of small rooms. Personalized service, excellent value. Closed Sat. lunch and Aug. AE, DC, V.

Casa Paco, Puerta Cerrada 11 (tel. 266 3166). This atmospheric old tavern is a perennial favorite and renowned for its steaks. Limited space and there is nearly always a line. Closed Sun. and Aug. DC, V.

El Cuchi, Cuchilleros 3 (tel. 266 4424). A colorful dinner awaits you in this fun-packed mesón with more than just a hint of Mexico to it; just off the Plaza Mayor, and the one place "where Hemingway *didn't* eat." AE, DC, MC, V.

Fuente Real, Fuentes 1 (tel. 248 6613). This stylish restaurant, tucked away between Mayor and Arenal, offers imaginative cuisine and original decor—it's half way between a turn-of-the-century private house and a museum packed with personal mementoes such as antique dolls, Indian figures, and Mexican Christmas decorations.

Hogar Gallego, Plaza Com. Morenas 3 just off Calle Mayor (tel. 542 5826). Galician restaurant specializing in seafood. Outdoor dining in summer. Closed Sun. evening and most of Aug.

Horno de Santa Teresa, Sta. Teresa 12 (tel. 419 0245). Traditional old-style restaurant famous for good service and classic cuisine. Closed Sat. and Aug. AE, DC, V.

House of Ming, Castellana 74 (tel. 261 1013). Excellent Chinese delicacies served up in a luxurious setting. Closed Aug. AE, DC, V.

La Taberna del Alabardero, Felipe V 6 (tel. 247 2577). Alongside the Teatro Real with atmospheric bar and several small dining rooms specializing in Basque and French dishes. Closed late-Aug. AE, DC, MC, V.

La Toja, Siete de Julio 3 (tel. 266 4664). Just off Plaza Mayor and specializing in seafood. A good place to try paella. Opens for dinner at 8. AE, DC, V.

Valentín, San Alberto 3 (tel. 521 1638). Longtime rendezvous of the influential and the famous, from bullfighters to literati. Intimate decor, good service, standard Spanish dishes. Close to Puerta del Sol. AE, DC, MC, V.

Inexpensive

La Bola, Bola 5 (tel. 247 6930). Plenty of old-world charm in this atmospheric restaurant that has been in the same family since the early 1800s. Closed Sun.

El Buda Feliz, Tudescos 5 (tel. 532 4475). Excellent Chinese restaurant near Plaza Callao. AE, DC, MC, V.

Casa Ciriaco, Mayor 84 (tel. 248 0620). An atmospheric old standby where the Madrid of 50 years ago lives on. Closed Wed. and in Aug.

Casa Ricardo, Fernando el Católico 31 (tel. 447 6119). One of Madrid's oldest *tabernas,* boasting bullfighting decor and excellent home-cooking. Closed Sun.

El Granero de Lavapies, on Calle Argumosa 10, near Lavapies metro (tel. 467 7611). Vegetarian restaurant, open for lunch only; closed Sun.

El Luarqués, Ventura de la Vega 16 (tel. 429 6174). Decorated with photos of the picturesque port of Luarca on the north coast, this popular restaurant is always packed with Madrileños who recognize its sheer good value. *Fabada asturiana* and *arroz con leche* among the Asturian specialties on the menu. Closed Sun. evening, Mon., and in Aug.

La Quinta del Sordo, Sacramento 10 (tel. 248 1852). An old favorite just off Calle Mayor, though it's rather overpatronized by budget tour groups. AE, DC.

Restaurante del Palacio de Anglona, Segovia 13 (tel. 266 3753). New fun eating house, open evenings only, and incredibly good value. V.

Terra a Nosa, Cava San Miguel 3 (tel. 247 1175). Typical Galician bistro near Plaza Mayor. Popular and crowded, with bags of atmosphere.

Outside Madrid

The following are all (E) and ideally suited for dinner on a summer's evening:

El Mesón, 13 km. (eight miles) out on C607, the road to Colmenar Viejo (tel. 734 1019). In an attractive rustic setting. AE, DC, MC, V.

Porto Novo, on the N-VI to Galicia, about ten km. (six miles) from Madrid (tel. 207 0173). Closed Sun. night. AE, DC, V.

Rancho Texano, on the N-II to Barcelona at km. 12 (tel. 747 4736). Very popular American steakhouse specializing in charcoal-grilled steaks and Baked Alaska. Closed Sun. evening. AE, DC, MC, V.

Los Remos, on the N-VI to Galicia, at km. 13 (tel. 207 7230). A long-time favorite with Madrileños. Superb fish and seafood, and some meat dishes too. This one is the best. Closed Sun. evening and last 2 weeks in Aug. AE, DC, V.

CAFETERIAS. For snacks a good place to go is one of the numerous cafeterias—by which we do not mean the self-service type of establishment found in the United States and Britain, but rather, smart cafes with table service. Here, you can order sandwiches, pastries, even simple meals, *platos combinados,* etc., and drink from a choice of fruit juices and other soft drinks, coffee—as well as beer, wine and liquor. Cafeterias are open from early in the morning until at least midnight. They are the best place for breakfast and mid-morning coffee, or for a meal outside restaurant hours. Reliable chains with branches all over Madrid are **California, Manila, Morrison** and **Nebraska.**

TRADITIONAL CAFES. Cafe Comercial, Glorieta de Bilbao 7. An old-time cafe that has not changed much over the last three decades; always crowded.

Cafe Gijón. Paseo de Recoletos 21. The best and most famous of the remaining cafes of old. It is still a hangout for writers and artists, carrying on a tradition dating back to the turn of the century, when the cafe was a meeting place of the literati. Tables outside on the main avenue in summer.

Cafe Lyon, Alcalá 57. Charming, old-fashioned decor; just up from Cibeles.

Cafe Metropolitano, Glorieta de Cuatro Caminos. Student atmosphere.

Cafe Viena, Luisa Fernanda 23. Done out like an old-time cafe, you can dine here evenings to the accompaniment of piano music.

The Embassy, corner of Castellana and Ayala. Elegant pastry shop and tearoom with a vast assortment of sandwiches, canapés and pastries.

La Mallorquina, on Puerta del Sol between Mayor and Arenal. An old-world pastry shop with a tea salon, where the incredible, probably doomed, tea ritual is enacted between 6 and 7 P.M.

FAST FOOD. American hamburger joints such as **McDonalds, Burger King** and **Wendy's** have mushroomed in Madrid over the last few years, and can now be found all over the city. In some cases, they have been obliged to keep to the traditional Spanish decor, which makes for some interesting not to say bizarre juxtapositions—the McDonalds on the corner of Montera and Gran Vía, and the Burger King on Arenal just off Puerta del Sol, are especially worth seeing. **Pizza Hut** also has a couple of branches, at Orense 11 and Plaza Santa Barbara 8. **VIPS** is a popular chain of cafes, much patronized by the young of Madrid, that serves hamburgers, club sandwiches, and ice cream into the small hours of the morning. It's Madrid's answer to the drugstore, and branches can be found all over town.

BARS AND CAFES. If you want to spend an enjoyable, typically Spanish, evening, then go bar-hopping in any of the following areas. You'll find many bars and cafes where you can sample the local wine, or have a glass of beer, and choose from any number of tapas. Stylish cafes with old-time piano music or chamber music are also very much in vogue, as are jazz cafes.

The **Plaza Santa Bárbara** area just off Alonso Martínez is currently one of the liveliest nighttime areas. Begin in the plaza itself, then stroll along any of the adjacent streets such as Santa Teresa, Orellana, Campoamor, Fernando VI or Regueros, and you will not be disappointed by the vast range of bars on offer. To mention just a few:

Café de Paris, Sta. Teresa 12. Stylish loud music bar currently very much in vogue.

Café Universal, Fernando VI 13. Very fashionable, serving good cocktails.

Cervecería Internacional, Regueros 8. A must for beer-lovers. A great selection of foreign beers and even a souvenir shop.

Cervecería Santa Bárbara, Plaza Sta. Bárbara 8. Atmospheric and very popular beerhall with a good range of tapas.

Bar Haddok, Orellana 14. Lively modern bar, very crowded at night.

Nicandra, Orellana 1. Smart bar ideal for a pre-dinner drink.

Rebote, Campoamor 13. One of the most popular in the area.

The **Malasaña** area around Bilbao and Fuencarral was the "in" place in the early '80s for Madrid's youth and it still boasts countless interesting cafes and bars open till the small hours around Plaza Dos de Mayo and Calles Ruiz, San Andrés and Vicente Ferrer. However, the area has become the center for Madrid's drug dealers and heroin addicts, and for this reason its popularity is now on the wane and it is best avoided, especially at night.

Not far away on the opposite side of the Glorieta de Bilbao, much of the action has now moved to the **Calle Cardenal Cisneros** which is packed with atmospheric tapa bars; the nighttime scene here is lively and much safer.

The **Huertas** area around Calle de las Huertas, leading from Paseo del Prado to Plaza del Angel, is another lively nighttime locale chockablock with cafes offering folk or chamber music and several colorful tapa bars.

El Elhecho, Huertas 56. Very popular. Turn-of-the-century decor with potted ferns *(elhechos);* evenings there's chamber or piano music.

La Fídula, Huertas 57. Another stylish cafe with (usually chamber) music nightly at 11.

The nearby **Calle Santa María** also has good bars such as **Café Ombu** at no. 3, **Harpo's** at no. 36, and **El Ratón** at no. 42.

The **Orense** development around the Azca Center has proved a magnet for the teenagers and the young of Madrid, who congregate here in the evenings in the many fast-food joints, discos, *whiskerías* and *coctelerías.* It is perhaps not worth making a special trip to, but if your hotel happens to be in the area, and you are young—or young at heart—then you could do worse than take a look.

The traditional mesones area just off **Plaza Mayor** on Cava San Miguel and Calle Cuchilleros has long been famous. Do the rounds of the mesones with names like the **Tortilla, Champiñón, Boquerón, Huevo,** etc., most of them named after their particular specialty, and on a busy night you may well come across someone playing the guitar and singing, or be serenaded by the wandering *tuna* minstrels.

For some of the oldest bars in Madrid, try the streets around the **Rastro.** Here you'll find such durable retreats as the **Mesón de Paredes, Jesús y María, Magdalena, Cascorro,** and **La Esquinita**—the latter, a bar with magnificent tapas, beer served in mugs, and roast chicken. The **Taverna de Antonio Sánchez,** at Mesón de Paredes 13, is an old mesón just off Plaza de Tirso de Molina, that first opened its doors in 1850 and was once a hangout for bullfighters. Its decor includes the head of the bull that killed Antonio Sánchez, son of the owner, and some drawings by Zuloaga.

The old, narrow streets between **Puerta del Sol** and **Plaza Santa Ana** are packed with crowded, colorful tapa bars. Wander along Espoz y Mina, Victoria, Cruz, Núñez de Arce, and Echegaray, and enter any bar that takes your fancy. Don't miss out on the alleyway, Pasaje Matheu, between

Victoria and Espoz y Mina, where there are several favorites. Here are but a handful of the many places on offer:

Cafe Central, Plaza del Angel 10. Atmospheric, old-style cafe with jazz, folk and classical music. Often has live jazz between 10 and midnight.

Cervecería Alemana, Plaza Santa Ana 6. Popular beer hall over 100 years old, originally founded by Germans. Once patronized by (who else?!) Hemingway, and now by tourists.

Cuevas de Sésamo, Príncipe 7. Popular basement piano bar.

Los Gabrieles, Echegaray 17. Magnificent old *bodega* with four bars whose superb ceramic decor has been expertly restored.

La Trucha, Manuel Fernández y González 3. Colorful and atmospheric, with strings of garlic and giant hams hanging from the ceiling. Specialties are *trucha navarra,* trout stuffed with ham and garlic, and *rabo del toro,* bull's tail.

Viva Madrid, Manuel Fernández y González 7. Beautiful old bar, currently one of Madrid's most popular meeting places.

NIGHTLIFE. Since Franco's death, the nightclub scene in Madrid has flung off all restraint and the city now throbs with shows featuring striptease, topless dancers, drag and every kind of no-holds-barred entertainment. Pick-up bars, ranging from the old-time standbys to flashy, elegant new places in the northern Castellana area, have multiplied enormously over recent years. Travelers who knew the tame Spain of a few years ago will be amazed by the change—all censorship has been discarded.

Florida Park, in Retiro Park (tel. 273 7804). Entrance opposite Calle Ibiza. You can have dinner here, and the shows often feature ballet or Spanish dance. Open from 9.30 to 3.30 in the morning, daily except Sun., with shows at 11.

Lola, Costanilla de San Pedro 11 (tel. 265 8801). The newest arrival on the Madrid night scene. Dinner at 9.30 followed by cabaret and dancing till around 4 A.M. The food is vastly superior to most nightclubs and the show has proved very popular.

Madrid's Casino, 28 km. (17 miles) out, on the N-VI road to La Coruña, at Torrelodones (tel. 859 0312). One of the largest casinos in Europe and offering French and American roulette, chemin de fer, baccarat, and blackjack. Three restaurants, six bars, and a nightclub with cabaret. Open 5 P.M. to 4 A.M. Free transportation service from Plaza de España 6.

La Scala, Rosario Pino 7, in Hotel Meliá Castilla (tel. 450 4400). Madrid's top nightclub, with dinner, dancing and cabaret at 8.30, and a second, less expensive, around midnight. Open till 4 A.M.

Discos. These are numerous and very popular in Madrid. Some charge an entrance fee, usually starting around 1,000 ptas., which includes your first drink; others just charge for your drinks. Most have two sessions: *tarde* from around 7.30–10.30, and *noche* from 11.30 onwards. Gay discos and transvestite clubs are also thick on the ground. For a complete listing, read the weekly *Guía del Ocio.* The following are just a few of the better-known ones:

Boccacio, Marqués de la Enseñada 16. A long-standing favorite and still very popular.

Joy Eslava, Arenal 11. Located in the old Teatro Eslava, and one of the liveliest and most popular discos in Madrid. AE, DC, V.

Keeper, Juan Bravo 39. Fashionable discothèque on three floors with all the latest in ultra-modern equipment.

Mau Mau, Padre Damián 23. In the *Hotel Eurobuilding* this is one of Madrid's smartest, and most expensive, discos.

Oh Madrid, Ctra. de la Coruña. Nine km. (five miles) out on the N-VI, this long-popular disco also offers a swimming pool and barbecue; very pleasant on a summer evening.

Pacha, Barceló 11. Another leading contender on the disco scene. Opened in 1980 in the old Teatro Barcelo; decorated like Studio 54 in New York. Open Wed. to Sun. only. AE, V.

Flamenco. Madrid offers the widest choice of flamenco shows in Spain and some of them are very good. While those uninitiated in the art of flamenco will most likely enjoy all the *tablaos,* the connoisseur will be disappointed at the extent to which shows are aimed right at the tourist market. Many clubs employ visiting rather than permanent artistes so quality can be variable. Dining is mostly mediocre, and very overpriced at 4,800–6,500 ptas. a head, but it ensures the best seats. If you are not dining, entrance including one drink varies between 2,000–3,500 ptas. Clubs serving dinner usually open around 9 or 9.30, those offering show only at around 11 P.M. Most clubs stay open until 2 or 3 A.M. Be sure to reserve.

Arco de Cuchilleros, Cuchilleros 7 (tel. 266 5867). Small, intimate club in the heart of old Madrid, just off Plaza Mayor. One of the cheapest and the show is good. No dining. Open 10.30–2.30 with two shows nightly.

Café de Chinitas, Torija 7 (tel. 248 5135). Well-known throughout Spain and abroad with some famous *cuadros.* The show is good, one of the best, and the dinner average. Open 9.30–3.

Los Canasteros, Barbieri 10 (tel. 231 8163). Show and drinks only, no dinner. Open 11–3.30.

Corral de la Morería, Morería 17 (tel. 265 8446). One of the best, owned by the famous Lucero Tena. Serves dinner. Open 9–3.

Corral de la Pacheca, Juan Ramón Jiménez 26 (tel. 458 1113). Right up in the northern part of town. A bit touristy but fun. Folk dancing and *sevillanas* as well as flamenco. Serves dinner. Open 9.30–2.

Torres Bermejas, Mesonero Romanos 11 (tel. 232 3322). Two shows nightly, the first with dinner which is expensive. Performances vary and some flamenco interpretations are not always too authentic. Open 9.30–2.30.

Venta del Gato, Avda. de Burgos 214 (tel. 202 3427). Seven km. (four miles) north on the road to Burgos. Authentic flamenco, and other flamenco dancers among the audience. The show begins at 11.30.

Zambra, Velázquez 8 (tel. 435 5164). A new club opened in 1987 in the Hotel Wellington by the former manager of *Las Brujas.* Smart ambience, jacket and tie are essential, and good show. Dinner is served from 10 P.M. to 4 A.M.

CITY TOURS. Tours of Madrid are run by the following three tour operators: *Pullmantur,* Plaza de Oriente 8 (tel. 241 1807); *Trapsatur,* San Bernardo 23 (tel. 266 9900); and *Juliá Tours,* Gran Vía 68 (tel. 270 4600). All three offer the same tours at the same prices and there is little to choose between them. In high season all tours (except bullfights) operate daily, but in low season the tours may be shared out among the three operators.

Tours are conducted in English as well as Spanish, and if need be, in French and other languages too. You can book your tours direct with the operators at the addresses above, or through any travel agency, or, in most cases, through your hotel. Departure points are from the above addresses, though in some cases you can be collected from your hotel.

Madrid Artístico. Morning tour of Madrid including visits to the Royal Palace and Prado Museum. Entrances included.

Madrid Panorámico. A panoramic drive around the city seeing all the main sights as well as some of the more outlying ones such as the University City, Casa del Campo Park, northern reaches of the Castellana and the Bernabeu soccer stadium. This is an ideal orientation drive for the first-time visitor to Madrid. It is a half-day tour, usually in the afternoons.

Madrid de Noche. This night tour of Madrid is available in various combinations. All begin with a drive through the city to see the illuminations of its monuments and fountains, followed either by dinner in a restaurant and a visit to a flamenco club; or by dinner and cabaret at Madrid's leading nightclub, *La Scala;* or by a visit to both a flamenco show and a nightclub.

Panorámica y Toros. Departures on days when there are bullfights (usually Sundays) 1½ hours before the fight begins. Panoramic tour of the city seeing the most important sights and an explanation of bullfighting before you arrive at the Ventas bullring to watch the *corrida.*

WALKING TOURS. Detailed walking tours of Madrid are run by the city hall but are conducted in Spanish only. For details, pick up a copy of the *Conozcamos Madrid* leaflet from the Municipal Tourist Office at Plaza Mayor 3, or contact the Tourist Office at Señores de Luzón 10 (tel. 248 7426), off Calle Mayor opposite the City Hall. Open Mon. to Sat. 9–1.

EXCURSIONS. Whole- or half-day excursions from Madrid to the places listed below are run by *Pullmantur, Trapsatur* and *Juliá Tours.* (For addresses and points of departure, see above under *City Tours.*) Tours can be booked through your hotel, travel agencies or at the tour operators' headquarters. Below we list only those tours which return to Madrid on the same day. Excursions to places further afield or involving overnight stays are also available; apply to any of the three operators for details.

Aranjuez. Half-day excursion in the afternoon, daily except Tues., Apr. to Oct. only, visiting the Royal Palace, gardens and the Casita del Labrador.

Avila, Segovia, La Granja. Full-day tour driving to Avila to see the medieval city walls, the cathedral and the Convent of Santa Teresa, birthplace of the saint. On to Segovia to see the 2,000-year-old Roman aqueduct, to visit either the cathedral or the alcázar castle, and lunch in a typical restaurant. Return via La Granja, once the summer residence of Spanish kings, to visit the palace and gardens modeled on Versailles. On Mon. the palace of Riofrío will be substituted for La Granja.

Cuenca. Full-day tour, Tues., Thurs. and Sat., May through Oct. Visits to the Enchanted City with its strange rock formations, and to the picturesque city of Cuenca, famous for its hanging houses, and where you will see Plaza Mayor, the cathedral, and the Museums of Archeology and Abstract Art. Lunch included. Book in advance.

Escorial and Valley of the Fallen. Half-day excursion, daily except Mon., visiting the Monastery of the Escorial, including the mausoleum of the Spanish kings since Charles V, and the Valley of the Fallen built to commemorate those who died in Spain's Civil War of 1936–39 and whose basilica houses the tomb of the dictator General Franco.

Rutas Verdes de Madrid. Tours through Madrid's countryside organized by the Madrid tourist authority and run by *Juliá Tours* and *Trapsatur*. Two itineraries operate on alternate Sat. The first route takes in the Sierra de Buitrago, the reservoir of Atazar and Torrelaguna, with a lunch stop in Buitrago. The second one covers La Cabrera, Valle de Lozoya, lunch in Rascafria, Puerto de Cotos and Villalba. Buses leave from outside the Tourist Office on Duque de Medinaceli, just off Plaza de las Cortes. Check availability with the Plaza de España Tourist Office first.

Salamanca and Alba de Tormes. Full-day tour, Mon., Wed. and Fri., May through Sept. Drive via the medieval walls of Avila to Salamanca where you will visit the ancient and prestigious university, the old and new cathedrals, the convents of San Esteban and Las Dueñas, and Spain's most beautiful Plaza Mayor. Then on to Alba de Tormes to visit the Carmelite Convent, which houses the remains of Santa Teresa of Avila. The trip includes lunch; book in advance.

Toledo. Whole- or half-day excursions (morning or afternoon) to this historic city visiting the cathedral, the Chapel of Santo Tomé to see El Greco's *Burial of the Count of Orgaz,* one of the old synagogues, the Church of San Juan de los Reyes, and a sword factory for a demonstration of the typical Toledo damascene work. The full-day tour also includes lunch in a restaurant and a visit to the Hospital de Tavera.

Toledo and Aranjuez. Daily except Tues. Full-day excursion to Toledo visiting places mentioned above (except Tavera), lunch, and on to Aranjuez on the banks of the Tagus, to visit the Royal Palace and the Casita del Labrador, "the laborer's cottage" modeled on the Trianon at Versailles.

Toledo, Escorial and Valley of the Fallen. Full-day excursion, daily except Mon., visiting Toledo (as above), lunch, the monastery of the Escorial and the basilica of the Valley of the Fallen. *Juliá Tours* and *Trapsatur* only.

EXCURSIONS BY RAIL. RENFE runs a popular series of rail trips at weekends in summer, from April through October. One-day excursions, mostly on Sundays and fiestas, include the *Tren de la Fresa* (Strawberry Train) to Aranjuez, the *Tren Murallas de Avila,* and the *Tren Doncel de Sigüenza.* Two-day excursions with departures on Saturdays and one night in a hotel included, are the *Tren de la Mancha, Tren Catedral de Burgos, Tren Plaza Mayor de Salamanca, Tren Ciudad Monumental de Cáceres,* and the *Tren Ciudad Encantada de Cuenca.* They cost 1,350 ptas. for a one-day trip and 10,000 ptas. for 2-day trips (1988 prices). Details from RENFE offices (p. 113) and stations, or call 228 3835 or 227 7058.

MUSEUMS. The opening times given below hold good at time of writing, but are subject to frequent change, so do check before making a journey. Most Madrid museums have different schedules for winter and summer months. *Patrimonio Nacional* (i.e. state-owned) museums are free to Spaniards with I.D., but make an entrance charge to visitors from abroad.

Museo del Aire (Air Museum), ten km. (six miles) out, on Paseo de Extremadura. Collection of planes and mementos illustrating the history of aviation and housed in Escuela de Transmisiones. Open Tues. to Sun. 10–2; closed Mon.

Museo de América (Americas Museum), Reyes Católicos 6. Excellent displays of Inca and Quinbaya treasures. Open Tues. to Sun. 10–7; closed Mon.

Museo Arqueológico Nacional (Archeology Museum), Serrano 13. Admirable collection including some particularly fine Greek vases and Roman artifacts, 180,000 coins, a good ceramics collection, the treasures of Iberian Spain—among them, the famous Dama de Elche and the Dama Ofrente del Cerro de los Santos—and a large display of medieval art and furniture. In its gardens you can visit a replica of the Altamira Caves, of particular interest now that exploration of the original is strictly limited. Open Tues. to Sun. 9–1.30; closed Mon.

Museo de Carruajes (Royal Coach Museum), Paseo Vírgen del Puerto. Can be visited on an individual ticket or on an all-inclusive ticket to the Royal Palace. Open Tues. to Sat., 10–12.45 and 3.30–5.15 in winter, 10–12.45 and 4–5.45 in summer; Sun. and fiestas 10–1.30 only. Closed Mon. and when official functions taking place in the Royal Palace.

Museo de Cera (Wax Museum), Paseo de Recoletos 41. One of the better examples of this specialized genre, with panels of scenes and personages out of Spanish history, as well as personalities ranging from Gary Cooper to President Kennedy. Open Mon. to Sun. 10.30–2 and 4–9.

Museo Cerralbo, Ventura Rodríguez 17. Tapestries, paintings, and some of the loveliest old porcelain to be seen anywhere, housed in the Cerralbo mansion. A good place to see the aristocratic setting of a turn-of-the-century villa. Open Tues. to Sat. 10–2 and 4–7, Sun. 10–2; closed Mon. and in Aug.

Museo de Ciencias Naturales (Natural Science Museum), Paseo de la Castellana 80. Zoological, geological and entomological collections. Open daily 9–2; closed Aug.

Museo del Ejército (Army Museum), Méndez Núñez 1. Vast but well-labeled collection of trophies, weapons and documents from wars in Europe and America, with a special section dedicated to the Civil War. Open Tues. to Sun. 10–2; closed Mon.

Museo de Escultura al Aire Libre (Openair Sculpture Museum). Situated beneath the overpass where Juan Bravo meets the Castellana. Contains the well-known *Sirena Varada* by Chillida.

Museo Español de Arte Contemporáneo (Museum of Contemporary Spanish Art), Avda. Juan de Herrera in the University City. Modern art and sculpture, with 375 paintings and 200 sculptures—including works by Picasso and Miró—set in pleasant gardens. Open Tues. to Sat. 10–6, Sun. 10–3; closed Mon.

Museo del Ferrocarril (Railroad Museum), Paseo de las Delicias 61 in the old Delicias station. Open Tues. to Sat. 10–5; Sun. and fiestas 10–2; closed Mon.

Museo Lázaro Galdiano, Serrano 122. One of the "musts" of Madrid, this museum is housed in an old, aristocratic mansion, and—besides containing a magnificent collection of paintings, furniture, clocks, armor, weapons, jewels, and artifacts—is a delight thanks to the tasteful arrangement of its treasures. There is a sizable collection of English paintings and the best display in Europe of ivory and enamel, as well as works by El

Greco, Zurbarán, Velázquez and Goya. Open Tues. to Sun. 10–2; closed Mon.

Museo Municipal (Municipal Museum), Fuencarral 78. Several rooms depicting Madrid's past, including a model of the city as it was in 1830. Open Tues. to Sat. 10–2 and 5–9; Sun. 10–2.30; closed Mon. and fiestas.

Museo Nacional de Artes Decorativas (National Museum of Decorative Art), Montalbán 12. Interesting collection of Spanish ceramics, gold and silver ornaments, glass, textiles, embroidery, furniture, and domestic utensils. Open Tues. to Fri. 10–3; Sat., Sun. and fiestas 10–2; closed Mon. and July through Sept.

Museo Nacional de Etnología (Ethnological Museum), Alfonso XII 68. Primitive artifacts and weapons from the Philippines, Africa, Asia and America, with several interesting mummies. Open Tues. to Sat. 10–2 and 4–7; Sun. 10–2; closed Mon. and Aug.

Museo Naval (Navy Museum), Montalbán 2. Ship models, nautical instruments, etc., with two rooms dedicated to the Battle of Lepanto and to the Discovery of America. The most famous exhibit is Juan de Cosa's original map, used by Columbus on his first voyage to the New World. Open Tues. to Sun. 10.30–1.30; closed Mon.

Museo del Prado, Paseo del Prado. The Prado is one of the world's greatest art collections. If your time is limited, the most priceless treasures—Velázquez, El Greco, Murillo, Zurbarán, and most Goyas—are one floor up and can be reached directly by a flight of steps from the outside, thus bypassing the ground floor and, incidentally, the long lines that often form at the lower entrance. Once inside, you have access to both floors, though not necessarily to special exhibitions which are charged separately. The Prado is always unbearably crowded, especially at weekends. Its modernization program involving the installation of airconditioning and better lighting is now well under way, but until it is completed some works are not on show while others have been moved to temporary locations and may be difficult to find. Open Tues. to Sat. 9–7, Sun. 9–2; closed Mon.

Admission to the Prado also includes entrance to the **Cason del Buen Retiro** annex, home of 19th-century Spanish painting and of Picasso's *Guernica* (entrance to latter is round the back in Alfonso XII). If you can't visit both on the same day, hang on to your ticket as it will still be valid for the part you haven't seen. Open same hours as Prado.

Another Prado annex, the **Palacio de Villahermosa,** Pza. de las Cortes 6, diagonally opposite the Prado across Pza. Cánovas del Castillo, is the new home of the great art collection of Baron Thyssen-Bornemisza, which the Baron loaned to Spain in 1988. Open same hours as Prado.

Museo Romántico (Romantic Museum), San Mateo 13. Designed and decorated like a 19th-century palace with paintings, furnishings and *objets d'art* from 1830–68. Open Tues. to Sat. 10–6, Sun. 10–2; closed Mon. and Aug.

Museo Sorolla, General Martínez Campos 37. The famous painter's house with a number of his works, as well as a good collection of popular art and sculpture. Open Tues. to Sun. 10–2; closed Mon.

Museo Taurino (Bullfighting Museum), Ventas Bullring at the end of Calle Alcalá. Bullfighting paraphernalia. Open Tues. to Sun. 9–3; closed Mon.

Real Academia de Bellas Artes de San Fernando (Fine Arts Academy), Alcalá 13. Splendid collection of works by great Spanish masters—Velázquez, El Greco, Murillo, Zurbarán, Ribera, and Goya. Open Tues. to Sat. 9–7; Sun. and Mon. 9–2.

PLACES OF INTEREST. Casa de Lope de Vega, Cervantes 11. The great playwright's house and garden, skilfully restored. Open Tues. and Thurs. 10–2; closed mid-July through mid-Sept.

Centro de Arte de Reina Sofía, Santa Isabel 52, off the Plaza Atocha. Huge art center in a converted 18th-century hospital. Leading art and sculpture exhibitions. Open daily, except Tues., 10 A.M.–9 P.M.

Ermita de San Antonio de la Florida and Goya Pantheon, Glorieta de San Antonio de la Florida. The hermitage dates from the end of the 18th century and was built by order of Charles IV. The ceiling of the church is covered in frescos by Goya of respectable court officials hobnobbing with less respectable ladies, though they are dimly lit. The church is now a kind of museum to Goya, and the artist's headless body is buried here. He died in France in 1828 and 60 years later his body, minus its head, was exhumed and brought to rest in Spain. Open 10–1 and 4–7 in summer; 11–1.30 and 3–6 in winter; closed Wed. and Sun. P.M.

Monasterio de las Descalzas Reales, Plaza de las Descalzas Reales 3. A 16th-century convent with superb and lavish ornamentation and a veritable wealth of jewels and religious ornaments, paintings including one by Zurbarán, and famous Flemish tapestries based on designs by Rubens. It won the European Museum of the Year award in 1988. Part of the building is still used as a convent. The entrance ticket (free to E.E.C. nationals) also includes a visit to the Monastery of the Incarnation not far away (see below). Open Tues. to Thurs. and Sat. 10.30–12.30 and 4–5.15; Fri. 10.30–12.30; Sun. and fiestas 11–1.15; closed Mon.

Monasterio de la Encarnación, Plaza de la Encarnación. Begun in 1611, this convent contains hundreds of paintings and frescos, but is in fact less interesting than the Descalzas Reales. Open Tues., Wed., Thurs. and Sat. 10.30–12.45 and 4–5.30; Fri. 10.30–12.45 only; Sun. and fiestas 11–1.15; closed Mon. Can only be visited on guided tours; free to E.E.C. nationals, and to everyone on Wed.

Palacio de Liria, Princesa 20. Contains an immense wealth of paintings by many great European masters, including Titian and Rembrandt, and a portrait by Goya of the 13th Duchess of Alba, believed to have been the model for his famous paintings in the Prado of *La Maja Vestida* and *La Maja Desnuda.* The palace can be visited by applying in writing in advance. Twelve of its rooms are open to the public. The guide who takes visitors round, though very informative, speaks only Spanish. Open Sat. only; closed Aug.

Palacio de El Pardo, in the village of El Pardo, 15 km. (nine miles) from Madrid. El Pardo is surrounded by woods which were much favored by the kings of Spain as hunting grounds. The palace was begun originally in the 15th century, but was mostly built by Sabatini during the reign of Charles III. It contains works by Titian, Bosch and Coello. The home of Franco from 1940 until his death in 1975, much of it now stands as a museum to that period of Spanish history. Open Mon. to Sat. 10–1 and 4–7, Sun. 10–1.

Palacio Real, Plaza de Oriente. The Royal Palace was begun in the reign of Charles III. Entrance is through the vast courtyard on the left of the palace, and then through the door to the right of the courtyard. Guided tours are compulsory. Admission varies depending on how much you want to see; you can visit just the State Apartments—or buy an all-inclusive ticket that includes the Royal Armory, Royal Library, Royal Pharmaceutical Dispensary and Coach Museum. Open Mon. to Sat., 9.30–12.45 and 3.30–5.15 in winter, 9.30–12.45 and 4–6 in summer; Sun. and fiestas 9.30–1.30. The palace is closed to the public when in use for official functions.

Real Basílica de San Francisco el Grande, Plaza de San Francisco. Madrid's most outstanding church. Open daily 11–1 and 4–7.

Real Fábrica de Tapices, Fuenterrabiá 2. A visit to the workshops of the Royal Tapestry Factory is recommended, and includes entrance to their exhibition of tapestries. Open Mon. to Fri. 9.30–12.30; closed Sat., Sun., fiestas and Aug.

Temple of Debod, in the Parque del Oeste. An ancient Egyptian temple given by the Egyptian government to Spain when its original site was flooded by the construction of the Aswan Dam. Open Mon. to Sat. 10–1 and 5–8, Sun. and fiestas 10–3.

PARKS AND GARDENS. Jardín Botánico, to the south of the Prado, between Paseo del Prado and Retiro Park. First opened in 1781. Over 30,000 different species from all over the world. Open daily 10–8.

Casa del Campo, across the Manzanares from the Royal Palace. Formerly the royal hunting grounds, the land was first acquired by Philip II in 1599. Shady walks, lakeside cafe, rowing boats on the lake, sports center (with pool), jogging track, zoo and amusement park, among the attractions. To reach the park, take subway to El Lago or Batan, or bus 33 from Plaza de Isabel II, or—the best idea—cablecar from Paseo Rosales.

Parque del Oeste, on western edge of Madrid, off Paseo del Pintor Rosales. A pleasant park containing the Temple of Debod and a pretty rose garden.

Parque del Retiro. This shady, once-Royal, retreat *(retiro)* makes the perfect refuge from Madrid's relentless heat. Embellished with statues and fountains, and a beautiful rose garden, the park is at its liveliest Sunday mornings with buskers, puppet theaters, and much of Madrid out strolling. You can hire a boat on the lagoon known as El Estanque or visit the temporary exhibitions held in the Crystal Palace or the Palacio de Velázquez.

MUSIC, MOVIES AND THEATERS. Music. The main concert hall is the old *Opera,* or *Teatro Real* as it is also known, located opposite the Royal Palace. Weekly concerts are given here, Oct. through Apr., by the Spanish National Orchestra and the National Radio and TV Orchestra, often under visiting conductors. Opera and ballet are also performed here Oct. to July.

The other main concert hall is the restored *Teatro Lírico Nacional de la Zarzuela* whose ground plan is identical to that of *La Scala* in Milan. An annual opera season is held here, so too are zarzuela performances, a colorful combination of operetta and folk dance.

Other concert venues include the *Sala Fenix,* Castellana 33, the *Salón del Ateneo,* Prado 21, and the *Fundación Juan March,* Castelló 77.

For program details, starting times and ticket prices, see the daily paper, *El País,* or the weekly leisure magazine, *Guía del Ocio,* available from newsstands all over Madrid.

Movies. Most foreign films shown in Spain are dubbed into Spanish, but there are about half a dozen cinemas in Madrid showing films in their original language with Spanish subtitles. Consult the local press, *El País* or *Guía del Ocio,* where these films will be marked "v.o." for *version original. El País* also lists cinemas showing subtitled films. A good cinema to try for films in English is the *Alphaville* (with four screens, entrance on Martín de los Heros) just off Plaza España. The official *Filmoteca* showing different films each day, always in their original language with Spanish subtitles, is in the Cine Torre, Princesa 1 just off the Plaza de España. Most movie houses have three performances a day at roughly 4.30, 7.30 and 10.30. Tickets cost 400–500 ptas. Madrid's International Cinema Festival, IMAGFIC, is held each year in March or April; details from the IMAGFIC office, Gran Vía 62 (tel. 241 5545).

Theaters. If your Spanish is not very good, the legitimate theater is likely to be a complete loss to you. However, you won't need Spanish to enjoy a *zarzuela* or a musical revue. They're good fun. The best bet for non-Spanish-speaking visitors is the *Zarzuela,* Jovellanos 4, where you may see the top dance groups, operas, operetta and, of course, *zarzuela,* if it's the season. The *Teatro Español* at Príncipe 25, on Plaza Santa Ana, shows Spanish classics, and the *Teatro María Guerrero,* Tamayo y Baus 4, the home of the state-sponsored *Centro Dramático Nacional,* regularly shows interesting plays. The *Centro Cultural de la Villa de Madrid,* the underground theater on Plaza Colón, is an exciting contemporary theater.

Most theaters in Madrid have two curtains, at 7 and 10.30 P.M. They close one day during the week, usually Mon. Tickets are inexpensive and on the whole easy to obtain. With a few exceptions it is not at all unusual to buy tickets on the night of the performance. Details of plays are listed in *El País* and in *Guía del Ocio.*

SPORTS. Bullfighting comes first to mind, though most Spaniards would not wish to see it classified as a sport. Madrid has two main rings, so be careful you get the right one. If you have the opportunity during your stay, try to visit the big Ventas bullring, which seats 25,000. A smaller bullring is the Vista Alegre in the Carabanchel Bajo region across the Manzanares river. The bullfighting season in Madrid runs from April through October. There's almost always a fight Sundays, and often on Thursdays, too. Tickets can be bought in advance from Calle de la Victoria, off Carrera San Jerónimo, or at the bullring itself on the afternoon of the fight. The average Sunday *corridas* are now little more than a tourist spectacle—and not very good at that—but if you are intent on seeing a really good fight, try to be in Madrid around the middle of May during the San Isidro festivals; this will be your chance to witness some of the best fights in Spain, and tickets may well be hard to obtain.

Pelota is a peculiarly Spanish game. It is the hardest, fastest ball game in the world. It is also a betting game, in which you get fast action for your money. If you want to try your luck, place your bet on Red or Blue and trust to luck. The handiest pelota court in Madrid is the Frontón Madrid, at Dr Cortezo 10, though it was closed for renovation at presstime.

Football (soccer) is Spain's number one sport and has far surpassed pelota or even bullfighting in popularity. It may be seen between September and May in the huge Santiago Bernabéu Stadium on the Castellana, home of Real Madrid, which holds 130,000 spectators, or in the Vicente Calderón Stadium, home of Madrid Atlético, near the Manzanares river. If you want to see **basketball** or even **baseball** (it's not unknown in Spain), check with your hotel porter on games that may be scheduled—depending of course, on the season. **Horse races** take place at the Hipodromo de la Zarzuela, on the Ctra de La Coruña, except in the summer months. **Car racing** at the Jarama Track, on the road to Burgos.

If you want exercise yourself, there is a fashionable and luxurious **golf** club, the Real Club de la Puerta de Hierro, on the Carretera de El Pardo. (Membership fees are prohibitively high, however.) Golf de Somosaguas, beside the Casa del Campo park, tel. 212 1647. Also Nuevo Club de Golf, at Las Matas at km. 26 on the Coruña highway, tel. 630 0820. For latter, membership not required, only a club card made out by your hotel. Club has pick-up service. There are plenty of places to **swim**—several of the 4- and 5-star hotels have pools, or you could try the Piscina El Lago, Avda. de Valladolid 37 or the Piscina Municipal, Avda. del Angel in Casa de Campo. You can play **tennis** also at the golf club, or at Casa del Campo, which has 15 all-weather courts.

Ice skating is at the Real Club in the Ciudad Deportiva, Paseo de la Castellana 259. There are two sessions daily, 11–1.45 and 5–11.45, and skates can be hired.

Greyhound racing is at the Canódromo Madrileño; buses leave from the Plaza Ramales. For **rowing,** there is the lake in the Retiro Park and the lake in the Casa de Campo, a much larger park across the Manzanares. In the winter, there is **skiing** in the sierra at Navacerrada. For **flying** enthusiasts, there exists the Royal Aero Club, with its airport at Cuatro Vientos; offices are at Carrera San Jerónimo 19.

SHOPPING. The large number of well-stocked stores sell everything imaginable. The glittering curio shops with their wares piled helter-skelter on dusty shelves, the richness and abundance of authentic works of art and, above all, the love and pride with which local goods are manufactured, make shopping in Madrid one of the chief attractions for anyone visiting this booming capital. Prices for clothes and shoes are generally higher than in the U.S. or Britain.

Main Shopping Areas. Madrid has two main shopping areas. The first is in the center of town where the principal shopping streets are Gran Vía, the Calles de Preciados, del Carmen and Montera and Puerta del Sol. The second, and more elegant area—and naturally more expensive—is in the Salamanca district bounded by Serrano, Goya and Conde de Peñalver. A fashionable boutique area is growing up around Calle Argensola off Calle de Génova. In the north of town the Azca Center betwen Calle Orense and the Castellana is a recent shopping development. The latest shopping center is *La Vaguada* or *Madrid 2,* in the northern suburbs. With 350 shops, two department stores, several cinemas, restaurants and cafes, it is well worth a visit and can be reached on the metro to Barrio del Pilar.

Department Stores. On the whole, visitors will generally find the best bargains in the department stores, in anything from souvenirs to furniture. Moreover, chances are you'll feel more at ease picking through the counters at your own speed than struggling to make yourself understood with the small shopkeepers. The department stores listed below all provide interpreter service for foreign clients, currency exchange desks (open when banks are closed), shipping services, and they operate tax refund plans for foreigners, though you'll need to spend 48,000 ptas. on any one item before refunds can apply.

Galerías Preciados is the longest-established department store in Madrid. Ask for its *Passport Service Card* at the Client Service Department which entitles foreign visitors to 10% discount on most purchases. Its main building is on Plaza Callao, right off the Gran Vía. Within the two seven-story buildings you'll find almost anything you may need. Another *Galerías* branch is located on Calle Arapiles near the Glorieta de Quevedo, and still another on Calle Goya, corner Conde de Peñalver. A few years ago *Galerías Preciados* took over the old *Sear's* department store on Calle Serrano, corner of Ortega y Gasset, and a brand new store is now open at La Vaguada. The Callao branch of *Galerías* is highly recommended for tourist souvenirs. Also outstanding are the Spanish ceramics, rugs, glassware and other handicrafts. Remains open throughout lunchtime.

El Corte Inglés in many ways is similar to *Galerías* and is its main competitor. There are four *Corte Ingleses* in Madrid: Calle Preciados, right near the Puerta del Sol; another one at the corner of Goya and Alcalá (also near the Goya *Galerías*); a third in the Urbanización Azca between the Castellana and Orense; and the fourth on the corner of Calle Princesa and Calle Alberto Aguilera. All have cafeterias. Quality of wares at the *Corte Inglés* is somewhat higher than that of *Galerías*. Best bet here, perhaps, are their leather goods. Remains open throughout lunchtime. The Preciados branch is probably the best. The Client Service Department for tax refunds and tourist discounts is on the 3rd floor.

Celso Garcia is a smaller, more intimate department store on Calle Serrano, corner of Ayala. Its goods tend to be of a higher quality and more exclusive taste. There is a huge new branch in the Azca shopping center on the Castellana.

Special Shopping Areas. One of the most interesting and colorful of the Madrid shopping areas is one you should save for a Sunday morning. It's the **Rastro** or Flea Market, which stretches down Ribera de Curtidores from El Cascorro statue, and extends over a maze of little side streets branching out from either side. Here, on a Sunday morning, you'll see an incredible display of secondhand odds and ends, spread out on blankets on the ground.

The central area, Curtidores, is more traditional. Here canvas booths have been set up to sell everything under the sun. Most of these, though, are cheap articles which are of little interest to the tourist, except for picture-taking.

If you want to try your hand at bargaining (which is a must here), there are booths selling everything conceivable. Buy with care, though, and don't carry money exposed. *Serious warning:* This place is an infamous hangout for pickpockets, who take advantage of the crowd's pushing and jostling. Women should leave pocketbooks behind and no one should take their passports or more money than they would mind losing.

From a buyer's viewpoint, the most interesting part of the Rastro is a series of galleries which line the street behind the booths. In dark shops built around picturesque patios, you can find all the antique dealers of Madrid represented. These shops, unlike the booths, are open all week during regular shopping hours, as well as on Sunday mornings. Here you can find old paintings and wood carvings, porcelain, furniture and jewelry. Also, in the *Nuevas Galerías,* Shop 45, you'll find a lapidary with unset precious, semi-precious and imitation gems which are well worth a look.

If you are a **stamp collector,** don't miss the *Stamp Fair,* held each Sunday and holiday morning from about 10 to 2 under the archways of Plaza Mayor.

Secondhand books can be bought all year round from the bookstalls on Cuesta Claudio Moyano, near Atocha railroad station. With a little browsing, you'll find curiosities and first editions. And if you're in Madrid at the end of May and the beginning of June, you can visit the National Book Fair, held in the Retiro Park from 10 A.M. to 10 P.M. daily. Here, Spanish booksellers offer both their newest releases and old standards—all at a 10% discount.

For **handicrafts** and **Toledo ware,** you will find literally hundreds of shops all over Madrid, many of which are reliable, some less so. Try the department stores first, particularly the *Corte Inglés* and *Galerías Preciados.* Then you might try *Artespaña,* the official Spanish government handicraft shop. They have branches at Gran Vía 32, Hermosilla 14 and Plaza de las Cortes 3. They have a wonderful assortment of all things Spanish— wood carvings, handwoven rugs, embroidered tablecloths, Majorcan glassware, attractive stone ornaments for gardens and rustic Spanish furniture. *Artespaña* will ship goods throughout the world, but be prepared for some high prices.

Toledo wares are particularly good at *Artesanía Toledana,* Paseo del Prado, and at *El Escudo de Toledo,* next door on Plaza Cánovas del Castillo. In both these stores you'll find a large selection of daggers, swords, chess boards, paintings, fans, Lladró porcelain, guns and leather wine bottles. For **Granada wares,** marquetry, inlaid mother of pearl and so on, try *Artesanía Granadina,* Marqués de Casa Riera.

Ceramics are a time-honored Spanish craft. Among the best examples are the exquisitely colored Manises lustrous glaze from Valencia, the blue and green designs from Granada, and the blue and yellow Talavera pottery and pretty greens from Puente del Arzobispo. They can be found in most of the large department stores where you can also find the famous Lladró porcelain. These delicate figures are made in the Lladró factory at Tabernes Blances just to the north of Valencia. Below are just one or two of the many shops you might try:

Original Hispana (O.H.1), Maestro Guerrero 1 behind the Hotel Plaza in Plaza de España. A vast and excellent display of Lladró.

Cántaro, Flor Baja 8 just off Gran Vía, specializes in ceramics from all over Spain and ironwork.

The following areas are good for **antiques:** the Rastro, Calle del Prado, Carrera de San Jerónimo, Plaza de las Cortes, Plaza de Santa Ana.

For **fans,** try either the department stores or, for really superb examples, try the long-established *Casa de Diego* Puerta del Sol.

Shoes. A chapter apart are Spanish shoes for both men and women. You'll find them made of sturdy yet flexible leather, handcrafted in the latest styles and colors. The Spanish last is long and narrow so be very sure of trying your choice on carefully. Prices have gone up considerably, so unless shoes are very comfortable, don't buy them. Take a stroll along Gran Vía, San Jerónimo or Calle Serrano, where numerous shoe shops vie for attention.

Books. An excellent bookshop for maps and guidebooks is the *Librería Franco Española,* Gran Vía 54. For books in English, go to *Booksellers, S.A.,* José Abascal 48 (tel. 442 7959) or *Turner's English Bookshop,* Génova 3 (tel. 410 2915).

USEFUL ADDRESSES. Embassies. *American Embassy,* Serrano 75 (tel. 276 3600). *British Embassy,* Fernando el Santo 16 (tel. 419 1528/0208).

Police station. To report lost passports, stolen purses, etc., go to the police station at Calle de los Madrazo 9 (tel. 221 9350).

Main post office. Plaza de Cibeles. Open *for stamps:* Mon. to Fri. 9–10; Sat. 9–8; Sun. 10–1. *Telephones, telex, telegrams:* Mon. to Fri. 8–midnight, Sat., Sun. 8 A.M.–10 P.M.

Main telephone office. Gran Vía 30 on the corner of Valverde. Open 24 hours.

Car hire. The most central offices of the main car-hire firms are: *Avis,* Gran Vía 60 (tel. 248 4203); *Europcar,* San Leonardo 8 (tel. 241 8892); *Hertz,* San Leonardo, corner of Maestro Guerrero just off Plaza de España (tel. 248 5803); *Ital,* Princesa 1 (tel. 241 2290). Central reservation numbers are *Atesa* (450 2062); *Avis* (457 9706); *Budget* (279 3400); *Europcar* (456 6013); *Hertz* (242 1000); *Ital* (402 1034).

Laundromats. *Lavomatic,* Bernardo López García 9 (tel. 241 5569), and *Lavomatic Electrodom,* Canillas 68 (tel. 416 1047), are both self-service coin-operated launderettes. *Yulienka,* on Calle Conde Duque, will do your washing and ironing for you.

Left-luggage facilities. *Estación Sur de Autobuses,* Canarias 17. There are coin-operated luggage lockers at Chamartín station and the underground Plaza Colón air terminal. Colón has the largest lockers.

Lost property. For items lost in city buses, Alcántara 26; in taxis, Alberto Aguilera 20; in the metro, the lost and found at Cuatro Caminos station.

American Express, Plaza de las Cortes 2 (tel. 429 7943/5775). Open Mon. to Fri. 9–5.30 and Sat. 9–12. American Express cash machine outside. Emergency numbers: 279 6200 or 459 9009.

Emergency phone numbers. Police 091; fire brigade 080; ambulances 230 7145 or 734 4794 (Red Cross).

Airline offices. *Iberia* has several offices around the city, the main ones being at Velázquez 130 (tel. 261 9100), Princesa 2 (tel. 248 6683) and Plaza de Cánovas del Castillo 5 (tel. 429 7443). The latter is perhaps the principal office and is the one you should go to if you are having problems with luggage lost on an Iberian flight. It is open Mon. to Fri. 9–7, Sat. 9–2. Ticket purchases on Sun. must be made at the airport. For 24-hour flight arrival and departure information, call *Inforiberia* on 411 2545. For international reservations, call 411 2011 (30 lines), and for national reservations call 411 1011, 8 A.M.–10 P.M. Iberia's general switchboard number is 585 8585.

British Airways is at Avda. Palma de Mallorca 43, 1st floor (tel. 431 7575), and Princesa 1 in the Torre de Madrid (tel. 248 7544/9574/2065). Open Mon. to Fri. 9–5 only. The B.A. sales office at Barajas is open daily 9–7. *TWA* is at Pza. Colón 2 (tel. 410 6012/6512/6007,8,9). Open Mon. to Fri. 9–5.30. TWA ticket sales office at airport is open daily 8–4. *Pan Am* is at Gran Vía 88 (tel. 241 4200/248 8535) beside the Plaza Hotel.

Colonia Güell—Gaudí

BARCELONA

The Catalan Capital

Barcelona, capital of Catalonia (Catalunya to the native Catalan speakers), is Spain's second largest city, with a population of over 3 million. It has long rivaled, even surpassed, Madrid in industrial muscle, business acumen, and as a leading cultural center. Though Madrid has now well and truly taken on the mantle of capital city, Barcelona has relinquished none of its former prowess and is currently in the throes of a massive building program in eager anticipation of the big event of 1992, its long-cherished goal of hosting the Olympic Games. It is also justly proud of its cultural heritage. For long Spain's most liberal and progressive city—the home of Gaudi, Miró, and, for a time, Picasso—Barcelona can claim Spain's only opera house and acknowledges with pride the contributions to the arts of native Catalans such as Pau (Pablo in Spanish) Cassals, the surrealist Salvador Dali, actor and director Nuria Espert, and opera singers Montserrat Caballe and Josep Carrers. The city also boasts of one of the world's most glamorous soccer clubs and a fashion industry hard on the heels of those in Milan and Paris. The natural excitement and drive of the city and its natives is summed up in the slogan for the 1992 Olympics—*Barcelona, Mes que Mai* ("Barcelona, more than ever").

Through the centuries Catalans, and especially the citizens of Barcelona, have forged a reputation for themselves in industriousness while remaining appreciative of the pleasures of life. Like the Basques, they take great pride in their own culture. The Catalan language (they will argue fiercely that it is *not* a dialect of Spanish Castilian or French) is commonly spoken in most households, more now than in the thirty-five years when

it was outlawed by the Franco regime. You will hear people speaking Catalan in the streets and shops, schooling is in Catalan, plays are put on in
Catalan, a newspaper is printed in that language, and there is a Catalan
radio and television station.

Though no-one would begrudge the Catalans the increasing use of their
language after almost four decades of repression, the tremendous zeal with
which this fiercely nationalistic people have embraced the legalization of
their own tongue has led to some confusion for the foreign tourist and
indeed for many non-Catalan speaking Spaniards (some 40% of Barcelona's population are not native Catalan speakers and the language barrier
has proved a big obstacle for the large migrant workforce from Andalusia).
Barcelona's streets are now known by both their Catalan and Castilian
names and the visitor with no knowledge of Spanish may encounter some
difficulty in relating the street name plaques to his street map.

The ordered cosmopolitanism of Barcelona will immediately be evident
to the tourist as he explores the city. Many streets are cobbled and lined
with trees as in France, and there are French-type cafés with glass-
enclosed terraces in the winter which invite you to while away an hour.
Drivers tend to be more careful than in Madrid, "zebra" crossings for pedestrians are usually respected and red lights not jumped. The food, too,
is essentially different from Madrid's. You'll often be served more imaginative dishes and desserts than in the rest of the Peninsula. Tea rooms and
pastry shops reminiscent of France and Germany lure afternoon idlers in
the elegant section of town. This polish, however, goes hand in hand with
a taste for local specialties in the portside taverns; the *paella* here rivals
any made in Valencia.

The city lies between two mountains, Tibidabo and Montjuïc, but
sprawls a good deal, so you will find yourself resorting to taxis, buses or
the Metro (subway). The Ramblas, the traditional main street, continues
to be a hive of activity at all hours of the day and night, but no really centralized section can be pinpointed; cinemas, clubs and restaurants are scat-
tered all around the city. The Passeig de Gràcia perhaps comes closest
to being an entertainment and shopping nexus.

As a large port city, there are the seamier sides as well, which makes
for greater diversity and contrasts than in cities of the interior. You can
opt for the luxury shops and restaurants on and off the Passeig de Gràcia
or plunge into the backstreet turmoil of the ancient quarter known as the
Barrio Gótico (Gothic Quarter).

The climate of Barcelona is extremely mild. In summer, weather can
be uncomfortably hot and muggy, and air-pollution is a mounting problem. Beaches near Barcelona are not recommended for bathers who value
their health, but north on the Costa Brava and south at Castelldefels and
Sitges, well-equipped but overcrowded resorts provide escape-valves.

A Little History

Barcelona's history dates back to its founding by the Phoenicians. This
Greek colony was subsequently occupied by the Carthaginians in 237 B.C.,
who called it Barcino (after the ruling House of Barca). Later the Romans
changed its name to Julia Faventia Augusta Pia Barcino and made it the
capital of the Roman province of Layetania. After a spell as capital of the
Goths, it was conquered in 713 by the Moors, who in turn were ousted

by the Franks. Under the Counts of Barcelona, starting in 874, the city attained its independence.

In the 11th century, Ramón Berenguer I compiled a sort of constitution, the *Usatges,* which proclaimed the region's autonomy and sovereignty, but in 1137 Catalonia became part of Aragón. During the 14th and 15th centuries the city prospered immensely thanks to its maritime trade, for Aragón then ruled over such Mediterranean colonies as the Balearics, Sardinia, and the Kingdom of Naples and Sicily. Finally, in 1474 when Isabella of Castile married Ferdinand of Aragón, Barcelona became part of united Spain, and ceased to be a capital.

However, the tradition of independence has always remained uppermost in the life of Catalans and on numerous occasions over the past centuries the region has revolted against the central authority of Madrid. Catalans have jealously guarded their language and culture and still only reluctantly think of themselves as Spaniards.

During the Civil War, Barcelona was a stronghold of the Republic, and base for many anarchists and communists. It resisted the approach of Franco's troops till very nearly the end of the conflict. Franco rigorously suppressed Catalan separatism and the Catalan language. But since the establishment of regional autonomy in 1979, the Catalans have been making headway in reinstating their customs and language. In 1980 Catalans voted for their first home-rule parliament since the Civil War and both then, and at the 1984 and 1988 elections, the Catalan Nationalist Party, led by Jordi Pujol, won a majority.

Exploring Barcelona

Barcelona offers the tourist a great variety of sights ranging from some excellent museums to the weird architectural vagaries of Antonio Gaudí, the leading figure in Barcelona's *art nouveau* movement which gripped the city from 1880 till the outbreak of World War I, and was known locally as *"Modernismo."* A good spot to start your wanderings is the Plaça de Catalunya, the large, somewhat amorphous square which is the intersection of several important streets.

The Ramblas

If you leave the Plaça de Catalunya by way of the Ramblas, you reach a section of the city which is a fascinating amalgam of earthy taverns and atmospheric squares and alleys. The Ramblas, which changes its name every block or so, is a lively, thronged promenade flanked by trees, running through the center of this area. It is lined with bookshops, flower stalls, and stands crammed with bird cages and fish tanks and is one of the most colorful streets in the whole country. The traffic roars down either side of it, while the middle section is happily still devoted to the needs of pedestrians. The Ramblas is always bustling with an endless stream of browsers, tourists, sailors and businessmen. The activity is such that you don't know where to look first, whether at the stalls, the crowd, the bootblacks and lottery-ticket sellers, the cafes, or at the venerable old buildings lining the street.

All the way along, cross streets beckon you to plunge deeper into the maze-like area. In contrast to the elegance of the section north of the Plaça de Catalunya, the Ramblas is lined mostly with inexpensive hotels, hooker clubs, snack bars and old cafes. Intermingled with these are historic monuments such as the church of Nuestra Señora de Belén on the right, on the corner of Carrer Carme, and opposite it the ocher-colored Baroque Palacio de Moya built in 1702. The colored paving stones of the Rambla de las Flores (or Sant Josep) were designed by the Catalan artist Joan Miró. Again on your right, notice the Casa Antigua Figueras, with its lovely mosaic façade and exquisite old fittings, and the Palacio de la Virreina, built by a viceroy of Peru in 1778. If you branch off to the right here for a couple of blocks you come to the ancient Hospital de la Cruz surrounded by a cluster of other 15th-century buildings which are today cultural and educational institutes, including the Central Library and a school for Catalan studies. You can wander through the courtyard of the Casa de Convalecencia which is particularly impressive with its Renaissance columns and its scenes portrayed in *azulejos,* and which in summer is sometimes used for outdoor concerts or theater performances. Return to the Ramblas and a little further down on the right, you reach a famous Barcelona landmark, the Liceo Opera House, one of the oldest and largest in Europe and long the pride of the city. It was built in 1845–7 and holds an audience of 5,000.

The Plaça Reial

One of the narrow side streets on the left leads to the Plaça Reial, a porticoed square in the Mediterranean style, where several tall palm trees in the center of the square add a touch of tropical voluptuousness. Take care here as the Plaça has sadly become a meeting place for drop-outs and drug addicts. The best and safest time to visit this lovely square is on Sunday mornings when the crowds gather to listen to the orators and peruse the popular stamp and coin stalls. Just behind the Plaça, on the Carrer Escudellers, is a cluster of bars and restaurants teeming with visitors and Spaniards of every description. Some of Barcelona's oldest and most atmospheric restaurants are located here, including Los Caracoles, famous since the turn of the century for its seafood, paellas and, of course, snails.

From the Carrer Escudellers down to the port you can plunge into the area of narrow streets known as the Barrio Chino, though the Chinese have long since departed. It swarms with somewhat shady nightclubs and single men usually get inviting nods from the ladies who frequent the little bars in the humid lanes. A word of warning at this stage: purse snatching is a big problem in Barcelona, especially in the narrow streets of the Gothic Quarter. The worst affected area is the lower regions of the Gothic Quarter between the Plaça Arc del Teatre and the port; you should take extra care at all times in this area. Best leave your purse and your camera behind if you are venturing below the Plaça Reial or Nou de la Rambla, and avoid the siesta hours when the streets are often deserted.

The Port

At the bottom of the Ramblas lies the Plaça del Portal de la Pau with its bronze statue of Columbus perched on a high column; ride the elevator to the top for a fine view of the port and the city. Anchored in the water nearby is a replica of the *Santa María,* Columbus's flagship, and on the right of the Ramblas is the excellent Maritime Museum chronicling the

BARCELONA

0 Miles   ½

0 Kilometers   ½

(NOT ALL STREETS SHOWN)

Points of Interest

Palau Centelles

1   Arc del Triomf
2   Barri Gòtic: Catedral;
     Museu Frederic Marés;
     Plaça del Rei
3   Basílica de la Mercè
4   Castell de Montjuïc:
     Museu del Exèrcit (Army Museum)
5   Fundació Joan Miró
6   Generalitat: Ajuntament;

7   Gran Teatre del Liceu
8   Hospital de la Santa Creu
9   La Llotja
10   Museu Arqueològic
11   Museu d'Art de Catalunya
12   Museu d'Art Modern
13   Museu Etnològic
14   Museu Marítim
15   Museu Picasso

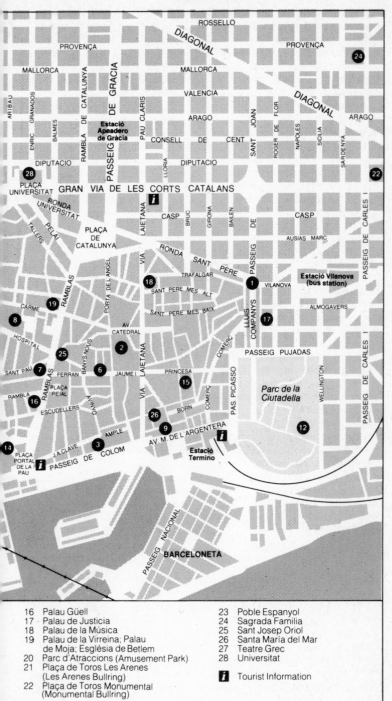

16 Palau Güell
17 Palau de Justicia
18 Palau de la Música
19 Palau de la Virreina; Palau
   de Moja; Església de Betlem
20 Parc d'Atraccions (Amusement Park)
21 Plaça de Toros Les Arenes
   (Les Arenes Bullring)
22 Plaça de Toros Monumental
   (Monumental Bullring)

23 Poble Espanyol
24 Sagrada Familia
25 Sant Josep Oriol
26 Santa María del Mar
27 Teatre Grec
28 Universitat

i Tourist Information

importance of Barcelona as a world port. The museum is housed in the medieval Reales Ataranzanas, one of Europe's oldest shipyards with the remains of a fort built by Jaime the Conqueror.

On the left, going down the wide Passeig de Colom which flanks the port where you can sometimes see battleships anchored, you come to the Plaça del Duc de Medinaceli, with a pretty fountain, and the Comandancia General, formerly the Convent of the Mothers of Mercy (1846), with a pretty patio. The facade dates from 1929. Behind it is the Baroque church of La Merced (1775), with a Renaissance portico from a previous church. La Merced contains the image of Barcelona's patron saint, the 16th-century Virgin of Mercy, whose feast day on September 24 is a local holiday and the occasion of much celebration. Further along the Passeig de Colom, on the corner of the Vía Laietana, is the main Post Office, built in 1926. Straight ahead lies the Avinguida Marquès de l'Argentera with the Lonja (Stock Market) rebuilt at the end of the 18th century on the site of the former Marine Exchange.

Barceloneta

Crossing over the busy Plaça Palau, you come eventually to the old quarter of Barceloneta, clustered onto the quay below Término station, which was built in 1755 and was traditionally the home of workers and fishermen. Today it is rather scruffy and run-down and many of its streets have a deserted, somewhat threatening air. But at lunchtime its main thoroughfare, the Passeig Nacional, or Moll de la Barceloneta, comes strikingly to life when the citizens of Barcelona flock here to feast on the delicious seafood of its numerous no-frills restaurants. As you walk past you will see people sitting outdoors, their plates piled high with shrimps, while others are digging into a paella.

The restaurants range from humble diners to traditional old favorites like Can Sole. On the Carrer Maquinista is a cluster of popular ones including the Pañol and Ramonet taverns. The latter is a lively haunt where the Catalans delight in ali-oli sandwiches (with tomato and garlic), smoked ham and *butifarra*. The rafters are so thickly hung with sausages and hams that the ceiling vanishes.

From the end of the Passeig Nacional, a cablecar *(teleférico)* crosses the port to Montjuïc Park offering some splendid views of the city. This cablecar can also be boarded at its halfway stage, the Torre de Jaume I on the Moll de Barcelona, only a short walk from the Columbus statue in Plaça Portal de la Pau.

The Cathedral

Another sightseeing route from our starting point of the Plaça de Catalunya is to walk down the Porta de l'Angel, past the Galerías Preciados department store, to one of the glories of Barcelona, its superb Gothic cathedral, one of the finest in the country. Just off the Plaça Nova, scene of an interesting antiques market on Thursday mornings, is a mural designed by Picasso for the College of Architects.

The cathedral is set in the so-called "Gothic" quarter of the city, a fascinating labyrinth of medieval streets and mansions, ideally suited for leisurely explorations. The present cathedral (known to the locals as La Seu) stands on the site of an earlier church, the Basilica of Santa Eulalia, which dated from A.D. 878. Work on the present structure was begun in 1298 under the kings of Aragón, and was completed around 1450. Such master builders as Jaime Fabré of Majorca and Master Roque are credited among its architects.

The two octagonal towers at either side of the transepts date from the 14th century, whereas the neo-Gothic facade on the Plaça Cristo Rei is modern (1892), as is the recent spire. The three rather somber naves measure 76 by 34 meters (249 by 111 feet), rising to a height of 23 meters (76 feet). The choirstalls by Matías Bonafe (the lower sections) and Lochner and Friedrich, two Germans of the late 15th century (for the upper sections) are astounding examples of the glories that wood-carving attained in the Middle Ages. See also the main altar, the crypt of Santa Eulalia, twenty-nine chapels and especially the magnificent cloister built in the Italian Renaissance style, finished by Roque in 1448, with capitals depicting scenes from the Bible.

Leaving the cathedral by the main door you come out into the Plaça Cristo Rei. On Sunday mornings in summer the citizens of Barcelona gather in the plaza to dance the traditional sardana, a living symbol of the tenacious regionalism of Catalonia. On Palm Sunday the mid-morning ceremony of the blessing of the palms on the steps in front of the cathedral is another spectacle well worth seeing.

The Gothic Quarter

Next, stroll through the Gothic Quarter, a warren of narrow streets with old churches and palaces dating from the 14th century. If you turn to your left on leaving the cathedral, you will pass the 15th-century Casa del Arcediano, home of the city's archives, before turning left again down the narrow Carrer Bisbe (Obispo) Irurita at the side of the cathedral towards the Plaça Sant Jaume (San Jaime). An alleyway off to the left leads to four Roman columns, remains of a temple dedicated to Augustus. On the west side of the plaza is the 15th-century Palau de la Generalitat, now the home of the Autonomous Government of Catalonia. Inside is an impressive courtyard with a beautifully balustraded staircase leading up to an arcaded gallery and the Patio de los Naranjos. Opening off this upper gallery is the Chapel and Salón de San Jorge—St. George being the patron saint of Catalonia—and the ornate Council Chambers. Facing it across the square is the Ajuntament, whose main facade dates from the 1840s, but just around the corner on Carrer Ciutat you can see one of its original facades dating back to 1400. Inside are the famous Salón de Ciento and the impressive mural of José María Sert in the Salón de Crónicas. Behind the Ajuntament, on the Baixada de Sant Miquel, you will come across the 15th-century Centelles Palace with a fine patio.

If on leaving the cathedral you turn instead to your right, you come face to face with the ancient Pía Almoina mansion, home of the Diocesan Museum and currently under restoration. Turn up the narrow street of the Comtes de Barcelona for a visit to the fascinating Federico Mares Museum. Across the museum's courtyard are the remains of the city's ancient Roman fortifications which can be visited on a ticket to the City of Barcelona Museum. Round the corner you will come upon the historic Plaça del Rei flanked by the Palacio Real; the Salón del Tinell, now an exhibition

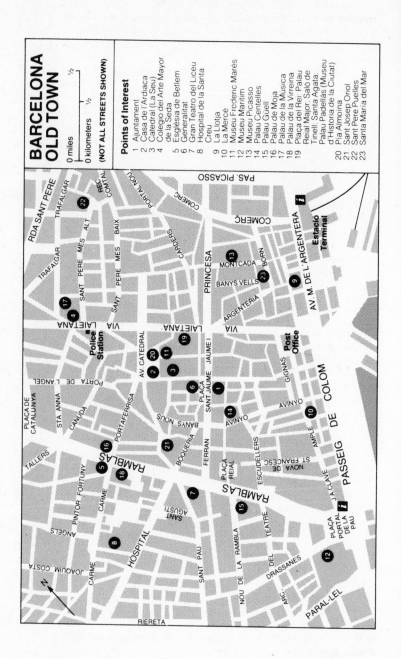

BARCELONA
OLD TOWN

0 miles   ½

0 kilometers   ½

(NOT ALL STREETS SHOWN)

Points of Interest

1 Ajuntament
2 Casa de l'Ardiaca
3 Catedral (La Seu)
4 Colegio del Arte Mayor
   de la Seda
5 Església de Betlem
6 Generalitat
7 Gran Teatro del Liceu
8 Hospital de la Santa
   Creu
9 La Llotja
10 La Merce
11 Museu Frederic Marés
12 Museu Marítim
13 Museu Picasso
14 Palau Centelles
15 Palau Güell
16 Palau de Moja
17 Palau de la Musica
18 Palau de la Virreina
19 Plaça del Rei: Palau
   Reial Major: Saló de
   Tinell: Santa Agata.
   Palau Padellas (Museu
   d'Historia de la Ciutat)
   Pia Almoina
20 Sant Josep Oriol
21 Sant Pere Puelles
22 Santa Maria del Mar

hall but originally a 14th-century banqueting hall where Columbus was received by the Catholic Monarchs upon his return from America; the 14th-century Chapel of Santa Agüeda built into the old Roman walls; and the Casa Padellás which houses the Museum of the City of Barcelona.

The Picasso Museum

Next make your way to the Plaça de l'Angel between Jaume I and Vía Laietana. Cross over the broad Vía Laietana, go down the Carrer de la Princesa and turn right at the Carrer Montcada, which takes you to the Picasso Museum. The collection has been added to over the years and is now one of the world's foremost museums on the artist who spent many of his formative years in Barcelona. In 1970, the artist donated some 2,500 works to the museum, despite pressures from the French government to keep the works in that country and in the early 80s the museum expanded into a neighboring palace. The collection includes paintings, engravings and drawings ranging over his entire creative life, some dating back as far as 1895 when Picasso was only nine years old. Of special interest are his variations on Velázquez's *Las Meninas* and his sketches of Barcelona.

On leaving the Picasso Museum, walk down the Carrer Montcada whose many splendid palaces, once the homes of rich and noble Barcelona families, now house museums (the Costume Museum in particular is well worth a visit), art galleries, poster stores, and trendy bars and cafés. Montcada opens out onto the Passeig del Born, a lively nighttime area, and adjoining it lies the church of Santa María del Mar, one of the loveliest churches in Barcelona. It was built between 1329 and 1383 though some of its portals and towers are of a later date, and was designed by Jaime Fabré, one of the architects of the cathedral.

The Museum of Modern Art and the Ciudadela Park

From the Passeig del Born it is only a short walk to the Ciudadela Park, containing a cluster of museums and an excellent zoo, home of Snowflake, the world's only albino gorilla. Within the park are the Geology, Natural History and Modern Art Museums as well as the seat of the Catalan parliament and an ornate fountain by José Fontseré on which the famous Gaudí worked as an assistant.

The Museum of Modern Art—something of a misnomer since most of its paintings are 19th- or even late 18th-century—has recently made more of a concession to modern art with the opening of rooms dedicated to contemporary artists. Most of the paintings are of local fame, but it is revealing to study the late 19th-century and early 20th-century works produced in Barcelona, which proved a transition period between the Impressionists and modern nonfigurative trends. Works by Fortuny, Rusiñol, Casas, Nonell, Zuloaga, and Sunyer evoke a golden period of painting and bohemianism in Barcelona, an age which saw Picasso living here, famous artistic *tertulias* in Els Quatre Gats, and the rise of the *modernista* movement. The whole museum in fact deserves far wider recognition and is well worth a visit.

From the Arch of Triumph to the Palau de la Música

Leaving the Ciudadela Park by way of the Passeig Lluis Companys, you will see on your right the Palacio de la Justicia, the law courts, and at the end a brick triumphal arch built for the exhibition of 1888. If here you turn left and plunge into the narrow streets of the old town along Rec Comtal, you will come to a small square joining the streets of Upper and Lower St. Peter's, on which stands the church of Sant Pere Puelles, one of the oldest medieval churches in Barcelona. Then continue along Sant Pere mes alt until you come to the city's main concert hall, the Palau de la Música, a fantastic and flamboyant building erected in 1908 by Luis Domenech y Muntaner in true Gaudiesque *modernismo* style. Try to attend a concert here if only to see the magnificent interior. Finally, as you come out once more onto the Vía Laietana, note the Colegio del Arte Mayor de la Seda, a fine plastered house built between 1759 and 1763 for the Guild of Silk Weavers. From here you can wander back into the maze of streets in the Gothic Quarter heading either for the Plaça Sant Jaume and the shops along Carrer Ferran, or alternatively wind your way back up past the cathedral to our starting point of the Plaça de Catalunya.

Montjuïc Park and Its Museums

Commanding a strategic position in Montjuïc Park, laid out in 1929–30 by Forestier for the International Exhibition, is the spectacularly positioned castle. The citadel was built in 1640 by those in revolt against Philip IV. It was stormed several times, the most famous assault being in 1705 by Lord Peterborough for the Archduke Charles of Austria. In 1808, the castle was seized by the French under General Dufresne during the Peninsular War. Later, in 1842, Barcelona was bombarded from its heights. Today the castle is home to the Military Museum and weapon collection of Federico Mares. Outside is a pleasant terrace commanding magnificent views of the city and its surroundings.

The Jardines de Miramar just beneath the castle can be reached by cablecar from the Passeig Nacional in Barceloneta. There is also a cog railroad up to Montjuïc from the end of Carrer Nou de la Rambla but as it runs only when the Montjuïc funfair is open and leaves from a very depressed part of the city, it's well worth taking a cab.

The most important of the cluster of museums in the Park of Montjuïc, which includes the Museo Arqueológico (Archeology Museum) and the Joan Miró Foundation, is the Museo de Arte de Cataluña (Museum of Catalan Art and Ceramics) in the Palacio Nacional. It contains an extraordinary collection of Catalan Romanesque and Gothic art treasures, such as can be seen nowhere else in the world. The murals—a superb collection—reredos and medieval sculptures represent the zenith of this genre in Spain. More conventional Baroque and Renaissance paintings, virtually all of a religious nature, are well represented too, but it is the Romanesque works which make a visit obligatory. Among the highlights is the concave fresco Pantocrator from the church of San Clemente de Tahull.

The exhibits in the Archeological Museum date from prehistoric times to the 8th century and include many artifacts found in the Balearics as well as some from the diggings at Ampurias, the large Greek and, later,

Roman colony on the Costa Brava. The Roman items are mostly frescos and mosaics. Classical plays are performed in the nearby Greek Theater in summer.

The Joan Miró Foundation designed by Josep Lluís Sert and opened in 1975 is one of Barcelona's most exciting contemporary art galleries. Its new extension by Jaume Freixa, a pupil of Sert, was opened by Queen Sofía in 1988, but it blends in so well with Sert's original that you're unlikely to notice it's there. The foundation puts on frequent temporary exhibitions as well as housing a comprehensive collection of sketches, paintings and sculptures by Joan Miró, the Catalan artist who was born in Barcelona in 1893 and who now lies buried in the cemetery of Montjuïc. Under the Franco regime which he strongly opposed, Miró had lived quietly for several years in a self-imposed semi-exile on the island of Mallorca. When he died on Christmas Day 1983 the Catalans gave him a send-off which amounted almost to a state funeral.

The Montjuïc stadium was built in 1929 for the Exhibition and with the intention of Barcelona's hosting the 1936 Olympics—later staged by Berlin. After twice this century failing to secure the Olympic nomination, Barcelona is now celebrating the capture of its long-cherished prize by renovating the semi-derelict stadium in time for 1992, when it will seat some 80,000 people.

Also on Montjuïc is the Pueblo Español, a miniature village, with each Spanish province represented. The Pueblo, created for the 1929 Exhibition, is a kind of Spain-in-a-bottle, with the local architectural styles of each province faithfully reproduced, enabling you to wander from the walls of Avila to the wine cellars of Jérez. Though, at present, it's little more than a tourist trap selling some grossly overpriced souvenirs, it's interesting up to a point. Plans are afoot, however, to inject a shot of new life into the village before 1992, and construction work is underway to build a theater, cinema, handicrafts center, convention hall, jazz and music bars, and a children's playground. An audiovisual *Barcelona Experience* center is also planned.

Just before the park's main exit you come to a huge fountain, one of the great prides of the city, which on festive occasions and weekends in summer is made to play colored fantasies while floodlights illuminate the large Palacio Nacional behind it. A wide esplanade leads past the fair buildings used for the many exhibitions and trade fairs which Barcelona hosts. The somewhat hideous fairground complex was created originally in the 1920s and '30s, but despite its monstrous architecture, it's not unimpressive. Coming out on the rather ugly Plaça de Espanya, you are face to face with Las Arenas bullring, built in Moorish style, though it is rarely used for bullfights now. From here you can take the subway or a bus back to the Plaça de Catalunya.

The Incomparable Gaudí

One of the major attractions of Barcelona is the work of the Catalan architect, sculptor and metalsmith, Antonio Gaudí, the leading exponent of the *Modernismo* movement, a Spanish and principally Barcelonan offshoot of Art Nouveau.

Born in Reus in 1852, Gaudí met his death in Barcelona in 1926 when he was run over by a tram, dying unrecognized in a hospital two days later.

He had become a virtual recluse, dedicating his life to work on his most famous building, the Templo de la Sagrada Familia (Church of the Holy Family), in whose crypt he is buried. Aided by public subscription, Gaudí began work on the Sagrada Familia in 1882. It was far from complete on his death but had already become something of a symbol to the people of Barcelona, and during the frenzy of church burning that took place after the outbreak of the Civil War in 1936, it was the only church, other than the cathedral, that was left untouched. Today work has once again begun on the church which at present resembles a building site rather than a place of worship. Amid much controversy, the work is being carried out following Gaudí's last-known plans; it is estimated it will take a further 50 years, but could take much longer if progress continues at the present pace.

If you have never seen any of his work you should make a visit to at least one of his buildings a must. The Catalan worked more as a sculptor than an architect, changing his ideas frequently as the work progressed; molding huge masses of material with a fluidity and freedom that turned towers into candles shrouded in molten wax, staircases into swooping parabolas, doorways into troglodytes' caves.

Other specimens of Gaudí's exciting architecture are the crypt of the Güell Colony in San Baudillo, two apartment buildings, the Casa Milá and the Casa Batlló on the Passeig de Gràcia, the street lamp and bench units that line the Passeig de Gràcia, the Casa Calvet on Caspe, the Casa Vicens on Carolines, and the Palacio Güell, off the Ramblas on the Carrer Nou de la Rambla, which is now a museum dedicated to the history of Barcelona's artistic past. Perhaps most fascinating, because you can inspect it at close range is the Parque Güell on a mountain in the northwest of the city, an art nouveau extravaganza where the strange shapes have been put at the service of a park-playground, with a mosaic pagoda, undulating benches and fantastic-shaped architectural effects.

Tibidabo Mountain

Finally you may like to make the trip to the top of Tibidabo Mountain behind the city, the spot for superb views. The summit is reached by car or cab in a 20-minute drive; alternatively, you can take Bus 58 from the Plaça Catalunya to the Avda. Tibidabo is where you catch the old *tramvía blau* (1901), which connects with the funicular (rack railroad). The view over Barcelona to the Mediterranean is indeed splendid, though a similar view can be had from the much prettier Parque Güell, and on clear days— and these can be few and far between in Barcelona—you can supposedly see inland to the jagged peaks of Montserrat and even as far as the Pyrenees. The entire site might easily be idyllic were it not spoilt by an over-commercialized church, a vast radio mast, and a rather brash fairground, a classic example of the misguided exploitation of a natural beauty spot.

PRACTICAL INFORMATION FOR BARCELONA

GETTING TO TOWN FROM THE AIRPORT. The least expensive way to travel from the airport into the city center is to take the airport train to Sants Central Station. From there taxis, city buses or the metro (subway) will take you quickly to your hotel. Trains leave the airport every 30 minutes between 6 A.M. and 11 P.M. The journey takes approximately 15 minutes, and there is only one intermediate stop. From the arrivals hall, follow the signs for RENFE. During the night, when trains are not running, RENFE provides a bus service into town. There is also a daytime bus service where you can take bus EA to the Plaça de Espanya; it runs from 7.15 A.M. to 9.15 P.M. At night bus EN runs to the Plaça de Espanya.

Alternatively, you take a taxi to your destination. The cab fare into town will cost you what is on the meter (approximately 1,400–1,800 ptas.) plus an airport supplement (about 150 ptas.) and extra for luggage. Make sure the driver starts his meter when you leave the airport.

TOURIST INFORMATION. Tourist Offices are located at **Sants-Central station** (tel. 250 2594), open daily 7.30 A.M.–10.30 P.M.; **Término station** (tel. 319 2791), open Mon. to Sat. 8 A.M.–8 P.M.; **Gran Vía Corts Catalanes 658** (tel. 301 7443), open Mon. to Fri. 9–7, Sat. 9–2; **Plaça Sant Jaume** in the Ayuntamiento (tel. 318 2525), open Mon. to Fri. 9–9, Sat. 9–2; in the **Columbus monument** in Plaça Portal de la Pau, open daily except Mon. 9.30–1.30 and 4.30–8.30; and at the **airport,** open Mon. to Sat. 8–8, Sun. 8–3.

TELEPHONE CODE. The area code for the city of Barcelona and the entire Barcelona province is (93). You need only dial the (93) if you are calling from outside Barcelona province, from anywhere within the province, just dial the number. When calling Barcelona from abroad, the area code is (3).

HOW TO GET AROUND. Modern Barcelona, north of the Plaça de Catalunya, is largely built on a grid system, though there is no helpful numbering system as in the U.S. However, the old part of town—from the Plaça de Catalunya to the port and ringed by the Rondas and Ciudadela Park—is quite different altogether. Here the narrow streets wind and twist in all directions. It is an area which can only be explored on foot, so before you plunge into this fascinating labyrinth, best arm yourself with a good street map.

There is a transport information kiosk in the Plaça de Catalunya (opposite Carrer Bergara and the Banco Bilbao), open 8–7 Mon. to Fri., 8–1 on Sat., which deals mainly with city bus transport. Here you can obtain maps of the bus and metro system.

By Metro. The subway system is already fairly extensive and is currently being further enlarged. This is the cheapest form of public transport and probably the easiest to use. You pay a flat fare of 60 ptas. no matter how far you travel; on Sundays and fiestas fares are 5 ptas. higher. Savings can be made by buying a *tarjeta multiviaje* from metro station ticket offices, branches of the Caixa de Pensions de Barcelona, or from the Plaça de Catalunya transport kiosk. Blue *tarjetas* cost 325 ptas. (1989 price) and are valid for 10 rides on the metro, tramvía blau, Montjuïc funicular, and Ferrocarrils de la Generalitat suburban trains. Pocket maps of the system are sometimes available from ticket offices.

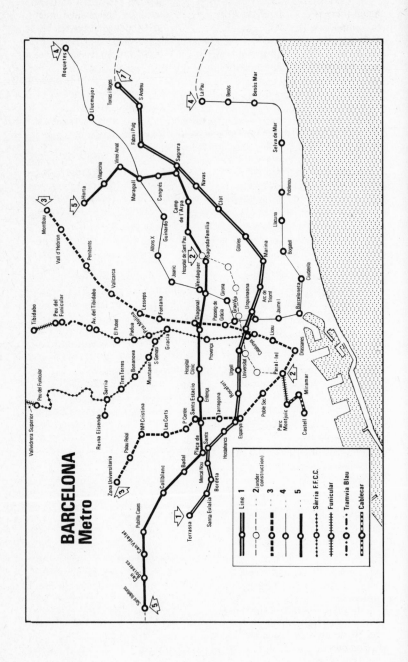

BARCELONA
Metro

By Bus. Most of the bus routes pass through the Plaça de Catalunya; again there is a flat fare system and again it's a little higher on Sundays (about 55 ptas. and 60 ptas.). A red *tarjeta multiviaje,* good for ten rides on buses as well as the metro, tramvía blau, Montjuïc funicular, and Ferrocarrils de la Generalitat trains, costs 360 ptas. (1989 price) from the Plaça de Catalunya kiosk and is the best all-inclusive ticket. Maps of the bus network are available from the kiosk or tourist offices. To go to the beach at Castelldefels, take the UC from outside the University.

By Taxi. Taxis in Barcelona have a much higher initial charge than in other Spanish cities, making short rides expensive whereas longer rides work out much the same as elsewhere. Taxis available for hire show a *Libre* sign in daytime and a small green lamp at night. When you begin your ride a standard charge of 210 ptas. will be shown on the meter. Supplements are 40 ptas. for suitcases, 55 ptas. for leaving a train station, and 200 ptas. to or from the airport. In Zone A fares are 50 ptas. a km. between 6 A.M. and 10 P.M., and 70 ptas. a km. from 10 P.M.–6 A.M. and on weekends. Zone B costs 70 ptas. a km. during the day and 80 ptas. at night and weekends (1989 rates). Make sure your driver turns down the flag when you start your journey.

RAILROAD STATIONS. Barcelona has three mainline railroad stations, the most important being **Barcelona Central** (or **Sants**) at the end of Avda de Roma, Europe's most modern station. Next comes the ancient **Estación de Francia** (or **Término**) on Avda. Marquès del' Argentera near the port. Trains to France leave from here. There is also an underground station, **Passeig de Gracià,** at the intersection of the Passeig de Gracià and Aragó. Many trains cross Barcelona stopping at all three stations but be sure to check which station you should board your train at.

For destinations outside the Barcelona area, buy your tickets well in advance from any of the three stations. Go to the windows marked *Venta Anticipada Largo Recorrido,* open approximately 8 A.M.–9 P.M. Trains to the airport leave from Sants Station. For destinations in Catalonia, local Ferrocarrils de la Generalitat trains leave from the underground stations in the Plaça de Catalunya and the Plaça de Espanya to Martorell, Igualada, Manresa and Berga. To the Costa Brava, from the Rodalies (Cercanías) Station at Término. Trains to Montserrat leave from the Plaça d'Espanya and connect with a teleférico (cable car) for the Monastery.

BUS STATIONS. There is no central bus depot in Barcelona though buses to most Spanish destinations leave from the old **Estación del Norte** on the Avda. Vilanova. For Montserrat, a *Juliá* bus runs daily at 9 A.M. from Plaça Universitat 12. The tourist office can help with bus schedules and we would advise you always to check your departure points well in advance of your journey. *Alsina Gräells,* Ronda Universitat 4, runs buses to Lérida, Soria and Andorra; *Juliá,* Ronda Universitat 5, to Zaragoza, Huesca and Montserrat (buses leave from Plaça Universitat 12); *Montesol,* Numància 63, to Bilbao, Jaen and Seville; and to Sitges from the Estación del Norte and the Plaça Universitat.

For buses abroad, *Iberbus,* Vergara 2, have services to Italy, France, Belgium, Holland and London. *Juliá,* Ronda Universitat 5 to France, Switzerland, Germany, Scandinavia and London. *Via Tourisme,* Pau

Claris 117 to Scandinavia, Holland, Belgium, France, Germany and London.

HOTELS. For a city of its size and importance, Barcelona has long been
underendowed with hotels, but, with the coming of the Olympics in 1992,
the city's hotel industry is having to think afresh. New hotels are going
up fast, international chains are vying for business, and of the existing hotels, many have either undergone, or will soon undergo, extensive renovation programs. At present most hotels in the downtown area around the
Ramblas and the Plaça de Catalunya are older style hotels whereas the
newer more modern hotels tend to be situated further out either along the
Diagonal or in the residential suburbs in the hills on the far side of it. When
an address is given as Gran Vía, this refers to Gran Vía de les Corts Catalanes.

Deluxe

Avenida Palace, Gran Vía 605 (tel. 301 9600). 211 rooms. Centrally
located between the Passeig de Gracià and Rambla Catalunya. An elegant,
old-style hotel which has been restored; rooms can be a little plain but
there are several interesting features. AE, DC, MC, V.

Duques de Bergara, Bergara 11 (tel. 301 5151). 56 rooms. A recently
opened hotel in a beautiful Modernista house (1898) just off Plaça de Catalunya; top marks for distinction and quiet elegance.

Meliá Barcelona Sarriá Avda. Sarriá 50 (tel. 410 6060). 314 rooms.
Near the Plaça Francesc Macià, and remodelled to cater for the business-
man's needs. AE, DC, V.

Princesa Sofia, Plaça Pius XII (tel. 330 7111). 505 rooms. Huge modern
hotel with pool and all amenities. Located quite a long way out on the
Diagonal close to the University City. Panoramic dining room on 19th
floor. AE, DC, MC, V.

Ramada Renaissance, Ramblas 111 (tel. 318 6200). 210 rooms. Formerly the *Manila,* this 4-star hotel has recently been renovated to high standards of elegance and comfort.

Ritz, Gran Vía 668 (tel. 318 5200). 197 rooms. One of the original hotels
founded by Cesar Ritz and still the grand old lady of Barcelona hotels.
Extensive refurbishment has restored its former splendor, luxury and comfort. AE, DC, MC, V.

Expensive

Arenas, Capitán Arenas 20 (tel. 204 0300). 59 rooms. Modern, in pleasant residential suburb. AE, DC, MC, V.

Balmoral, Vía Augusta 5 (tel. 217 8700). 94 rooms. Comfortable, functional hotel just off Diagonal. AE, DC, MC, V.

Barcelona, Caspe 1 (tel. 302 5858). 64 rooms. Good modern hotel very
centrally located just off Rambla de Catalunya and only a short distance
from Plaça de Catalunya.

Castellnou, Castellnou 61 (tel. 203 0554). 29 rooms. A new hotel out
in the residential Sarrià district.

Colón, Avda. Catedral 7 (tel. 301 1404). 161 rooms. In the Gothic Quarter overlooking cathedral square. An older, cozy hotel with a charm and
intimacy of its own, though the cathedral bells can be disturbing. AE, DC,
MC, V.

Condes de Barcelona, Passeig de Gracià 75 (tel. 215 0616). 100 rooms. Recently opened in a superb *modernista* house; stunning decor and currently one of the most fashionable hotels in town. Top rates. AE, DC, MC, V.

Condor, Vía Augusta 127 (tel. 209 4511). 78 rooms. Parking and good amenities. In smart residential area just beyond Diagonal. AE, DC, MC, V.

Cristal, Diputació 257 (tel. 301 6600). 148 rooms. Good location close to center on corner of Rambla Catalunya. AE, DC, MC, V.

Derby, Loreto 21 (tel. 322 3215). 116 rooms. Smart modern hotel not far from Plaça Francesc Macià; a sister hotel to the more expensive Gran Derby. AE, DC, MC, V.

Gala Placidia, Vía Augusta 112 (tel. 217 8200). 31 rooms. A luxurious apartment hotel, though officially classed as 3-star. AE, DC, MC, V.

Gran Derby, Loreto 28 (tel. 322 3215). 39 rooms. A plush suites-only hotel with novel decor and high standards close to the *Sarria Gran* and *Derby* hotels. AE, DC, MC, V.

Gran Hotel Calderón, Rambla Catalunya 26 (tel. 301 0000). 244 rooms. Long a leading contender, a recent refit has given it a bright new image. Pool, sun terrace; one of the best. AE, DC, MC, V.

Hesperia, Los Vergós 20 (tel. 204 5551). 144 rooms. In the residential district of Sarriá. AE, DC, MC, V.

Majestic, Passeig de Gracià 70 (tel. 215 4512). 344 rooms. Well-renovated traditional hotel with pool. AE, DC, MC, V.

Park Putxet, Putxet 68 (tel. 212 5158). 125 rooms. Recently opened apartment hotel in the Lesseps area beyond the Diagonal; high rates. AE, DC, MC, V.

Presidente, Diagonal 570 (tel. 200 2111). 161 rooms, pool. Elegant 5-star hotel on corner of Muntaner in Plaça Francesc Macià area. AE, DC, MC, V.

Regente, Rambla Catalunya 76 (tel. 215 2570). 78 rooms. An older-style hotel with pool on the corner of Valéncia. AE, DC, MC, V.

Royal, Ramblas 117 (tel. 301 9400). 108 rooms. Conveniently located near the top of Ramblas, the Royal has recently undergone a thorough facelift.

Moderate

Astoria, París 203 (tel. 209 8311). 109 rooms. Functional '50s-style hotel near Diagonal between Aribau and Enric Granados. AE, DC, MC, V.

Bonanova Park, Capitan Arenas 51 (tel. 204 0900). 60 rooms. In fashionable residential area in the hills beyond the Diagonal. AE, DC, MC, V.

Covadonga, Diagonal 596 (tel. 209 5511). 76 rooms. Stylish older hotel close to Plaça Francesc Macià. AE, DC, MC, V.

Gran Vía, Gran Vía 642 (tel. 318 1900). 48 rooms. Elegant old hotel between Passeig de Gracià and Pau Claris.

Habana, Gran Vía 647 (tel. 301 0750). 65 rooms. Genteel and old-fashioned establishment on a smart central street. AE, DC, V.

Mitre, Bertrán 15 (tel. 212 1104). Small hotel quite a way from center in residential suburb. 57 rooms. AE, DC, MC, V.

Montecarlo, Rambla dels Estudis 124 (tel. 317 5800). 73 rooms. Some of the public rooms have retained their charming turn-of-the-century decor, but bedrooms are only functional; good location on Ramblas.

Oriente, Ramblas 45 (tel. 302 2558). 142 rooms. Barcelona's oldest hotel, opened in 1843. Its public rooms are a delight; the ballroom and dining room have lost none of their 19th-century magnificence, though the bedrooms have undergone featureless renovation and the hotel tends to cater to budget tour groups. AE, DC, MC, V.

Regencia Colón, Sagristans 13 (tel. 318 9858). 55 rooms. A somber but comfortable annexe to the Colón, close to cathedral. AE, DC, MC, V.

Rialto, Ferrán 40 (tel. 318 5212). 128 rooms. Stylish old-world hotel in heart of Gothic Quarter just off Plaça Sant Jaume. AE, DC, MC, V.

Suizo, Plaça de l'Angel 12 (tel. 315 0461). 50 rooms. A cozy old favorite on the edge of the Gothic Quarter just off Vía Laietana and overlooking Jaume I metro. AE, DC, MC, V.

Terminal, Provença 1 (tel. 321 5350). 75 rooms. Recent hotel on 7th floor of a modern block opposite Sants Station. Pleasant service and comfortable, functional rooms. AE, DC, MC, V.

Tres Torres, Calatrava 32 (tel. 417 7300). 56 rooms. Small hotel in the residential area of Tres Torres on the hill beyond the Diagonal. AE, DC, MC, V.

Wilson, Diagonal 568 (tel. 209 2511). 52 rooms. An older and traditional hotel on the Diagonal on corner of Bon Pastor and Muntaner. AE, DC, MC, V.

Inexpensive

Cataluña, Santa Anna 22 (tel. 301 9150). 40 rooms. Small hotel in the old town between Ramblas and the Porta de l'Angel just below the Plaça Catalunya.

Continental, Rambla Canaletas 136 (tel. 301 2508). 30 rooms. A deluxe hostel in a stylish old house with elegant canopies, at the top of the Ramblas near the Plaça Catalunya. Friendly reception and a long-standing favorite.

Cortes, Santa Anna 25 (tel. 317 9212). 46 rooms. Under the same management and a sister hotel to the *Cataluña.* AE, MC, V.

Internacional, Ramblas 78 (tel. 302 2566). 62 rooms. Friendly old-fashioned hotel right opposite Liceo Opera House. AE, DC, V.

Moderno, Hospital 11 (tel. 301 4154). 57 rooms. Pleasant hotel on corner of the Ramblas near Boqueria market; very popular with Spaniards.

Nouvel, Santa Anna 18 (tel. 301 8274). 76 rooms. Simple but in a charming old-fashioned house close to the *Cataluña* and *Cortés.*

Urbis, Passeig de Gracià 23 (tel. 317 2766). 61 rooms. Excellent deluxe hostel, very popular with Spaniards.

Villa de Madrid, Pza. Villa de Madrid (tel. 317 4916). 28 rooms. Modestly priced 3-star hotel in small square in Gothic Quarter just off Ramblas.

Youth Hostels. Barcelona has four Youth Hostels: the **Albergue Verge de Montserrat,** Mare de Déu del Coll 41–51 (tel. 213 8633), nearest metro: Lesseps, or buses 25 or 28; the **Albergue Pere Tarres,** Numància 149 (tel. 230 1606) not far from Sants Station; the main one is the **Albergue de Juventud** on Passeig Pujadas 29 (tel. 300 3104) near the Ciudadela Park; **BCN-Xatrac** Youth Hostel, Pelai 62, overlooking the Plaça de Catalunya.

RESTAURANTS. Barcelona is well endowed with fine restaurants. Catalan cooking is wholesome with hearty portions. You'll find good paellas here and snails are also a specialty. Pasta, too, is more popular here than elsewhere in Spain. The seafood is also excellent. Other local specialties are *butifarra,* a typically Catalan sausage, and *rovellons,* an earthy-tasting mushroom. *Espinacas a la catalana* (spinach with garlic, pine nuts, and raisins) makes a tasty appetizer, and *music* is a typically Catalan dessert of dried fruits with a glass of moscatel wine. Barcelona has long been a notorious port; should you come across street walkers near any of our recommended restaurants, rest assured, they—the restaurants!—are quite respectable inside.

Many Barcelona restaurants are closed on Saturday night and Sunday, so do check in advance. Many also close for a month in summer, usually in August.

Deluxe

Eldorado Petit, Dolors Monserdá 51 (tel. 204 5153). Considered one of Barcelona's very best restaurants; exquisite cuisine and beautiful setting in a private villa. Closed Sun. and two weeks in Aug. AE, MC, V.

Finisterre, Diagonal 469 (tel. 239 5576). International dishes served in great style. Especially recommended are the *steak tartare* and the sweet *soufflés* for dessert. Closed in July and Aug. AE, DC, MC, V.

Orotava, Consell de Cent 335 (tel. 302 3128). This fashionable spot has a high reputation for its elegant setting and *haute cuisine.* Its seafood and game specialties are outstanding. Closed Sun. AE, DC, MC, V.

Reno, Tuset 27 (tel. 200 9129). An elegant restaurant on the corner of Travessera de Gracià much famed for its *haute cuisine* and especially well recommended for business entertainment. The *Menu Reno* is a wise choice allowing you to sample several of the best dishes. AE, DC, MC, V.

Vía Veneto, Ganduxer 10 (tel. 200 7244). Highly recommended for the best in food and professional service. Splendid decor. AE, DC, MC, V.

Expensive

Agut d'Avignon, Trinidad 3 (tel. 302 6034). Hidden at the end of the first alley on the right off Avinyó leading out of Ferran in the Gothic Quarter. Rustic atmosphere; a favorite with politicians. Catalan cuisine and game specialties in season. Reservation essential. Closed Sun., Easter Week. AE, DC, MC, V.

Ara-Cata, Dr. Ferran 33 (tel. 204 1053). Located in the residential suburb of Pedralbes, its strange name is an abbreviation of Aragón-Catalonia, the owner being Aragonés and his wife Catalan. Outstanding food. Closed Sat. and in the evenings of fiestas, Easter Week and Aug. AE, DC, MC, V.

Azulete, Vía Augusta 281 (tel. 203 5943). One of the most beautiful restaurants in Barcelona, the dining room in an old conservatory, filled with flowers and plants. Highly imaginative cooking, a mixture of Catalan, French and Italian with an interesting blend of traditional and new dishes. Closed Sat. lunch, Sun. and fiestas, and first two weeks of Aug. AE, DC, MC, V.

La Balsa, Infanta Isabel 4 (tel. 211 5048). Up in the hills just above Plaça Bonanova, this fabulous chic restaurant won an award for its architecture; original cuisine, and great outdoor terrace. Closed Sun., and Mon. lunch. AE, DC, V.

Botafumeiro, Major de Gracià 81 (tel. 218 4230). One of Barcelona's best seafood restaurants. Closed Sun. P.M., Mon., and Aug. AE, DC, MC, V.

La Cuineta, Paradis 4 (tel. 315 0111). Intimate small restaurant in 17th-century house just off Plaça Sant Jaume; specializes in Catalan cooking. Good service. Closed Mon. AE, DC, MC, V.

La Dorada, Travessera de Gracià 44 (tel. 200 6322). Under same ownership as the Madrid and Seville *La Doradas,* this one too serves top fish and seafood flown in daily from Andalusia. Closed Sun. and Aug. AE, DC, V.

Florián, Bertrand i Serra 20 (tel. 212 4627). A prestigious restaurant famed for unusual cuisine. The menu changes daily depending on fresh market produce, and includes international delicacies such as caviar and more humble local produce like sardines. Closed Sun. and two weeks in Aug. DC, MC, V.

La Font del Gat, Passeig Santa Madrona (tel. 325 3698). Magnificently set on Montjuïc in a large villa with patio—dining among fountains and flowers. Expensive but worth it. Catalan specialties. AE, DC.

Gorria, Diputació 421 (tel. 232 7857). Highly rated for its excellent Navarre-style cooking, good wine list, and professional service; four blocks south of Sagrada Familia. Closed Sun. and Aug. AE, DC, MC, V.

El Gran Café, Avinyó 9 (tel. 318 7986). Stylish turn-of-the-century decor in heart of Gothic Quarter; dining to piano music. Closed Sun., Easter week, and Aug. AE, DC, MC, V.

Guria, Casanova 97 (tel. 253 6325). Luxurious Basque restaurant with outstanding cuisine and service; currently one of the highest rated restaurants in town. Closed two weeks in Aug. AE, DC, MC, V.

Jaume de Provença, Provença 88 (tel. 230 0029). One of Barcelona's highest rated restaurants. Ideal for business lunches. *Haute cuisine* specialties often include baby eels rolled in smoked salmon. Closed Sun. evening, Mon., Easter Week and Aug. AE, DC, MC, V.

Neichel, Avda. de Pedralbes 16 bis (tel. 203 8408). Luxurious and elegant decor; one of Barcelona's most highly-thought-of restaurants. Closed Sun. and fiestas, Easter Week and Aug. AE, DC, MC, V.

La Odisea, Copons 7 (tel. 302 3692). Inventive restaurant near cathedral. After your meal there is a pleasant coffee lounge with piano music. Closed Sun., Easter Week and Aug. AE, MC, V.

Quo Vadis, Carme 7 (tel. 302 4072). One of Barcelona's "musts". Highly original dishes; much praised. Closed Sun. and Aug. AE, DC, MC, V.

El Tunel de Muntaner, Sant Màrius 22 (tel. 212 6074). A popular restaurant on the hills behind the city not far from the Avda. Tibidabo. Its menu combines *haute cuisine* with popular home-cooking. There is a good bar at the entrance and a well stocked "boutique" for wine buffs. Closed Sat. lunch, Sun., fiestas and in Aug. AE, DC, MC, V.

Tinell, Frenería 8 (tel. 315 4604). In the heart of the Gothic Quarter just behind the cathedral. Friendly service and a delicious *sopa de ajo.*

La Venta, Plaça Dr. Andreu (tel. 212 6455). Delightful turn-of-the-century spot with tiled floors, marble-topped tables and pot-bellied stove. In a splendid setting with outdoor terrace, right beside the Tibidabo funicular. Closed Sun. DC, MC, V.

Vinya Rosa Magi, Avda. de Sarrià 17 (tel. 230 0003). Pleasant small restaurant convenient to the *Sarrià* and *Derby* hotels, specializing in Catalan and French dishes. Closed Sun. AE, DC, MC, V.

Moderate

Brasserie Flo, Jonqueres 10 (tel. 317 8037). Excellent French restaurant just off the top of Via Laietana; well decorated and good value. AE, DC, MC, V.

Can Culleretes, Quintana 5 (tel. 317 6485). This picturesque old restaurant began life as a *pastelería* in 1786 and is located on a narrow street between Boquería and Ferran just off Ramblas. Three dining rooms, walls hung with photos of visiting celebrities, it's a find and serves real Catalan cooking. Do not be put off by the hookers outside, this is a popular family restaurant. Closed Sun. evening, Mon., and two weeks in June or July.

Can Isidre, Les Flors 12 (tel. 241 1139). Long-standing tradition just off the Paral-lel and popular with artists, writers and actors. Traditional and imaginative cuisine making use of fresh produce bought daily in the Boquería market. Very highly rated but go by cab as the area's not the best. Closed Sun., Easter Week and mid-July to mid-Aug. AE, V.

Can Leopoldo, Sant Rafael 24 (tel. 241 3014). Famous for its seafood for over half-a-century; in the heart of the old town and best reached by taxi. Closed Sun. night, Mon., Easter Week and Aug. AE, MC, V.

Can Solé, Sant Carlos 4 (tel. 319 5012). Plenty of old-world charm with a nice tavern atmosphere in Barceloneta. Specializes in seafood. Closed Sat. night and Sun. Closed first two weeks of Feb. and first two weeks of Sept.

Los Caracoles, Escudellers 14 (tel. 301 2041). Famous Barcelona restaurant with wonderful decor and atmosphere. Specialty is snails. AE, DC, MC, V.

Casa Quirze, Laureà Miró 202 (tel. 371 1084). Justly famous restaurant serving mainly French-style dishes quite a long way out in Esplugues de Llobregat off the far end of the Diagonal. Closed Sun. night, Mon. and Easter Week. AE, MC, V.

La Dida, Roger de Flor 230 (tel. 207 2391). A well-recommended restaurant with atmospheric decor in the vicinity of the Plaça Joan Carlos and not too far from the Sagrada Familia church. Closed in the evening on Sun. and fiestas, and on Sat. from mid-June thru Sept, and Easter Week. AE, DC, MC, V.

Hostal Sant Jordi, Travessera de Dalt 123 (tel. 213 1037). Serving Catalan and French food of a consistently high standard; the house menu is a good choice. Closed on Sun. evenings and in Aug. AE, DC, V.

A la Menta, Passeig Manuel Girona 50 (tel. 204 1549). Atmospheric tavern serving good grilled meat. Best to reserve a table. Closed Sun. evenings and all day Sun. during Aug. AE, DC, V.

Network, Diagonal 616 (tel. 201 7238). This ultramodern cafe won a design award, and concentrates on everyday favorites—American, Mexican, and Italian—at value-for-money prices. Open till 2.30 A.M. AE, V.

Senyor Parellada, Argentería 37 (tel. 315 4010). In vogue Catalan restaurant just off Vía Laietana. Closed Sun. AE, DC, MC, V.

Sete Portes, Passeig Isabel II 14 (tel. 319 3033). Delightful restaurant going strong since 1836 and with lots of old-world charm; on the edge of the port. Open from 1 P.M. through 1 A.M. continuously. Very popular and crowded on Sundays and fiestas. AE, DC, MC, V.

Sopeta Una, Verdaguer i Callis 6 (tel. 319 6131). Delightful small restaurant with old-fashioned decor and intimate atmosphere, near Palau de

la Música. Specializes in Catalan cuisine. Closed Sun. and Mon. lunch.
v.

Tramonti 1980, Diagonal 501 (tel. 410 1535). Excellent Italian restaurant just beyond Plaça Francesc Macià. Its range of pastas and Italian cheeses is superb. AE, DC, MC, V.

El Tunel, Ample 33 (tel. 315 2759). An old stand-by with good old-fashioned service and reliable cooking, in the lower reaches of the Barrio Chino just off the Passeig Colom. Closed Sun. night, Mon. and mid-July thru mid-Aug.

Inexpensive

Agut, Gignàs 16 (tel. 315 1709). Good value Catalan cooking in the heart of the Barrio Chino. This simple restaurant, founded in 1914, serves only food and wine, no coffee or liquor. Closed Sun. P.M., Mon., and in July.

El Caballito Blanco, Mallorca 196 (tel. 253 1033). Long-standing popular restaurant offering a good choice of simple cooking and good selection of cheeses. Closed Sun. night, Mon., and Aug.

Del Teatre, Montseny 47 (tel. 218 6738). Located in the Teatre Lliure, this restaurant serves some original and imaginative dishes and is very good value. Closed Sun., Mon. and in Aug. AE.

Egipto, Jerusalem 3 (tel. 317 7480). Small, friendly restaurant hidden behind the Bonquería market; well known to locals for its incredible value, good home cooking, and huge desserts.

Flash Flash, La Granada 25 (tel. 237 0990). Serving every imaginable kind of omelet—over 101 choices—with arty black-and-white decor. Open till 1.30 A.M. AE, DC, MC, V.

Mesón de las Ramblas, Ramblas 92 (tel. 302 1180). Pleasant bistro popular with tourists and which starts serving dinner early.

La Morera, Plaça Sant Agusti 1 (tel. 318 7555). Just off Ramblas between the market and Liceo. Smart decor and very good value.

La Ponsa, Enric Granados 89 (tel. 253 1037). A family-run restaurant serving Catalan food at very moderate prices; something of a budget institution in Barcelona. Closed Sat. night, Sun., and mid-July to mid-Aug.

Racó d'en Jaume, Provença 98 (tel. 239 7861). This is the old Jaume de Provença now reopened and serving down-to-earth good Catalan home cooking. Well worth a visit for insight into the way Catalan families eat at home. Closed Sun. night, Mon., and Aug.

Rey de la Gamba 1, 2 and 3, all on the Passeig Nacional in Barceloneta. Nothing pretentious but very popular with the locals. Great seafood and *pan tomate* at low prices.

Self Naturista, Sta. Anna 13. Popular self-service vegetarian wholefood restaurant; very cheap with long lines forming at lunchtime.

FAST FOOD. Burger King, at top of the Ramblas. The **Chicago Pizza Pie Factory,** Provença 300. A little bit of Chicago in Barcelona serving American-style pizzas, carrot cake, cheeses and garlic bread, good selection of cocktails, with American music, video and decor. **Compañía General de Sandwiches,** Santaló 153 and Moyá 14. Great selection of sandwiches—over 100 varieties—and canapés to take away. Closed Sun. **El Drugstore,** Passeig de Gracià 71, open from early morning till very late at night for snacks and self-service meals. **Drugstore David,** Tuset 19 off the Diagonal. Every kind of hamburger, pizzas and Spanish meat dishes. Popular with the young set. **Fontanella 5,** on the corner of Fontanella and Plaça Catalunya. Pizzas and sandwiches. **Kentucky Fried Chicken,** Aribau 16, Rambla de Catalunya 113, Sants 136, and Fontanella near Plaça Catalunya. **McDonalds,** Pelai 62 on the corner of Ramblas and on Ramblas corner of Ferran. **New Kansas,** Passeig de Gracià 65 bis. Pizzas and good selection of sandwiches. **Niridia,** Diagonal 616. Pizzeria and fast food. **La Oca,** Plaça Francesc Macià 10. Smart trendy cafe serving *platos combinados,* club sandwiches and pastries; also take-away snacks. **Pizzería Samoa,** Passeig de Gracià 101. **Tropeziens,** Passeig de Gracià 83. Pizzeria and cafeteria. **Pokins** take-away hamburger chain, at Porta de l'Angel 1 and 27, Pelai 52, and Pza Francesc Macià 3.

BARS AND CAFES. Barcelona abounds in colorful old tapas bars, smart, trendy cafes where you can go for coffee and a pastry or for *platos combinados* and snack meals, jazz cafes, piano bars, and a whole range of stylish in vogue bars glorifying in the titles of *coctelerías, whiskerías* or *champanerías.* Below we list just a few of these places but, on the whole, it is best simply to wander at will and sample any which take your fancy; of one thing you can be sure—there are hundreds to choose from.

Tapas Bars. The most colorful are found in the old narrow streets on either side of the Ramblas, around the Plaça Reial, and in the area around the Picasso Museum along Carrer Princesa and surrounding the Carrer Montcada. In the port area of Barceloneta, in Carrer Maquinista the **Ramonet** and **Pañol** taverns with their garlic- and ham-strung ceilings are well worth a visit. Two well known bars very popular for their tapas are:

Alt Heidelberg, Ronda Universitat 5. Colorful bar with German beer on tap and a great variety of German sausages and tapas.

Cervecería, at the top of Ramblas opposite the Hostal Continental. Popular beerhall with a vast variety of tapas and especially good seafood.

Bars. Boadas, Tallers 1 on the corner of Ramblas. Going strong for over 50 years, this popular meeting place is famed for its cocktails.

Dry Martini, París 102. *The* place to go if your tipple is Martini. The barman has over 80 different gins with which he concocts his special martinis, and there is a *Martini del Día* on offer every day. Also a selection of whisky. Even the paintings on display are related to the Martini theme. Closed Sun. and last two weeks in Aug.

Ideal Cocktail Bar, Aribau 89 on the corner of Mallorca. A well-known cocktail bar first opened in 1931 and with some remnants of its original *Art Deco* style still there. It serves a good selection of whisky, including malts, amongst other liquors and fruit based *aguardientes,* and there are tapas and canapés to accompany your drinking. Closed Sun. and last two weeks in Aug.

Merbeye, Plaça Dr. Andreu. Next to the Tibidabo funicular, its pleasant terrace with palm trees is ideal for a coffee or early evening drink. The inside bar is very fashionable with the young and stays open till 3 A.M. Closed Sun.

Nick Havanna, Rosselló 208. Lively cocktail bar claiming to be "the ultimate bar."

Otto Zutz, Lincoln 15. One of the latest "in" places where people go to be seen. Loud, lively and open till the wee small hours.

El Paraigua, Pas. de l'Ensenyança 2, on Plaça Sant Miquel in heart of Gothic Quarter. Stylish turn-of-century style cocktail bar with classical music.

Els Quatre Gats, Montsió 5. A picturesque *tertulia* bar in the heart of the Barrio Gótico, a reconstruction of the famous original *Els Quatre Gats* which opened in 1897 and was the cafe associated with the *Belle Epoque Modernista* movement, where Picasso had one of his first shows, Albeniz and Granados played their piano compositions, Maragall read his poetry and for which Ramon Casas painted two famous murals.

Jazz Cafes. Abraxas Jazz Auditorium, Gelabert 26. Large venue with live and recorded music, mostly jazz. Well known Spanish and foreign bands. Closed Mon. and in Aug.

La Cova del Drac, Tuset 30, off the Diagonal. Bar famous for its live music, usually Catalan singing or jazz. Closed Sun.

Passeig del Born. This is one of the best streets for exciting bars and cafes and definitely one of the "in" places for the young. **Berimbau** at no. 17 has Brazilian music; **El Born** at no. 26 is a pleasant cocktail bar with a buffet; **El Copetín** at no. 19 has exciting decor and some good cocktails; **Miramelindo** at no. 15 offers a large selection of herbal liquors, fruit cocktails, pâtés and cheeses with music, usually jazz.

Champanerías. Brut, Trompetas 3 in the Picasso Museum area. A popular after-the-theater-or-cinema bar serving cocktails and champagne specialties.

La Cava del Palau, Verdaguer i Callis 10, close to the Palau de la Música. Good selection of wines and champagne cocktails served with home-made canapés and sandwiches. Wide choice of Catalan *cavas*.

La Folie, Bailén 169. One of the city's best known wine and champagne bars with good atmosphere and pleasant decor.

La Xampanyeria, Provença 236 on the corner of Enric Granados. This was the first, and is still one of the best, champanerías to open in Barcelona. Open from 7 P.M. until 2.30 A.M. and serving over 50 different Catalan wines.

Cafés and Tea Salons. Café de l'Opera, Ramblas 74. This traditional gathering place right opposite the Liceo is one of the great cafes of old; an ideal place at any time of day for a coffee or a drink.

Café Zurich, corner of Pelai and Plaça Catalunya. Barcelona's best-known meeting place, and a good place to relax and watch the world go by.

Oriente, Ramblas 45. The outdoor terrace of the Oriente hotel right on the Ramblas itself is the perfect place for a coffee or cocktail and to watch the ever-lively promenade.

Salón de Te Llibre i Serra, Ronda Sant Pere (San Pedro) 3. Exquisite tea room in a pastry shop which dates from 1907. Some 25 kinds of tea are served accompanied by sweet and savory delicacies. Closed Sunday afternoons.

Salón de Te Mauri, corner of Rambla de Catalunya and Provença. Typical tea room atmosphere and a good selection of pastries.

CITY TOURS. Tours of the city are run by *Juliá Tours,* Ronda Universitat 5 (tel. 317 6454) and *Pullmantur,* Gran Vía de les Corts Catalans 635 (tel. 318 0241). You can book these tours direct with the head offices above, or through any travel agency, or, in most cases, through your hotel.

City Tour. A half-day tour in the morning visiting the Plaça de Catalunya, the cathedral and Gothic Quarter, the City Hall (Ayuntamiento), the Passeig Colom, Montjuïc for a view over the city, and the Pueblo Español (Spanish Village).

City Tour and Picasso Museum. A half-day tour in the afternoon visiting Gaudi's Sagrada Familia and the Picasso Museum.

Panorámica y Toros. On days when there are bullfights only (usually Sundays). A drive through the city along the Diagonal, past the Church of the Holy Family, to the Monumental bullring. Seats for the bullfight and an explanation of bullfighting by the guide are included.

Night Tours. These come in various combinations including *Panorámica y Flamenco,* a panoramic drive through the city to see the illuminations followed by a flamenco show with drink included; *Gala en Scala,* cabaret show at La Scala with either dinner or just a drink; *Noche Flamenca,* dinner in a restaurant followed by visit to a flamenco show.

EXCURSIONS. These are run by *Juliá Tours* and *Pullmantur* and are booked as above.

Montserrat. Half-day excursion (morning or afternoon) to the famous Benedictine monastery of Montserrat 50 km. from Barcelona. Excursion includes a guided visit of the monastery, time to see the shrine of the Black Virgin and listen to the famous La Escolanía choir (mornings only), or a funicular ride to the top of one of the peaks of the strange saw-edged mountains (afternoons only).

Costa Brava. A full-day trip leaving Barcelona at 9 A.M. to the Costa Brava resorts including a boat cruise to Lloret de Mar. May to Oct. only, daily except Sun.

Andorra. A full-day trip, on Mon., Wed. and Fri., leaving Barcelona at 6.30 A.M. to the independent Principality of Andorra situated high in the Pyrenees between Spain and France. Lunch is included and Andorra is a mecca for tax-free shopping. Weekend trips with Sat. night in an hotel are available year round.

NIGHTLIFE. Barcelona has long had a reputation as a center of wild and wooly nightspots and there is no shortage of places putting on gay, transvestite or just plain pornographic shows. What are hard to find, however, and surprising for a city of its size, are many high-class nightclubs along the lines of, say, Paris' *Lido* or *Crazy Horse.* The places listed below should not, we hope, offend in any way, but beware the seedier night spots of the Barrio Chino and Paral-lel. *Belle Epoque* and *La Scala* are probably the best bets.

Nightclubs. Belle Epoque, Muntaner 246 (tel. 209 7385). Beautifully decorated music hall putting on good shows. Closed Sun. AE, DC, MC, V.

Gran Casino de Barcelona, 42 km. south in Sant Pere de Ribes near Sitges (tel. 893 3866). 19th-century casino with Black Jack, Boule, Roulette etc., restaurant, dancing and shows on some nights.

El Mediévolo, Gran Vía 459, between Rocafort and Calabria (tel. 325 3480). Medieval feasts and entertainment; much geared to tourists but fun.

Regine's, Av. Joan XXIII, in the Princesa Sofia hotel. Barcelona's top in-vogue club combines fashionable disco, bar, and restaurant; definitely one of the places in which to be seen, but call the hotel first to check on membership rules.

Scala Barcelona, Passeig Sant Joan 47 (tel. 232 6363). Barcelona's leading nightclub with two shows nightly, the first with dinner and cabaret, the second, around midnight, with drinks, dancing, and cabaret. Closed Mon. AE, DC, MC, V.

Flamenco. Catalans often consider this Andalusian spectacle anti-Catalan so Barcelona is not richly endowed with flamenco spots and those that there are, are aimed right at the tourist market. However, Barcelona's large Andalusian community from which many of the performers come, should offer a touch of authenticity.

Andalucía, Ramblas 27 (tel. 302 2009). Dinner from 8.30–10 followed by flamenco and Spanish dancing.

El Cordobés, Ramblas 35 (tel. 317 6653). This is the one visited by most tour groups, but it is fun and colorful.

Las Sevillanas del Patio, Aribau 242 (tel. 209 3524). Sevillanas rather than flamenco are performed here, often with audience participation.

Los Tarantos, Plaça Reial 17 (tel. 317 8098). Good flamenco show twice nightly at 10 and midnight, popular with tourists and locals.

Discos. Barcelona is very much a disco city with new and sophisticated places springing up each year. As in most Spanish cities, there are usually two sessions, *tarde* from around 7 P.M.–10 P.M., which is geared very much to the young and is usually cheaper, and *noche* beginning at 11 or 11.30 P.M. and continuing until 2 or 3 A.M. The "in" place to go changes frequently, but the following have proved reliable bets. Entrances vary from 1,000–2,000 ptas. and one drink is usually included in the price.

Duetto, Consell de Cent 294. A very popular disco appealing to a wide range of tastes with bars on three floors, videos and live shows.

Studio 54, Paral-lel 54. One of the biggest and with some "spectacular" shows which draw the crowds; lots of action. Open Fri., Sat. and Sun. only.

Trauma, Consell de Cent 228. A pleasant spot with a wide range of music and modest prices.

Up and Down, Numància 179. Very smart and fashionable (men must wear jacket and tie). Definitely one of the "in" places with loud music on the downstairs dance floor and upstairs a quieter, more sophisticated, even "snob" atmosphere. There is also a restaurant. Call 204 8809 to check membership rules.

MUSEUMS. Barcelona is well endowed with museums, the most outstanding being the Museum of Catalan Art and the Picasso Museum. Many of the best museums are now free, others have a free day on either

Sundays or Wednesdays, and holders of ISI cards, and in some cases, senior citizens, are often entitled to free entrance. Most museums close on Mondays.

Fundación Joan Miró, in Montjuïc Park. Center for the Study of Contemporary Arts founded by the artist Joan Miró and designed by Josep Lluis Sert. Collection of paintings and sculptures by Miró. Open Tues. to Sat. 11–7 (11–9.30 on Thurs.); Sun. and fiestas 10.30–2.30. Closed Mon.

Museo Arqueológico, in Montjuïc Park. Roman mosaics and displays of finds from Ampurias. Open Tues. to Sat. 9.30–1 and 4–7, Sun. 10–2 only; closed Mon.

Museo de Arte de Cataluña, in the Palacio Nacional on Montjuïc. Houses the world's greatest collection of Catalan Romanesque art. In the same building is a delightful **Ceramics Museum** which can be visited on the same ticket. Open 9–2. Closed Mon. Partially closed at presstime for renovation; check with tourist office.

Museo de Arte Moderno, in Ciudadela Park. Worthwhile collection of paintings from the late 18th century to early 20th including works by the Catalan artists Casas, Fortuny, Miró, Tàpies and Russinyol. Several rooms are now dedicated to the works of contemporary Catalan artists. Open Tues. to Sat. 9–7.30, Sun. 9–2, Mon. 3–7.30.

Museo de Autómatas del Tibidabo, in the Amusement Park on Tibidabo. Fairground automatons, mechanical dolls, electric trains, magical wizards, etc. Open Mon. to Fri. 12–2 and 3–5.45, Sat. to Sun. 12–3 and 4–7.45.

Museo de Calzado Antiguo, Plaça Sant Felip Neri in the Gothic Quarter. Museum of the history of shoes and shoe-making. Includes shoes donated by Pablo Casals. Open Sat., Sun. and fiestas only, from 11–2.

Museo de Carruajes, in the Pedralbes Palace on the Diagonal. Coach and carriage museum with a small collection of weapons and uniforms. Open Tues. to Fri. 10–1 and 4–6, Sat. and Sun. 10–2 only.

Museo de Carrozas Funebres, Sancho de Avila 2. Collection of funeral carriages dating from the middle of the 19th century onwards, and related funeral paraphernalia. Open 9–2. Closed Sun.

Museo de Cera, Pasaje de la Banca 7, at the port end of Ramblas. Wax Museum with over 300 historic and contemporary figures. Open daily 11–1.30 and 4.30–7.30.

Museo de la Ciencia, Teodoro Roviralta 55. Science Museum, including a Planetarium. Open 10–8. Closed Mon.

Museo Etnológico, Passeig Santa Madrona in Montjuïc Park. Exhibits from early civilizations worldwide. Open Tues. to Sat. 9–8.30, Sun. 9–2, Mon. 2–8.30.

Museo Federico Marés, Comtes de Barcelona 10. In the Palacio Real in the heart of the Gothic Quarter, this museum houses an important collection of religious sculpture including several wooden crucifixes, and upstairs, the personal collection of the sculptor Federico Marés, a wonderful array of *bric-à-brac* of all sorts; a fascinating museum. Open Tues. to Sat. 9–2 and 4–7, Sun. 9–2. Closed Mon.

Museo de Geología, in Ciudadela Park. Municipal Geology Museum (Martorell Museum). Open Tues. to Sun. 9–2. Closed Mon.

Museo de Historia de la Ciudad, in the Casa Padellás in the Plaça del Rei. The history of Barcelona throughout the ages with traces of the Roman city in the basement. Open Mon. 3–8, Tues. to Sat. 9–8, Sun. 9–1.30.

Museo de la Indumentaria Manuel Rocamora, Montcada 12. Interesting Costume Museum with costumes from the 16th to 20th centuries installed in one of the old palaces near the Picasso Museum. Open daily 9–2.

Museo Marítimo, Reales Atarazanas at the bottom of Ramblas. Outstanding Maritime Museum containing replicas of the galley used by Don John of Austria at the Battle of Lepanto, the first submarine, and a nautical map by Amerigo Vespucci. Open Tues. to Sat. 10–2 and 4–7, Sun. 10–2. Closed Mon.

Museo Militar, in Montjuïc Castle. Well arranged collection of arms and military uniforms from various countries and a collection of miniature soldiers. Open Tues. to Sat. 10–2 and 4–7, Sun. 10–7. Closed Mon.

Museo de la Música, Bruch 110. Musical instruments, manuscripts, scores and mementoes of great musicians. Open 9–2. Closed Mon.

Museo Picasso, Montcada 15. Important collection of sketches and paintings, donated originally by the great man himself. Open Tues. to Sun. 10–7. Closed Mon.

Museo Taurino, Plaza de Toros Monumental, Gran Vía 749. Bullfighting paraphernalia, bulls' heads, suits of light, etc., situated in the Monumental Bullring on the corner of Gran Vía and Passeig Carles I. Open 10–1 and 3.30–7; on days when there are bullfights 10–1 only.

Museo Zoología, Passeig dels Tillers in Ciudadela Park. Natural History museum in a building known as the Castle of the Three Dragons designed by Domènech i Montaner for the 1888 Exhibition. Open 9–2. Closed Mon.

HISTORIC BUILDINGS AND SITES. Antiguo Hospital de la Santa Cruz, Hospital 56. One of the principal complexes of Gothic buildings in the city with a splendid patio. Amongst the many cultural institutes housed here is the **Sala Miguel Soldevila,** with a collection of the artist's enamels. Open 10–1 and 4–8. Closed Sat. and fiestas.

Basílica de la Vírgen de la Merced, Placa de la Merced off the Passeig Colom. Baroque church containing the image of Barcelona's patron saint. Open 7 A.M.–8 P.M.

Casa Batlló, Passeig de Gràcia 43. Built for the textile manufacturer Josep Batllo in 1875–77, Gaudi gave it a splendid facelift in 1904–06 so it could outshine its neighbor, the Casa Amatller at no. 41 by Puig i Cadafalch. Now used as offices but open to visitors 8–10 A.M.

Casa Milá or **La Pedrera,** Passeig de Gràcia 92. Gaudi's splendid "stone quarry" was built in 1906–10 for Pedro Milá, Batllo's business partner. Now owned by an insurance company, which extensively cleaned and renovated it in 1988, its patio is open to visitors. You can visit the roof at 10 A.M., 11 A.M., and 12 noon, or have a drink in the **Amarcord** bar inside the building.

Gran Teatro Liceo, Ramblas 61. Begun in 1845, this is one of the grandest Opera Houses in Europe. Tours of the Opera House are conducted at 11.30 and 12.15 on Mon., Wed. and Fri. in winter, and daily Mon. to Fri. in summer.

Iglesia de Santa María del Mar, Plaça de Santa María. Beautiful early Gothic church with huge single vault and unusual columns. Open 8–1 and 4–7.30.

Iglesia del Pí, Plaça del Pí. 14th-century Gothic church of San José Oriol in delightful small square just off Ramblas. Open 8–1 and 6–9.

Lonja, Passeig de Isabel II. Neo-Classic Palace of the Exchange housing the 14th-century Gothic *Salón de Contrataciones,* The Stock Exchange, the Chamber of Commerce and Navigation and the Royal Academy of Fine Arts.

Monasterio de Pedralbes at the end of Passeig de Reina Elisenda de Montcada. Convent founded by Queen Elisenda, wife of Jaime II, in 1326. Beautiful chapel with 14th-century stained glass, rose windows and the tomb of Queen Elisenda. Important paintings and murals by the Sienese school with outstanding murals by Ferrer Bassa (1436). A rich collection of works of art. Open 10–1; closed Mon.

Palacio del Ayuntamiento, Plaça Sant Jaume. Gothic City Hall with a neo-Classical facade. Inside is the splendid *Salón de Ciento* and the *Salón de las Crónicas* with murals by José María Sert. Open during business hours.

Palacio de la Generalidad (Palau Generalitat), Plaça Sant Jaume. Gothic patio and stairway, the famous *Patio de los Naranjos,* and the Chapel and *Salón de San Jorge* with murals by Torres García. Open on Sundays only from 10–1.

Palacio Güell, Nou de la Rambla. This is one of the few of Gaudí's buildings it is possible to go inside as it houses the **Museu de les Arts de l'Espectacle,** a museum of the history of Barcelona's theater, cinema and dance. Open Mon. to Sat. 11–2 and 5–8.

Palacio (Palau) de la Música, Amadeo Vives 1, just off Vía Laietana. Magnificent concert hall by Lluis Doménech i Montaner built in *Modernista* style. Can be visited on Mondays and Fridays at 11.30.

Palacio de Pedralbes, out along the Diagonal. Temporary art exhibitions. Open Mon. to Fri. 10–1 and 4–7, Sat. and Sun. 10–2, but call 203 7501 to check.

Palau de la Virreina, Ramblas 99 on corner of Carme. Built by a viceroy of Peru in 1778 for the wife he left behind, it now serves as a major exhibition center; check to see what's showing. Open 9.30–1.30 and 4.30–9; closed Mon.

Parque Güell in which there is a house which has been turned into a **Gaudí Museum.** The museum is open on Sundays only from 10–2 and 4–6.

Pueblo Español in Montjuïc Park. The Spanish Village built in 1929 by Miguel Utrillo and Xavier Nogués for the International Exhibition. Houses, streets and plazas showing the different architectural styles of each region of Spain. Of the many small industries and crafts that used to be demonstrated here, today only a glass blowers and a printing press remain. Incorporates two museums, the **Museum of Graphic Arts** and the **Museum of Popular Arts and Crafts,** both open Tues. to Sun. 9–2; closed Mon. The village is open daily 9–7.

Reales Atarazanas, in the Porta de la Pau off Passeig Colom. 14th-century Royal shipyards built by Pedro el Grande and Pedro el Ceremonioso; the only remaining one of its kind in Europe. The **Maritime Museum** is housed here.

Sagrada Familia, between Mallorca-Provença, and Marina-Sardenya. Gaudí was first recommended as the architect of the Sagrada Familia in 1883, and after 1911 when he stopped work on the Parque Güell, he dedicated the rest of his life to this great building in whose crypt he now lies buried. Construction is still going on but you can visit part of Gaudí's original building. The site is open daily 9–8.

PARKS AND GARDENS. Parque de la Ciudadela is the closest to the city center. Its name means "Citadel Park" and the citadel, built in 1716 by Philip V, was pulled down in 1868 and replaced by public gardens laid out by Josep Fontseré. In the park are the Geology and Natural History Museums, the Museum of Modern Art, a zoo, aquarium and the Catalan Regional Parliament. The gardens, with their statues and fountains, make a pleasant place to stroll or relax.

Parque Güell, in the northwest of the city is a delightful place to visit. It was begun by Gaudí whose idea was to build a kind of garden city development to demonstrate his ideas on town planning. The project was never finished and only a few early constructions can be seen, but these constitute a superb Art Nouveau extravaganza. Not only does the park have Gaudí's incredible mosaics but also magnificent views over the city to the Mediterranean. The park is open daily, but the Gaudí Museum in one of its houses is open only on Sundays. The park has recently been undergoing restoration and although open to the public may not be seen to its best advantage; so check with the Tourist Office before you set out. To reach the park, take Metro Line 3 to Lesseps or Vallcarca and then walk—it is quite a steep climb; or alternatively take buses 24 or 28 from the Plaça de Catalunya, which go right by the park.

Parque de Montjuïc. Its name, meaning "hill of the Jews," comes from the time when Barcelona's Jewish community lived on its slopes. The gardens surrounding the hill were laid out for the International Exhibition of 1929. The Jardines de Miramar offer a splendid view over the city and the park is the home of six museums—Catalan Art, Ceramics, Archeology, Military, Ethnological and the Joan Miró Foundation—as well as the Pueblo Español, the model Spanish village, the Teatre Grec where open-air performances are held in summer, a huge amusement park and a magnificent fountain whose colored illuminations are a memorable sight on summer weekends or fiestas. There are several ways of reaching Montjuïc. Probably the most spectacular is to take the aerial cable car which runs from Barceloneta to the Jardines de Miramar. There is also the funicular from the end of Nou de la Rambla but this is more often than not out-of-order. Bus no. 61 from the Plaça de Espanya runs through the park passing the Pueblo Español, the Joan Miró Foundation and the Amusement Park every half hour on the hour and half past until 8 P.M. Bus 13 from the San Antonio Market on Borrell runs to the Plaça Espanya and on to the Pueblo Español. But public transport here is often misleading, and it's best just to walk from Plaça d'Espanya or else hail a cab.

Tibidabo. This mountain lying behind Barcelona is 1,745 ft. high and can be reached either by funicular (rack railroad) or by a winding road affording spectacular views of the city and Mediterranean. Atop the mountain is a basilica and a brash fun fair, but the view is breathtaking. To take the funicular up to the top, first take bus no. 58 or the subway (F.C. Sarrià line) to the Avda. de Tibidabo, then take the *tramvía blau,* the only remaining one of the blue trams of old, which runs to the funicular station. The funicular runs every half hour from 7.15 A.M. to 9.45 P.M.

MUSIC, MOVIES AND THEATER. To find out what is on in Barcelona, look in the daily press *(La Vanguardia, Correo Catalan, Diario de Barcelona),* or better still in the weekly *Guía del Ocio* available from newsstands all over town.

Music. Barcelona has one of the world's finest opera houses, the **Gran Teatro del Liceo** seating some 5,000 people, and which many consider to be second only to Milan's *La Scala*. The Liceo stands on the Ramblas on the corner of Sant Pau (San Pablo). The box office for advance bookings is down the side of the building in Sant Pau 1 (tel. 318 9277), open Mon. to Fri. 8–3, Sat. 9–1. Tickets for performances on the day are on sale in the Ramblas entrance (tel. 301 6787) from 11–1.30 and from 4 onwards. The main opera season runs throughout the winter from November till March, but performances may often be seen much later into the spring. The ballet season is usually April thru' May. Famous opera singers perform here frequently and the Liceo is especially well known for its Wagnerian performances. Tickets are not expensive by international standards and, if you are content with the cheaper seats, can usually be obtained right up to the day of performance itself.

The main concert hall is the **Palau de la Música,** Amadeo Vives 1, just off the Vía Laietana. Its ticket office opens Mon. to Fri. 11–1 and 5–8, Sat. 5–8 only. Tickets for performances on the day are only available from 5 P.M. onwards. Its Sunday morning concerts are a very popular Barcelona tradition. Best known amongst Barcelona's musical groups and orchestras is the *Orquesta Ciudad de Barcelona* (Barcelona City Orchestra) and the *Orfeó Català* (Catalan Choral Society). In summer concerts are sometimes held in the patio of the Antiguo Hospital de la Santa Cruz on Carrer Hospital. An *International Music Festival* is held in Barcelona in September during the city's celebrations for the feast of the Merced (around Sept. 23).

Movies. Barcelona has plenty of movie theaters but the majority of foreign films are dubbed into Spanish. Some theaters also show films in Catalan. However, if you have the patience to go through the *Guía del Ocio* looking for films marked *V.O. Subtitulada* this means that the films are being shown in their original language (often English) with Spanish subtitles. The official **Filmoteca** is on Travessera de Gracià 63 on the corner of Tusset, and shows three films a day in their original language.

Theater. Catalonia is well known for its mime theater and two well known mime troupes are *Els Joglars* and *La Claca*. An *International Mime Festival* is held most years as is a *Festival de Títeres* (Puppet Festival). One of the best known theaters is the **Teatre Lliure** which specializes in experimental theater and satirical reviews, but as with many other Barcelona theaters, many of its performances are in Catalan. There is an open-air summer *Theater Festival* in July and August when plays, music, song and dance performances are held at the **Teatre Grec** in Montjuïc Park.

SPORTS. Bullfights. These are normally held from the end of March thru' October, usually on Sundays and for fiestas. The main ring is the **Monumental** on Gran Vía and Carles I. **Las Arenas** ring in the Plaça de Espanya is used only rarely. Tickets can be bought at the rings themselves or from the advance ticket office at Muntaner 24.

Soccer (fútbol). Barcelona's famous team, known as Barça, is one of the world's richest and grandest soccer teams. Matches are played, usually on Sundays, at the Camp Nou Stadium off Avda. Arístides Maillol which is being enlarged to hold 125,000 for the 1992 Olympics. Matches are also played at the **Sarrià Stadium,** Avda. Sarria 120.

Golf. There are five golf clubs in the area around Barcelona. The **Sant Cugat Club** about 14 km from the center; the **Prat de Llobregat Club,** the **Sant Andreu de Llanvaneres Club;** the **Vallromanes Club** and the **Terramar Club** in Sitges.

Tennis. For tennis there are the following clubs: **Barcino,** Passatge Forester 2; **Pompeia,** Travessera de Gracià 13; **La Salut,** Verge de la Salut 75; **Real Club,** Bosch i Gimpera; and the **Club Deportivo Laietano,** Sant Ramón Nonato. Rental courts at Andrés Gimeno off the highway in Castelldefels, and at Can Melich at Sant Just Desvern (take bus SJ from the Plaça Universitat for the latter).

Bowling. At the **Boliche Bolera,** Diagonal 508 and the **Bolera Novedades,** Casp 1.

Ice skating. At the **Skating Club,** Roger de Flor 168 and another at the **Palau Blau-Grana,** at the Barcelona Fútbol Club stadium, Avda. Arístides Maillol.

Swimming. Several of the 4- and 5-star hotels have pools and there are public pools on Avda. Sarrià 84, the **Piscina Montjuïc** on Avda. Miramar and the **Piscina Bernardo Picornell** in Montjuïc Park.

SHOPPING. The best shopping streets are the Passeig de Gracià (the Fifth Avenue of Barcelona); the Rambla de Catalunya; the Gran Vía between Balmes and Pau Claris; and on and around the Diagonal in the area between Ganduxer and Passeig de Gracià where there are several small boutiques in the Carrer Tusset area. For more old-fashioned, typically Spanish-style shops, explore the area between Ramblas and the Vía Laietana, especially along Carrer Ferran (Fernando). There are also lots of young fashionable stores and trendy gift shops in this area bounded by the Ramblas, Ferran, Porta de l'Angel and the Plaça Catalunya—try especially the narrow streets around the Placeta del Pi from Boquería to Portaferrisa and Canuda.

If you're feeling adventurous, you might wander over to the Major de Gracià area just above the Passeig de Gracià. This is really a small, almost independent pueblo within a large city, a warren of small, narrow streets, changing name at every corner, and filled with tiny shops where you'll find everything from old-fashioned tin lanterns to real feather dusters.

For **antiques** your best bet is to wander around the cathedral in the Barrio Gótico. Carrer de la Palla and Banys Nous have one antique shop after another. There you'll find old maps, books, paintings and furniture. And don't forget the antiques fair held on Thursday mornings in the Plaça Nova in front of the cathedral. You might also just come across some bargains at the Els Encants flea market. On the Passeig de Gracià at no. 57, the Centre d'Antiquaris, has some 75 antique stores.

Department stores. The main department stores are *El Corte Inglés* on the Plaça de Catalunya, with a newer and much bigger one on the Diagonal near the metro stop María Cristina; and the *Galerías Preciados* on Porta de l'Angel just off Plaça Catalunya, in the Plaça Françesc Macià on the Diagonal, and at Meridiana 352. All are open 10–8. Enquire about tourist discount plans.

Markets. Antiques Market. Held in the square in front of the cathedral on Thursday mornings. Antiques are often of high quality, especially the silver.

For a typical and very colorful food market, you should go to the **Boquería Market** just off the Ramblas between Carme and Hospital on any day of the week except Sunday.

Els Encants. Barcelona's flea market held on Mon., Wed., Fri. and Sat. at the end of Dos de Maig on the Plaça Glories Catalanes. Junk of all kinds; fascinating and picturesque.

San Antonio Market, held on Sunday mornings in the old market building with beautiful tiled stalls on the corner of Urgell and Tamarit at the end of Ronda Sant Antoní. Fascinating collection of second-hand books, old magazines, postcards, press cuttings, lithographs, prints, etc.

Stamp and Coin Market, held on Sunday mornings in the Plaça Reial.

Artists' Market. Paintings are on sale on Saturday mornings in the Placeta del Pi alongside the church of San José Oriol in the Gothic Quarter.

USEFUL ADDRESSES. Airlines. The *Iberia* air terminal is in the Plaça de Espanya, and the main *Iberia* office at Passeig de Gracià 30 (tel. 301 3993) on the corner of Diputació 258; open Mon. to Fri. 9–1.30 and 4–7, Sat. 9–1. For national reservations, call 301 6800; for international reservations, call 302 7656; for flight arrival and departure information, call *Inforiberia* on 301 3993. The airport number is 370 1011.

British Airways are at Passeig de Gracià 85, 4th floor (tel. 215 2112), open Mon. to Fri. 9–5. *Pan Am* are handled by *Transtur,* Avda. Drassanes 6 (tel. 301 7249). *TWA* are at Gran Vía de les Corts Catalans 634 (tel. 318 0031).

Consulates. U.S. Consulate, Vía Laietana 33 (tel. 319 9550). British Consulate, Diagonal 477 (tel. 322 2151).

Police. The main Police Station is on Vía Laietana 49 (tel. 301 6666). In an emergency, dial 091.

Car Hire. *Atesa,* Balmes 141 (tel. 237 8140); *Avis,* Casanova 209 (tel. 209 9533) and Aragó 235 (tel. 215 8430); *Hertz,* Tuset 10 (tel. 237 3737); *Ital,* Travessera de Gracià 71 (tel. 321 5141), and all are represented at the airport.

Travel Agents. *American Express,* Rosselló 257 on corner of Passeig de Gracià (tel. 217 0070), open Mon. to Fri. 9.30–6, Sat. 10–12. *Wagon Lits Cooks,* Passeig de Gracià 8 (tel. 317 5500).

Main Post Office. Plaça Antoní López at the bottom of Vía Laietana.

Telephone Exchange. Carrer Fontanella on the corner of Plaça Catalunya, open Mon. to Sat. 8.30 A.M.–9 P.M., closed Sun.

Hospital Evangélico (or of the Foreign Colonies), Alegre de Dalt 87 (tel. 219 7100).

American Visitors' Bureau, Gran Vía 591, 3rd floor (between Rambla de Catalunya and Balmes) (tel. 301 0150/0032). Services include packing and shipping of personal effects or purchases. Open 9–1.30 and 4–7, Sat. 9–1 only.

SPAIN AND THE SPANIARDS

A Changing Image

by
HARRY EYRES

Harry Eyres has lived, and traveled extensively, in Spain, both as a student and as the Spanish correspondent of the London Spectator, *for which he still writes on Spanish affairs.*

Spain—to risk one of the few generalizations that can be made about a land of such diversity—is the most individual country in Europe, and the Spanish are the most individualistic people. In fact, they are so individualistic that they find it difficult to accept the existence of anything as totalitarian as the Spanish nation. Spain has preserved its regional differences and identities better than other European nations, which gives it both the advantage of variety and the danger of disunity. It is a land of nationalisms rather than nationalism. The most violent, of course, is that of the Basques, with their strange prehistoric language and their terrorist independence movement, E.T.A. But the Basques are not the only Spaniards with their own language and pretensions to independence. Six million people on the east coast and in the Balearic islands speak Catalan, a language related to old Provencal, quite separate from Spanish, (which incidentally is known in Spain as Castilian), and equally rich in culture, history and tradi-

90

tion. Away in the wet northwest corner of the peninsula, the Galicians speak Gallego, which is related to Portuguese, and nurture their less vigorous dreams of an independent Galicia.

These complications should intrigue rather than disturb the visitor. Catalan street signs in Barcelona may be hard to decipher at first, but Catalans will speak Castilian if you ask them politely. Though E.T.A. have taken to planting bombs on beaches, they have so far confined their killing to the National Police and the Civil Guard.

Galloping Modernity

Indeed some visitors may prefer to forget altogether about political problems, relying on traditional images of bullfights and castanets, or beaches and sangría. Such things can be found, though the romantic idea of Spain is very much based on the South, and Andalusia in particular. Young Spaniards will not thank you for expecting them to conform to stereotypes of the torero or the haughty señorita. Among the more educated people there is a very strong wish to get away from all that paraphernalia, partly because it was promoted so strongly during the long repressive regime of Franco, whose belief in the immortal essence of Spain involved much artificial preservation of tradition. Most Spaniards now want to be modern and West European, not, as the Spanish Tourist Board used to say, "different."

There can be no denying that they have moved a very long way to that end in an extremely short space of time. What was still in the 1930s a rural and agricultural society has become predominantly urban and industrial, or even post-industrial. Ten years after the death of Europe's second last surviving Fascist dictator, Spain has a democratic system headed by a sane and tactful constitutional monarch, and a socialist government—voted in by an enormous majority—for the first time since the short-lived Second Republic of 1931–36.

That earlier period of democracy ended in the carnage of the Civil War, which seemed for a long time (its memory was fostered by Franco) to have reaffirmed the Black Legend of Spain's tragic destiny. Spaniards now do not like to talk about it, but more out of a wish to forget a time of appalling waste than because of unhealed wounds. When Lt. Col. Tejero of the Guardia Civil walked into the Cortes (Parliament) brandishing a pistol on 23 February 1981, it appeared for a short time as if Spain's renascent democracy had been ended once again by a military coup. When this attempt failed, however, almost entirely because of King Juan Carlos's firm and immediate appeal to the army to remain loyal to him as its commander-in-chief, it proved instead that the new democracy in Spain had been strengthened by its first serious ordeal. Future threats from the Armed Forces, the only real danger to the democratic system, had become suddenly less credible.

The final confirmation, for most Spaniards, that their country has shrugged off its persistent image of backwardness, is Spain's acceptance into the European club, the E.E.C. What benefits this will bring remain to be seen—and there are some who even dare to doubt that it *will* bring substantial benefits—but its psychological importance cannot be doubted. Fernando Morán, then Spanish Foreign Minister, summed it up when he said after terms had been agreed in March 1985: "now at last Spain can hold her head high once more in international relations."

Perhaps even more important than this political modernization is the drastic liberalization which has occurred in Spanish society. From being one of the most conservative countries in Western Europe, Spain has suddenly become, in certain respects, one of the most liberal. The taking of some soft drugs, for example, is now permitted, even if their sale is not (though the vendors of so-called "chocolate" at the entrance to the arcaded Plaça Reial in Barcelona do not seem to be aware of this). It must be said that many people are linking the rise in crime on the streets with the availability of drugs, and there are signs of the government backpedalling on this issue. Abortion is now legal, though only for medical reasons or after rape—and here too there are signs of a conservative backlash, because the Constitutional Court recently (1985) ruled against the Socialist government's pro-abortion legislation—though only on a technicality. Pornography, banned for so long under the "muy católico" Generalissimo Franco, is back on the streets, and it seems to be making up for lost time. Pornographic comics, strangely combining strip (in both senses) cartoons with radical politics are popular with the student generation, who have been going through all the styles, fashions and movements which Spain missed out on from the '50s to the '80s, rock'n'roll to punk, in an accelerated rampage. Toplessness is rife on the crowded beaches, despite the disapproval of the Catholic organization Opus Dei and the right-wing daily paper *A.B.C.*

The Spanish Landscape

Despite all this evidence of Spain's modernity, however, it may still be that it is the anachronistic and, dare one say, "different" elements of the country which will interest and attract the visitor most. Under this heading come history, culture and many aspects of the way of life in Spain which still contrast (and we at least may be grateful for it) with the increasingly homogenized world outside. One thing not much affected by modernization is the landscape, or at least its more permanent features, the mountains, the light, the sea—if we forget for the moment the ghastly ribbon development which has spoilt so much of what Rose Macaulay in the 1950s could still call its "fabled shore."

Spain is a large country by European standards, only slightly smaller than France, twice the size of Britain, and it contains an extraordinary variety of geography and, above all, climate, which goes far towards explaining the strength of regional character and identity noted earlier. It might be better to think of Spain as a subcontinent than a country. Certainly the idea of a uniformly "sunny Spain" is misleading, but not as misleading as the English ditty "The rain in Spain falls mainly on the plain," which, if you take the plain to mean the central tableland or meseta, is precisely the opposite of the truth. This plateau (about 2,000 feet high) which covers two-fifths of the peninsula is parchingly arid for most of the year, as are large stretches of the eastern coastal region and the southwestern region of Extremadura. The northwestern "nationality" of Galicia, on the other hand, is wetter than Ireland, with which it has much in common. This excess of humidity is very much the exception in Spain, and it is a costly irony of fate that rainfall should be highest in areas where the soil is poorest. Aridity is the keynote, and nowhere is this brought home more vividly than at the historic pass of Roncesvalles, where Roland made his last stand, which connects the French *département des Pyrenées Occidentales* with the little Spanish kingdom of Navarre. In summer, looking from the Spanish side, you see a bank of cloud like smoke rolling through the defile from the damp deciduous forests of beech and chestnut which cover the French western Pyrenees, then dissolving into blue sky as it reaches the great golden-tawny expanse of the Navarrese plain.

Such a color can only be produced by long hours of burning sun. The summer sun in Spain is often more awesome than, as the tourist brochures stupidly reiterate, pleasant and sexy. It is capable of obliterating all activity and reducing one to utter torpor. Unlike that of northern countries, Spanish sun can have a negative or destructive value. It ages people prematurely and etches bitter lines in those faces which we picturesquely associate with Picasso peasants. On the other hand, it relaxes the muscles and dissolves away many of the neuroses which afflict people from sunless lands. A Spanish Edvard Munch is inconceivable. In winter, spring and autumn the extra light and heat which the northerner will experience can only be a bonus. I have breakfasted outside under the lemon tree on my patio in Barcelona on Christmas Eve with the thermometer standing at 70°, and throughout November and December there will be days, in the low-lying areas at least, when it is as warm as high summer in England. Even in January and February, when the temperature often falls below zero in Madrid, the weather is frequently bright and cloudless, and the crystalline light of Castile exhilarating, however cold the air.

Apart from the sun-baked dryness, the most striking feature of the Spanish landscape is its ruggedness. This is, after Switzerland, the second most mountainous country in Europe, containing its highest roads and villages. This means ample opportunities for skiing in ranges like the Pyrenees, the Sierra Nevada, the Guadarrama and the Picos de Europa. It also means innumerable remote and lovely valleys, often deserted by nearly all their former inhabitants in the drift towards the towns, where those who favor adventurous holidays can hunt, fish, walk, or just find an almost overwhelming peace camping in the open or sleeping in derelict farmhouses. Such relics of paradise exist, for example, three hours drive from Barcelona in the Catalan hinterland, where you can find yourself quite literally in another world. The experience can be disorientating, but will not be easily forgotten.

Early History

To some people this romantic notion of getting away from it all and communing with nature will seem nostalgic, unrealistic, or simply boring. Human activity, which in its more memorable forms means culture and history, will be the focus of their attention. Spanish culture and history have of course been decisively influenced by geography. The three features of that geography to note here are the barrier of the Pyrenees, neatly isolating Spain from the rest of Europe, the proximity to Africa (indeed W.H. Auden described Spain as "that fragment nipped off from hot Africa soldered so crudely to inventive Europe"), and the outlook westwards to the Americas.

Not that the Pyrenees have ever been an impassable barrier—first the Carthaginians, to attack the Romans, then the Romans, to defeat the Carthaginians, found it possible to cross them repeatedly. In the end Spain, or rather two Spains, Hispania Citerior and Hispania Ulterior (and the plurality may be significant) became part of the Roman empire: they produced four emperors as well as literary figures as distinguished as the Senecas, Martial and Lucan. The most important evidence of Roman dominion is the language, or languages (again plural)—Castilian, Catalan and Gallego, but not of course Basque, are all members of the Romance family—but there are also imposing physical remains like the aqueduct at Segovia and the theater and other ruins in the Extremaduran city of Mérida. No question then that Spain was very much part of Western Europe.

The Moorish Inheritance

It did not stay that way. In 711 the troubled period of Visigothic rule ended when Spain was invaded by Arabs from North Africa, who overran the country in an astonishingly short space of time. The Moorish rule which prevailed throughout much of the peninsula for the next seven-and-a-half centuries was generally tolerant—far more tolerant, most historians consider, than the Christian rule which followed—and it produced peaks of civilization which Spain has since rarely, if ever, surpassed.

The influence of the Moors on Spain is a huge subject which can only be touched on here. It is certainly not confined to the 4,000 odd Arabic words (including nearly all those beginning "al," like "alcalde," "alcázar," "albañil" and so on), or the beautiful remains of Moorish architecture, but persists in ethnic and, more interestingly, social characteristics which are the legacy of those 750 years of intermingling. Still, the architecture is what most tourists will want to see. It is difficult to say anything new about the Alhambra at Granada, but it *is* delicate and superbly civilized and one of the few wonders of the world in which you could want to live. Personally I prefer the Generalife, with its famous gardens but also less restored and therefore more evocative buildings. Manuel de Falla's *Nights in the Gardens of Spain* (one of the few great pieces of Spanish music not written by a Frenchman) is a wonderful recreation of its atmosphere of delicate and sensual beauty.

The most amazing Moorish building in Spain is not of course in Granada, but in Córdoba: the grand mosque or Mezquita, whose vast interior supported by over 800 columns, as Richard Ford rightly and simply said in the first handbook to Spain, "cannot be described, it must be seen." Hidden away in this forest or labyrinth of striped marble is a fair-sized Christian cathedral. It was ordered to be built by the Emperor Charles V, who also knocked down part of the Alhambra to construct a Renaissance palace, vilified by most guide writers, but to me a telling contrast to its surroundings. Charles however was not pleased when he saw how his orders had been carried out in Córdoba, and he rebuked the clerical authorities in resonant words which convey his generous appreciation of the culture he was annihilating: "You have built here what you, or anyone, might have built anywhere else; but you have destroyed what was unique in the world."

He and his successors did not take this message to heart. Andalusia has never recovered the prosperity it enjoyed at the height of Moorish rule.

The Conquest of the Americas

Having rooted out the cultured Moors and the rich and industrious Jews from their own land, the Catholic Kings turned their attention overseas. The colonization of Central, South and parts of North America was an astonishing feat, carried out, like the unification of Spain itself, in just one generation. Whether it had an altogether positive value, either for the colonies or for Spain itself, is debatable: in our post-colonial, post-imperial age the destruction of the Aztec, Maya and Inca cultures is likely to seem more shameful than heroic, especially when the Spanish administrations which replaced them have become the byword for seediness and corruption. However, Hispano-America still exists, and forms a kind of cultural commonwealth with Spain of which Spaniards at least feel proud, and is now showing signs of sloughing off its centuries-old apathy and emerging into the modern world. Its literary culture, revived by such figures as Borges, García Márquez and Vargas Llosa, is at the moment second to none.

For Spain herself, the colonization of the Americas was both her greatest achievement and the cause of her long decline. Instead of stimulating the economy, Peruvian gold and Bolivian silver encouraged indolence and produced inflation. At the same time religious dogmatism and at times fanaticism (the Inquisition is not entirely a legend) gave rise to costly religious wars, and then isolation from Protestant Europe. The first centralized state in Europe put unity above everything else, and kept itself together, just, at the cost of the prosperity which the rising capitalist system was bringing to other parts of Europe. The naturally bourgeois, trading, capitalist Catalans resented this, tried to break away, and were crushed in two bloody wars which have not been forgotten to this day. The Catalans' heyday had been in the 13th, 14th and 15th centuries when their mercantile empire extended as far as Athens and they produced literature, art and architecture to match any in Europe. The *barrio gótico* (including the cathedral with its idyllic cloister full of trees and geese) and the church of Santa Maria del Mar in Barcelona, as well as the majestic cathedrals of Palma and Gerona, still bear ample witness to the glories of Catalan Gothic.

Art and Culture

From the late 16th century onwards, Spain, ruled by introverted monarchs like Philip II, turned in on herself. Her architecture, after the rich Plateresque period when stone was treated like gold or silver, acquired a somber austerity, epitomized by Philip's grey granite monastery, which looks more like a Ministry, the Escorial. In painting, as well as fine devotional artists of widely different character like the ascetic Zurbarán and the gentle Murillo, Spain in the 17th century produced the first of her indigenous, isolated universal geniuses in Velázquez. The Velázquez rooms in the Prado are a must for anyone interested not just in Spain but in European culture, and in themselves make a nonsense of Kenneth Clark's omission of Spain from his personal view of civilization.

The next great Spanish pictorial genius was Goya, and it would not be much of an exaggeration to say that he was the next thing of any real interest to happen in Spain after Velázquez's death in 1660. Once again the

Prado is the place to appreciate the full range of this extraordinary artist who managed to combine vitality and grace with horror and despair.

Goya ended his days in Bordeaux, and exile or emigration became a familiar fate of Spanish artists and intellectuals from his day until very recent times. The rest of the 19th century was not a happy time for Spain (though it produced two great novelists in Pérez Galdós and Leopoldo Alas), and the century ended, symbolically, with the loss of her remaining colonies in the disastrous wars of 1898. In fact, the annus terribilis of 1898 became a symbol not just of military defeat but also of intellectual regeneration. Chastened by the events of that year, which seemed to indicate a near-terminal decline from the days of national greatness, a group of writers, of whom Unamuno and Ortega y Gasset are the most famous, set about examining the state of the nation's soul.

The first three decades of this century were altogether an astonishingly vital creative period in Spain. Apart from the poets there were the painters Picasso, Gris and the Catalans Miró and Dalí, and Dalí's friend and Surrealist collaborator the film director Luis Buñuel. Picasso and Miró have their own museums, both beautifully housed, in Barcelona, and Dalí has his idiosyncratic one in his native town of Figueras. These men were experimenters at the forefront of the avant-garde impetus of European art at that time, which went so far beyond the present that looking at it now one feels passé. Equally modern, but in a different, highly religious spirit, is the work of the Catalan architect Antoni Gaudí. His church of the Holy Family (Sagrada Familia) in Barcelona, which looks like a cross between a Gothic cathedral and a flight of rockets, is still not finished, and will not be for a century or two, but it is still one of the world's most impressive buildings. How tragic then that all this creative exuberance, fostered by the relatively benign dictatorship of Primo de Rivera in the 1920s, then the Republic of the 1930s, was dissipated by the Civil War. It is only now, after 40 years of stifling repression under Franco, that culture can breathe again in Spain. Some exciting work is certainly being done—filmmakers like Victor Erice and Carlos Saura have at last provided a worthy succession to Buñuel—and Madrid now considers itself to be the cultural capital of Europe.

The Art of Living

There is a sense in which all this talk of culture and history is beside the point—the point being that Spain's special strength has always been in popular culture rather than high culture, the art of living rather than fine art. Spain's ultimate art-form is the fiesta, a popular religious celebration which turns into a street party, and embraces dance, processions, masquerade and bullfight. The fiesta is not a piece of phoney folklore artificially preserved for tourists, but an integral part of Spanish life. Fiesta is also the ordinary Spanish word for party. The biggest one of all takes place every July in Pamplona—ten solid days of drinking, dancing, bull-running and bullfighting, called the Sanfermines after the town's patron saint (who may never have existed). The whole affair, despite the religious processions, is profoundly pagan and bacchanalian. Many tourists take part in it, but they are easily absorbed into the mass of Spaniards who come from all parts of the peninsula, thieves and beggars as well as aficionados, swelling the population of Pamplona to twice its normal size of 150,000. It is a joyful, liberating and totally exhausting experience (not to go to bed, at night anyway, for the duration of the fiesta is a point of honor), and the real heroes are the waiters who maintain an incredibly professional 24-hour service against all odds. The would-be heroes are those who run with the bulls every morning through the narrow Calle Estafeta to the bullring armed only with a rolled-up newspaper. As several people get gored every year, and fatalities are not uncommon, this is a sport best left to the local lads, who know what they are doing. As for the bullfights themselves, by all means go to one, with Hemingway at your side (though you will find queueing for seats in Pamplona a frustrating exercise), for they are a genuine and unique part of Spanish popular culture, but if you are like me you will find them not so much revolting as ultimately boring.

Every night of the Sanfermines a band plays in the Plaza del Castillo until four A.M., and the locals, dressed in white with red sashes, dance with a grace which makes the foreigner feel ashamed and envious. All Spanish people seem able to dance well, no matter what age they are, and every part of the country has preserved its indigenous traditional dances. These range from the statuesque Sardana of Catalonia, with its strong nationalistic overtones, to the passionate, very unEuropean flamenco of Andalusia.

Eating Well

I described the waiters as the heroes of the Sanfermines, and waiters are perhaps the most important professional group in Spain. The enormous success of tourism in Spain must be largely owing to them, and the fact that there is no other country in Europe at least where one can eat and drink in so civilized a manner at so modest a cost. The sheer number of bars and restaurants is staggering, but even more important is the flexibility they offer in terms of one's being able to eat or drink anything one wants from eight in the morning until two the next, and above all the ease of atmosphere which makes eating and drinking out seem the most natural thing in the world.

As for the food and drink themselves, I have never understood why Spanish cuisine has such a dubious reputation. The abundance of good ingredients, fresh fish (available everywhere), olive oil, tomatoes, cheese from La Mancha, and the very limited encroachment of fast food, make eating a constant pleasure even at a simple level. In the smart restaurants of Madrid and Barcelona, you can enjoy genuine haute cuisine at a fraction of what it costs in France. Spanish wine, even if it cannot reach the heights of the finest from France and Germany, offers the best value in Europe. I lived happily for months on a mellow Valdepeñas which cost 70 pesetas a bottle; excellent Riojas and Penedes wines can be had for only three or four times that amount, as can sherry and delicious bubbly (now that Spain is in the E.E.C. it can no longer be called champagne) from San Sadurní de Noia. Brandy is perhaps too cheap, and if it wants to tackle the problem of alcoholism, the Spanish government should consider raising the duty on hard liquor, which until recently stood at 1 peseta a bottle.

I have left until last what I consider the best thing Spain can offer, and that is an evening spent going round bars or "tascas" eating tapas. Tapas are small dishes, usually eaten to the accompaniment of equally small glasses of wine or sherry, and they consist of things like fried fish or shellfish (any number of different varieties), slices of cured ham, olives and dev-illed eggs. Each bar in tapa centers like the Calle Echegaray in Madrid, the Parte Vieja of San Sebastián or the Calle de la Merced in Barcelona has its own specialty. I would like to leave you in one of those places, where you will encounter a heartwarming openness and hospitality, as you get to know the generous people of Spain, and conclude for yourself whether their country is different and romantic, or modern and European, or just, as they will often tell you, a disaster. Few visitors will agree with that: most will want to return.

SPAIN'S HISTORY AND ART

Land of Contrast

by
AILSA HUDSON

Spain, the crossroads between Africa and Europe, the Atlantic and the Mediterranean, is a country of striking contrasts. On the one hand, this gigantic peninsula offers a welcoming coastline of natural harbors and fertile foreshores, but on the other, for those who penetrate it more deeply, it throws up barriers of high sierras and plateaux, with a rude climate and sparse resources. The coastal fringe seems to turn its back on the central mesetas, and mirrors the history of Spain—a ceaseless struggle between the will to unite and the tendency to dispersion and isolation, still seen today in the struggle of the Catalans and the Basque separatists.

The history you see in the coastal Greek and Roman remains at Ampurias, the Moorish palaces and mosques of Granada and Toledo in the south, and the splendid royal residences of the interior, has been largely determined by the diverse physical background of the country.

To grasp some understanding of the peoples and culture which greet you today, it is essential to know something of the colorful and often turbulent past which has shaped them.

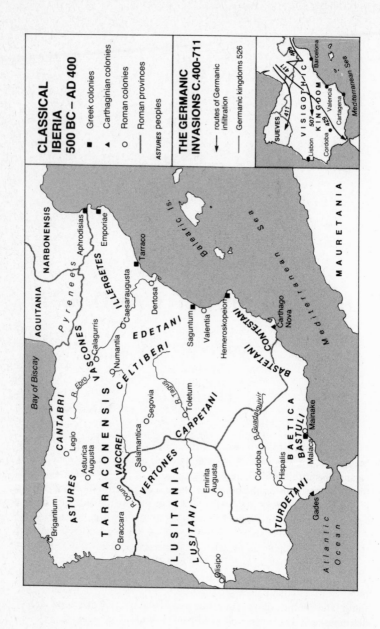

From the Phoenicians to the Visigoths

c. 1100 B.C.	Earliest Phoenician colonies, including Cádiz, Villaricos, Almuñécar and Málaga
c. 650	Beginning of Greek colonization of the eastern seaboard
237–206	*Carthage v. Rome*—237 Carthaginians land in Spain; c. 225 Cartagena founded by Hasdrubal as capital of the Carthaginian colony; 219 Hannibal's successful siege of Sagunto, a Roman ally, precipitates the Second Punic War; 218 The Romans under Scipio Calvus land at Ampurias to assault Carthaginian supply lines in Spain; 212 Romans capture Sagunto; 209 Scipio Africanus captures Cartagena and uses it as his base for the defeat of the Carthaginians in Spain; 206 Carthaginians expelled from Spain
138	Roman conquest of Galicia
121	Roman conquest of the Balearic Islands
29–19	The Cantabrian War brings the whole of Spain under Roman domination
A.D. 67	St. Paul is said to have visited Spain
74	The Edict of Vespasian extends rights of Roman citizenship to all Spaniards
200s	Christian communities established throughout Spain
380	Emperor Theodosius I, a Spaniard, proclaims Christianity the only tolerated religion throughout the empire
409	The first wave of Germanic invaders, the Sueves and the Vandals, reach Spain, signalling the end of the period of classical culture. Settling in Iberia by treaty with Rome, they set up a series of kingdoms broadly based on the old Roman colonies

The settlement of Spain dates from an early age. Paleolithic remains have been found in abundance at many sites, including the famous caves at Altamira painted with animals and hunting scenes, the "Sistine Chapel of Prehistoric art." During the second millennium B.C. the northern, western and southern parts of the Iberian peninsula shared a copper age culture with much of northwest Europe, characterized by megalithic structures, passage graves and extensive mineral exploitation. Mineral wealth led to Spain's early emergence as a trading and exporting centre, and during the first millennium B.C. it attracted Phoenician, Greek and eventually Carthaginian traders and settlers. The remains of their towns and cities still scatter the eastern seaboard.

By this time the native inhabitants can be broadly divided into the Iberians in the south, the Basques in the western Pyrenees, and the Celts who had colonized much of northern Iberia.

The influence of the Mediterranean colonists upon the native peoples was limited to the coastal zones, but some fine examples exist of hybrid sculpture, such as the *Lady of Elche* (Archeological Museum, Madrid).

Carthaginian aggression finally provided their rivals, the Romans, with a pretext for resuming open warfare. During the Second Punic War (219–202 B.C.), despite Hannibal's successes in Italy, Rome thrust out at

Spain. By the end of the war Carthaginian forces had been totally expelled from Spain, and Rome with its usual ruthless efficiency proceeded to conquer the interior and the west.

The coastal regions of Spain were quickly Romanized, but resistance elsewhere was fierce and the invasion took over 75 years to complete. The Romans brought with them their institutions, their language, law and order, tailor-made local government, roads and, in later years, Roman citizenship and Christianity, all of which left an indelible mark. They rapidly exploited Spain's natural resources, lead, silver, iron ore, tin and gold being mined unceasingly during the first two centuries A.D. Andalusia became Rome's granary, and wine, olive oil and horses were other major exports. The peninsula soon became the pre-eminent colony outside Italy, and indeed a number of outstanding Roman figures were born in Spain, including the emperors Trajan and Hadrian, and the writers Seneca, Martial and Quintilian.

The extent and permanence of Roman colonization is demonstrated by the wealth of remains which are still visible throughout Spain today. These include many towns and cities, such as Tarragona, Sagunto (near Valencia), Itálica (near Seville) and Mérida (near Badajoz), and remarkable civil engineering feats, such as the 128-arch aqueduct at Segovia and the bridge at Alcántara. Ampurias has Greek and Roman remains side by side.

The beginning of the fifth century A.D. brought the gradual decline of Roman dominance in Spain, as the infiltration of Germanic peoples which had occurred elsewhere in the empire finally reached the Iberian peninsula. The Sueves, Alans and Vandals crossed the Pyrenees in 409 and within two years had established themselves in separate kingdoms, ending the endurance and continuity of the classical era.

Christians and Muslims

419	Visigoths establish themselves in northern Spain, creating a large kingdom with its capital at Toulouse
507	Toledo becomes Visigothic capital
558	Extension of Visigothic rule to include much of the south, and the kingdom of the Sueves in the west
587	Visigothic king Reccared embraces Catholicism: enforced baptism of Jews follows
711	Invasion from North Africa by Muslim Berber armies. King Roderick defeated and Visigothic kingdom destroyed
712	Muslim invasion completed, Visigothic resistance isolated in a strip of Christian states across the north of Spain. Muslim capital established at Córdoba, and the territory administered as an emirate of the Ummayad Caliphate of Damascus
718	Pelayo, successor of Roderick, creates the kingdom of Asturias; the Christian reconquest of Spain is launched
732	Muslim expansion north of the Pyrenees halted by the Franks at Poitiers; Muslims withdraw to Iberia
756	Abd al-Rahman I establishes semi-independent Ummayad dynasty in Spain

777	Frankish invasion of Spain under Charlemagne checked at Zaragoza
778	Charlemagne's retreat shattered at Roncesvalles, but Franks establish rule over Spain north of the Ebro
837	Muslim suppression of Christian and Jewish revolts
899	Miraculous discovery of remains of St. James the Greater, foundation of the church of Santiago de Compostela
912–961	Reign of Abd al-Rahman III, the apogee of Ummayad culture. Reorganization of government, navy, agriculture and industry
c.930–970	Rise of Count Fernán González of Burgos, establishing Castile as autonomous Christian power
970–1035	Sancho the Great unites Castile and Navarre and begins the conquest of León
976–1009	Reign of Hisham II, effectively deposed by Hajib al-Mansur whose brilliant administrative reforms and successful campaigns against the Christian kingdoms briefly revives flagging Ummayad power
1002	Death of al-Mansur, followed by power struggles, civil war and the disintegration of centralized Ummayad authority

Despite the barbarian name-tag, the peoples who settled in the northern and western regions of the later Roman empire saw themselves for the most part as successors to and preservers of Roman culture and the resident Hispano-Romans (who out-numbered the Visigoths five to one) continued to exist much as before. Prior to the baptism of Reccared and the reforms of Receswinth, the Visigoths maintained their own religion and civil code, but with the extension of their territory throughout the peninsula a centralized system of law, religion and government became necessary. Something of the classical heritage was revived and preserved, reflected in the encyclopedic works of Isidore of Seville, and in the Visigothic architectural decoration in Córdoba cathedral and the church of San Juan de Baños de Cerrato, near Palencia, built by Receswinth.

However, the economic and strategic importance of Spain encouraged attempts at invasion by the Franks and the Byzantines. The third such attempt, by the Islamic Berbers, was successful. Within seven years Iberia was conquered, and Christian resistance limited to pockets in the north. Islamic expansion was finally checked by Charlemagne, but with the Ummayad dynasty in firm control of Spain south of the Ebro a period of cultural blossoming began. In many ways the Arabs were the heirs to classical culture. They were largely tolerant of Christians and Jews living in their realm. They embellished and improved much of the legacy of Roman civilization, introducing new plants and agricultural techniques, reinvigorating manufacturing and trade and introducing distinctive styles and motifs still traceable in modern ceramics, carpets and folk music. They built palaces, mosques, libraries and schools; many of those buildings which survive in Andalusia were built much later, but the 850 columns elaborating the mosque at Córdoba and the smaller mosque at Toledo testify to the magnificence of early Moorish architecture. The distinctive characteristics of this style are the horseshoe arches and extensive geometric and floral patterns intermingled with Kufic script.

The polyglot nature of Moorish society permitted the fertile intermingling of many groups and factions—there was exchange and respect between the localised groups of each faith, as well as intermittent revolts and power struggles. It was against this backdrop, in the first half of the eighth century, that a substantial Christian state developed in Asturias. The moral strength of the Christian north was boosted considerably by the apparent discovery of the remains of St. James the Greater, and the foundation of the cathedral of Santiago de Compostela, which has remained an important pilgrimage centre. By the tenth century, mainly under the leadership of Castile, the Christian states rallied sufficiently to begin the long task of reconquest.

The Reconquest

1065–1109	*Reign of Alfonso VI of Castile* who led the revival of the Christian reconquest of Spain; 1085 Toledo captured by Alfonso VI; 1086 The Almoravids enter Spain to help combat the Christians. Alfonso VI defeated at Zallaka; c.1091 Muslim Spain integrated with the Almoravid empire; 1087–88 Rodrigo Díaz de Bivar, known as El Cid (Lord), re-enters the service of Alfonso VI. A knight of Burgos (in whose cathedral he and his wife are buried), he served under Sancho II of Castile. Exiled in 1081 he returned to help the Christian assault, but subsequently served the Muslim ruler of Zaragoza. He eventually ruled Valencia. After his death (1099) Valencia was regained by the Almoravids
1126–57	*Alfonso VII of Castile* takes the Christian offensive; 1137 Aragón unites with Catalonia, forming a new Christian power centered on Zaragoza; 1144 Christian attacks on Andalusia; 1146 The Almohades come to the defence of Moorish Spain, eventually taking complete control
1158–1214	*Reign of Alfonso VIII of Castile* who leads a series of successful campaigns against the Moors; 1195 Alfonso VIII defeated by the Moors at Alarcos, but, supported by Pope Innocent III he prepares for a major assault; 1212 Victory at Las Navas de Tolosa by united Christian armies. Almohades expelled from Spain and Moorish power limited to the kingdom of Granada; 1214 Catalonia secured from the Franks by the Aragonese at Muret
1213–76	Reign of Jaime I the Conqueror of Aragón who regained the Balearics (1229–35), Valencia (1238) and Murcia, which he ceded to Castile
1230–52	Reign of Ferdinand III (St. Ferdinand) of Castile and León, who conquered Córdoba (1236) and Seville (1248)
1252–84	Reign of Alfonso X the Wise of Castile, scholar, astronomer, poet, historian and codifier of the law
1270	End of the main period of the Reconquest, as Portugal concentrates on control of the Atlantic coast, Aragón seeks power in the Mediterranean, and Castile enters a period of dynastic power struggles

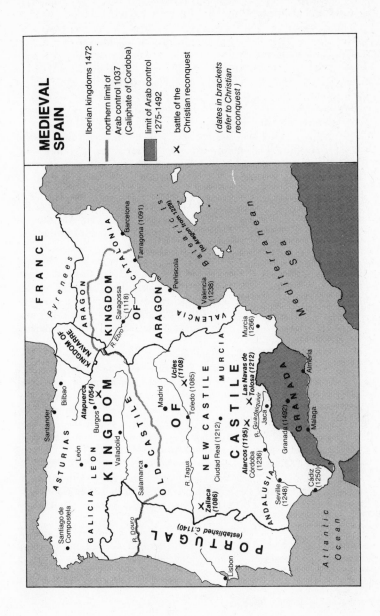

MEDIEVAL
SPAIN

— Iberian kingdoms 1472

— northern limit of
Arab control 1037
(Caliphate of Cordoba)

— limit of Arab control
1275–1492

× battle of the
Christian reconquest

*(dates in brackets
refer to Christian
reconquest)*

FRANCE

Pyrenees

KINGDOM OF NAVARRE

ARAGON

KINGDOM OF ARAGON

CATALONIA

Barcelona (1091)

Tarragona (1118)

R. Ebro

Saragossa (1118)

Peñiscola

Valencia (1238)

VALENCIA

Balearic Is (to Aragon from 1229)

Mediterranean Sea

ASTURIAS

Santander

Bilbao

Atapuerca (1054) ×

Burgos

León

GALICIA

LEON

Santiago de Compostela

Valladolid

OLD CASTILE

KINGDOM OF CASTILE

Salamanca

Madrid

Uclés (1108) ×

Toledo (1085)

NEW CASTILE

MURCIA

Murcia (1266)

Ciudad Real (1212)

R. Tagus

Las Navas de Tolosa (1212) ×

Alarcos (1195) ×

Jaca

R. Guadalquivir

Granada (1492)

GRANADA

Almería

Zallaca (1086) ×

Cordoba (1236)

Seville (1248)

ANDALUSIA

Cádiz (1250)

Malaga

R. Douro

PORTUGAL (established c.1140)

Lisbon

Atlantic Ocean

Although this period saw the gradual decline of Moorish power and the establishment of three increasingly distinct and secure Christian states in Portugal, Castile and Aragón, the Christian states remained almost continually under arms, while the Muslims saw the establishment of two powerful dynasties, the Almoravids and Almohades, both marked by considerable cultural achievements. The Alcázar and the Giralda still dominate Seville today and, with the Alhambra at Granada (completed in the 14th century), are unique in Islamic architecture, a true fusion of Moorish and local styles.

Arabic scholasticism continued to advance, with the first major universities being founded at Valencia (1209) and Salamanca (1242). The work of outstanding Arabic scholars provided a direct link with the classical past long after the Reconquest was complete. Idrisi the geographer and the philosopher Averroes were both active in the 12th century. So too was the great Jewish philosopher Maimónides who translated Arabic medical texts and Sarasorda who introduced Muslim mathematics to the West. One aspect of the intermingling of Islamic and Christian cultures was the development of lyrical poetry and the art of the troubadour. The exploits of El Cid were a popular subject and probably first recorded in the 12th century in the *Cantar de Mio Cid*.

Throughout the period the strength of the Church remained stable. Carolingian and then Romanesque architecture, derived from southern French models, was developed most spectacularly at Santiago de Compostela. Later, the High Gothic style made its appearance in the building of the cathedrals of Toledo (c.1230), Burgos (1126) and León (c.1230). Catalan Gothic can be seen in the cathedrals of Barcelona (1298) and Gerona (1312).

The Reconquest also had a lasting effect on the social structure of Spain. The Christian kingdoms developed a nobility based on military achievement and as the Reconquest proceeded south such figures were granted substantial domains—some still owned by their descendants. At a slightly lower level were the wealthy knights—*infanzones* and *hidalgos*—a class which was created by and lived for force of arms. It was this chivalric brotherhood which carried Spanish might overseas to Holland, the Americas and the Indies after the Reconquest—but which also provided the model for Don Quixote.

However, the gradual process of Reconquest also held back the development of feudalism, and the long tradition of guerrilla warfare in Castile led to a concentration of the population in towns, and an impoverishment of agriculture which still exists today.

Minority groups, including Jews and non-belligerent Muslims, continued to live unhampered in the Christian states. The piecemeal granting of communal sovereignty still influences local politics, and forms the spine of the arguments for separatism voiced today.

The High Middle Ages

1282   Peter (Pedro) III adds Sicily to the Aragonese kingdom; Aragón becomes the principle power in the western Mediterranean

1295	Frederick I of Sicily establishes dynasty independent of Aragón
1340	Alfonso XI of Castile ends the threat of the Moroccan Muslims at Rio Salado
1374	Peace of Almazan between Castile, and Portugal and Aragón
1409	Martin of Aragón reunites Aragón and Sicily, ending a period of dynastic struggle
1435	Alfonso V of Aragón and Sicily conquers Naples and southern Italy, transferring the center of power away from the Spanish mainland to Italy
1454–74	Reign of Henry IV of Castile, during which the rivalry and anarchic power of the nobility reaches its height
1469	Marriage of Isabella, princess of Castile, to Ferdinand, heir to the throne of Aragón; this marriage becomes the key to Spanish unity
1474	Isabella succeeds to the Castilian throne
1478	Establishment of the Inquisition
1479	Ferdinand succeeds to the throne of Aragón, Catalonia and Valencia. The rule of the combined Catholic crowns restores royal power in Castile
1492	Conquest of the last Moorish outpost of Granada makes Ferdinand and Isabella rulers of all Spain. Attempted conversion of Muslims and Jews follows; subsequent expulsion of all Jews; first voyage of Christopher Columbus, under the patronage of Isabella, discovers the West Indies. Further voyages (1493, 1498 and 1502) establish the existence of the Americas
1494	Treaty of Tordesillas whereby Portugal and Spain divide the non-European world into two spheres of influence. Almost all of the known Americas and the Philippines fell under Spanish rule in the 16th century
1502	Uprising of Moors in Castile leads to forcible conversion on pain of expulsion for all Muslims
1504	Death of Isabella; her daughter Joanna with her husband Philip try in vain to claim Castilian inheritance. Philip dies and Joanna is locked away, insane
1509–11	A series of military expeditions under Cardinal Cisneros in North Africa conquer Oran, Bougie and Tripoli
1512	Conquest of Navarre by Ferdinand
1516	Death of Ferdinand. Cardinal Cisneros becomes regent until the legal heir, Charles I (son of Joanna and Philip) arrives from Flanders

Played against the backcloth of the later stages of the Reconquest was the drama of the struggle for political maturity of the great kingdoms of Castile and Aragón.

Aragón largely abandoned the fight against Islam, and turned instead to the development of a west Mediterranean empire to rival the Holy Roman Empire of central Europe. In this it was largely successful, acquiring Sicily and the southern part of the Italian peninsula. However, rapid population growth, the overworking of the land, plague and an unstable economy led to widespread agrarian revolts and eventually to open civil war (1462–72), dominated by a nobility dissatisfied with the monarchy and yet unwilling to relinquish its historical rights.

A greater stability marked the development of Castile. The effects of the Great Plague (1347) were less devastating than in Aragón and a major economic advance was the granting of privileges to the Mesta, a guild of cattle and sheep herders, who were permitted almost unrestricted access to seasonal pasture. Not only the massive increase in wool production, but also the regular annual movement around the kingdom of an increasingly prosperous group stimulated economic growth, although uncontrolled grazing of the mesetas eventually proved destructive. Castile also developed on two maritime fronts: to the north on the Atlantic seaboard centered on Cádiz, and in the south building up a trading zone on the northern and Atlantic coasts of Africa.

With the unification of the kingdoms of Aragón and Castile by the marriage of Ferdinand and Isabella the monarchy assumed firm political control. The powers of the nobility and the clergy were contained, and the Catholic kings found their most extreme voice in the creation of the Inquisition and the subsequent conversion or expulsion of Muslims and Jews.

During this period Spanish Gothic architecture reached its peak, producing the most ornate and decorated examples of the style in Europe. A fine example is the cathedral at Seville. The intensely decorative element of Spanish Gothic was to persist for some centuries, being applied to the Italian Renaissance style which appears at the end of the 15th century, and evolving into a hybrid mannerist form known as Plateresque.

Similarly, Moorish architecture reached an apogee of stylistic refinement and decorative elaboration in Granada with the completion of the Alhambra, while the combination of three styles—Moorish, Gothic and Renaissance in the cathedral at Granada reflects the exact historical moment of the completion of the Reconquest. As the Reconquest proceeded, and the Moorish urban craft populations became absorbed by the Christians, a unique hybrid style came into being, known as *mudéjar*. Intricate working in wood, ivory, enamel, silver and gold as well as mosaics, leatherwork and ceramics reached a peak in Toledo, especially in the art of damascening—inlaying steel with gold and silver. Examples of this work are still produced in the region today. Mudéjar architecture extended this tradition on a large scale, finding expression in elaborate brickwork in towers and apses and ornately carved wooden *(artesonado)* ceilings.

The development of Castilian ecclesiastical painting underwent two distinct foreign influences—firstly that of the Italian school of Giotto and then, with the visit of Jan van Eyck (1428), that of the Flemish school.

By the end of the 15th century Castile had entered the mainstream of European culture and had a thriving literary tradition of its own. Outstanding in this period were: Juan Manuel (1282–1348) who collected fables in *El Conde Lucanor;* Juan Ruiz, who wrote the *Libro de Buen Amor;* and later the popular dramatist Juan del Encina (c.1469–1529). The advent of printing in 1474 led to the wide circulation of contemporary literary works and among these was the first Spanish novel, *La Celestina,* (c.1499) a novel in dialogue attributed to Fernando de Rojas.

The crusading energy of the Reconquest found its vocation after the fall of Granada during the reign of Ferdinand and Isabella when the Spanish attempted to find a westward route to Asia. By the time of Magellan's successful discovery of such a route, Spain had established firm control of the Caribbean and was poised to take hold of the greatest treasure hoard in man's history—the Americas.

The Habsburgs

1519	Charles I, the founder of the Spanish Habsburg dynasty, elected as Holy Roman Emperor, thereby becoming Charles V. He inherits the Spanish Netherlands and Franche-Comté from his father; Cortés conquers the Aztec empire in Mexico
1519–22	Magellan rounds Cape Horn, traverses the Pacific and claims the Philippines for Spain, dying there. The first circumnavigation completed by his lieutenant Elcano
1521	War with France; decisive victory for Charles at Pavia (1525)
1531	Pizarro conquers the Inca empire in Peru
1535–51	Territorial wars with France
1554	Charles' heir, Philip, marries Queen Mary of England
1556	Charles abdicates in favour of his son Philip II, who inherits Spain, Sicily and the Netherlands; the Holy Roman Empire is conferred on Charles' brother Ferdinand
1560	Capital established at Madrid
1563	Construction of El Escorial begins
1567	The beginning of the Dutch Revolt, a prolonged struggle for an independent Protestant Netherlands
1569	Revolt of the Moriscos (supposedly converted Muslims): brutally suppressed
1571	Battle of Lepanto, the climax of naval rivalry between Spain and the Ottomans. Spain, with the aid of Venice, destroys the Ottoman fleet
1580	Philip inherits the Portuguese throne
1587	Spanish fleet destroyed by the English fleet at Cádiz
1588	The Spanish Armada. The Reformation, English aid to the Dutch rebels, rivalry in the Atlantic and Caribbean and finally the execution of Mary Stuart provoke Philip to attempt to destroy Protestant rule in England. The fleet meets with disaster, and Anglo-Spanish hostility continues until 1603
1589–1600	Involvement in French religious wars
1598	Philip II dies; Philip III's shyness and piety lead to an increase in nobility and church power and estates, and a marked agricultural and economic decline
1609	Expulsion of the Moriscos
1618	Spain's Habsburg interests draw her into the Thirty Years' War
1621–65	Reign of Philip IV whose minister, Count-Duke Olivares, attempts to modernize government by centralization and increased royal power
1622	Beginning of lengthy territorial war with France
1640–59	Catalonian revolt; Republic declared and recognized by France, lasting 12 years

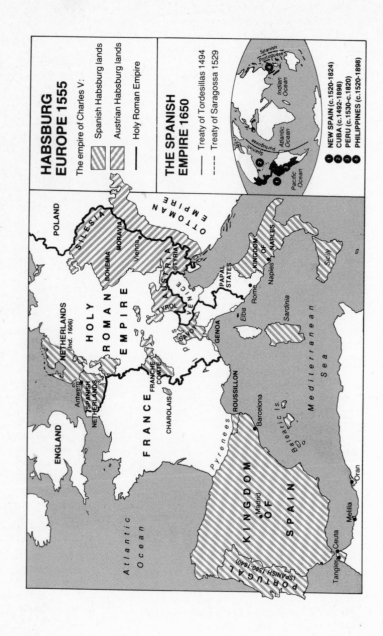

HABSBURG EUROPE 1555

The empire of Charles V:

Spanish Habsburg lands

Austrian Habsburg lands

—— Holy Roman Empire

THE SPANISH EMPIRE 1650

—— Treaty of Tordesillas 1494

- - - Treaty of Saragossa 1529

1. NEW SPAIN (c.1520-1824)
2. CUBA (c.1492-1898)
3. PERU (c.1530-c.1820)
4. PHILIPPINES (c.1520-1898)

1648	Peace of Westphalia, ending the Thirty Years' War, brings independence to Holland
1659	Treaty of the Pyrenees ends both the war with France and Spanish ascendancy in Europe
1665–1700	Reign of Charles II; last of the Spanish Habsburgs
1674	Spain joins coalition against France
1678	Treaty of Nimwegen; Spain cedes further European territories to France
1698	First partition treaty between England, Holland and France; an attempt to resolve in advance the problem of the succession to Spain and her empire
1700	Charles names Philip of Anjou, Louis XIV's grandson, as his heir

The accession to the Spanish throne of Charles I, bringing the Netherlands which he inherited from his mother, and his subsequent (partly rigged) election as Holy Roman Emperor made Spain the most powerful country in Europe.

Another factor also altered the balance of European power in Spain's favor; with the rapid exploration and exploitation of new lands overseas the axis of European power swiftly moved from the central Mediterranean to the Atlantic seaboard, dominated by Portugal, Spain and the Netherlands. The simultaneous rise of France and England made them fractious contenders for Atlantic honors, and their skirmishes punctuate the period of Habsburg ascendancy.

Thus Spain accrued great wealth, and an economy underwritten by global trade, overseas plantations (using native slave labor) and silver looted and mined by the Conquistadores in the Americas.

The Reformation had little effect on Spain; it remained part of the Catholic core, and during Philip II's reign played a great part in the Counter-Reformation, assuming an ideological offensive against the Dutch separatists and the English. The blood shed in the Netherlands and during the heyday of the Inquisition is notorious, and the crusade was carried overseas (often forcibly) by the Jesuit Order, created by the Spanish soldier Ignatius de Loyola (1491–1556). Another great figure of the period was St. Teresa of Avila (1515–82) who reformed the Carmelite nunneries, but whose great contributions were her autobiography (which includes descriptions of divine visions) and her *Castillo interior* which greatly influenced Catholic mysticism.

The Habsburg monarchs could afford to exercise patronage on a grand scale, and the 16th and 17th centuries were the Golden Age of Spanish culture. El Escorial, the royal residence and monastery near Madrid, is their greatest monument, but reflects the somber religious tastes of Philip II. The Counter-Reformation throughout the Catholic countries produced a reinvigoration of devotional art. One of the most distinctive painters of the period lived and worked in Toledo—the Cretan-born El Greco (1541–1614). His unique fluency in both line and color created an ecstatic visionary world—a realization in paint similar to the revelations of St. Teresa. However, the Spanish Baroque school was principally created by the work of a group of painters who had studied in Italy: Navarrete (c.1526–79), Ribalta (1565–1628) and the morbid Ribera (1588–1652).

The handling of devotional subjects in the 17th century was to become softer and more Italianate in the works of Murillo (1617–82) and Zurbarán (1598–1664). But the master of Spanish painting at that time was Velázquez (1599–1660) whose work was predominantly concerned with contemporary life—genre scenes and portraits—and found its fullest expression in his work as court painter to Philip IV. His careful compositions, unique handling of form and light and in later years his color sense imbue his subjects with a heroic but immediate stature.

It was, however, in literature that Spain took the cultural lead in Europe. Poets thrived in the age of humanism inaugurated by Ferdinand and Isabella, including Garcilaso de la Vega (1503–36), the mystical poet Juan de la Cruz (1542–91) and the theologian Luis Ponce de Léon (b.1528). Later outstanding poets were Quevedo (1580–1645) and Góngora (1561–1627). Lope de Vega (1562–1635), responsible for over 2,000 plays, is regarded as the father of modern drama; however, the dramatic tradition was brought to its highest point in the work of Calderón (1600–81) whose most famous play *La Vida es Sueño* ("Life is a Dream") is still performed today throughout Europe. The other towering literary figure of the period is Miguel de Cervantes (1547–1616) whose *Don Quijote* is an unsurpassed ironical portrait of contemporary Spain. An elegaic view of the lost cause of Spanish chivalry, it is one of the world's greatest novels.

Cervantes had been wounded at the battle of Lepanto, one of Spain's last significant victories in Europe. The weakening of the Spanish monarchy after Philip II's reign was due to a number of factors, not least the ascendancy of France and the Protestant states of the north. Economically Spain was unable to compete with the latter; its creative medieval mercantile classes—Jews and Muslims—had been expelled, and the nobility were reluctant to invest their substantial wealth in anything but property. By the end of the Habsburg period Spain and its empire were increasingly viewed by the rest of Europe as a glittering cadaver ripe for profitable dismemberment.

The Bourbons

1701–14	*The War of the Spanish Succession*—three legal claimants exist—Louis XIV; Leopold I, a German Habsburg and the electoral prince of Bavaria; and Philip of Anjou who is supported in Spain and becomes the first Bourbon ruler as Philip V; 1704 Gibraltar captured by the British; 1709 Menorca captured by the British; 1713 Treaty of Utrecht whereby Philip is recognized as the king of Spain on condition that France and Spain remain separate; 1714 Treaty of Rastatt in which Spain cedes Flanders, Luxembourg and Italy to the Austrian Habsburgs. The special privileges of Catalonia and Valencia are abolished
1717–18	Spanish seize Sardinia and Sicily
1720	Treaty of the Hague settles Habsburg and Bourbon claims in Italy
1727–29	War with Britain and France
1733–35	Spanish invasion of Habsburg Naples and Sicily
1739–41	War of Jenkins' Ear against the British

1756	Spanish recovery of Menorca during the Seven Years' War
1759–88	*Reign of Charles III* who promotes economic and administrative reform—1761 War with France against Britain; 1762 Treaty of Paris; Spain cedes Menorca and Florida to Britain, and in compensation receives Louisiana from France; 1779 Spanish support for the Americans in the War of Independence; regains Florida and Menorca
1788–1808	*Reign of Charles IV*—1793 Revolutionary France declares war on Spain; 1795 Treaty of Basel ends the Franco-Spanish war. Spain now allies with France against Britain; 1797 Franco-Spanish fleet defeated by the British at Cape St. Vincent; 1805 Spain and France defeated by the British at Trafalgar; 1807 Treaty of Fontainebleau; Napoleon's influence becomes manifest. Spanish invasion of Portugal with French support; 1808 Abdication of Charles IV in favor of Joseph, Napoleon's brother. Portugal invaded by the British. Napoleon personally leads a French invasion, defeating the Spanish at Burgos and Espinosa, taking Madrid in December. The British invade northwest Spain
1809	Defeat of the British at Corunna
1809–14	Gradual conquest of Spain by the British forces, and restoration of the Bourbons under Ferdinand VII (reigned 1814–33)
1833	Ferdinand deprives his brother Don Carlos of direct succession to the throne in favour of his infant daughter Isabella (reigned 1833–68), her mother María Cristina becoming regent upon Ferdinand's death
1834–39	First Carlist War: Don Carlos, with conservative and regional separatist support, contests the crown
1836	*Progresista* revolt in Andalusia, Aragón, Catalonia and Madrid. Restoration of the 1812 constitution
1840	María Cristina forced into exile by the rebellion of General Baldomero Espartero, who becomes dictator
1842	Republican separatist revolt in Barcelona bloodily suppressed
1843	Coalition of moderates and *progresistas* ousts Espartero and declares Isabella of age. General Narváez creates the Guardia Civil
1854	Revolution led by General Leopoldo O'Donnell and Espartero; Liberal alliance formed
1864	Narváez becomes premier; period of reactionary policy
1868	Death of Narváez places absolutist regime in jeopardy. Admiral Juan Topete, supported by liberals, topples the crown. Provisional government formed under Marshal Serrano
1873	First Spanish Republic declared in the midst of Carlist uprisings
1875	Alfonso XII, son of Isabella, restored to the throne. Continuation of the Carlist War
1885	Regency of Alfonso's widow María Cristina
1890	Universal suffrage introduced

1895   Cuban revolution
1898   Spanish-American war results in the loss of the remaining
              Spanish empire in Cuba and the Philippines.

The succession to the Spanish throne of Philip of Anjou brought European tensions and rivalries to a head; the War of the Spanish Succession affected the whole of Europe, and although Philip finally won, Spain lost
further territories and the promise of a future union with France.

During the 18th century there was considerable growth and expansion
within Spain and by the turn of the century the growing economy and
weak monarchy seemed to make Spain an attractive and relatively easily
acquired property within Napoleon's scheme for a new Europe. Napoleon
effected the abdication of Charles IV and invaded the peninsula. He had
correctly identified a historical moment in Spain's cultural development—a clash between a modern vitality and the lingering ghosts of the
past represented by the Church (and the Inquisition) and the Crown. This
moment is most brilliantly captured in the work of the Aragonese artist
Francisco de Goya (1746–1828); on the one hand he portrayed the joy
and vitality of everyday Spanish life—the *fiestas, majas* and bull fighting;
on the other he was a passionate satirist of the Inquisition and the futility
of war. Even his royal portraits betray a knowing recognition of a doomed
family. Late in life the darker side of his preoccupations rose to the surface
in the *Caprichos* and the horrific murals in his house of black sabbaths
and abominations—echoes of Spain's medieval heritage.

A prerequisite of the Bourbon restoration in 1814 was a constitution
carefully constructed to limit the powers of the Crown. Ferdinand immediately rode roughshod over it, setting an example to his nominated successor, Isabella, selected in illegal preference to the heir, his brother Don
Carlos. The monarchy was irrevocably split, and the way open for ambitious statesmen—such as Espartero, Narváez and O'Donnell—to seize
power. The age of the *pronunciamiento*—of successive coups and changes
of government—had arrived. It reached its climax in 1898; Spain's attempt
violently to suppress independence movements in Cuba and the Philippines provoked American intervention and outbursts from intellectuals
and Basque and Catalan separatists at home. The eventual loss of the colonies undermined royal power for good.

A century of such vigorous polemic breeds fine literature. The Romantic
movement in drama was led by José Zorrilla (1817–93), best known for
his play *Don Juan Tenorio,* which is still performed today. The epic quality
of Byron can be traced in the work of the poet José de Espronceda
(1808–42) and the melancholy vein of Romantic poetry was developed by
Gustavo Adolfo Bécquer (1836–70). The later radical development of Ro-
manticism—Realism—was most fully realised by Benito Pérez Galdós
(1843–1920), Spain's Dickens, whose novels include *Doña Perfecta* and
Fortunata y Jacinta; he also wrote an impressive cycle of historical novels,
the *Episodios Nacionales.* Vicente Blasco Ibáñez (1867–1928) took realism
a step further in his powerful social novels, the best known being *La Barraca,* and the original which became the film *Blood and Sand.*

The leading composers of the 19th century, Isaac Albéniz (1860–1909)
and Enrique Granados (1867–1916) also worked in the Romantic style.
But by 1898 social and cultural differences had crystallized, and a more
politicized consciousness accompanied Spain's entry into the 20th century.

Republicanism and the Right

1902–31   *Reign of Alfonso XIII*—1909 Conscription of troops for Mo-
           rocco provokes a general strike in Barcelona. Uprising
           spreads to other Catalonian cities, convents are burned
           and clergy massacred before it is violently suppressed. The
           king calls a Liberal ministry and invites the participation
           of all political parties; 1910 Liberals in power; 1912 Assas-
           sination of anti-clerical Liberal premier José Canalejas;
           1913 Conservatives return to power; 1914 Spain declares
           neutrality in the First World War; 1921 Massive defeat
           of Spanish forces in Morocco during the Rif revolt; 1923
           Army mutiny at Barcelona precipitates the military coup
           of General Manuel Primo de Rivera who, with royal sup-
           port, proclaims national martial law; 1925 Primo de Rive-
           ra becomes prime minister of a largely military cabinet,
           ending his dictatorship; 1927 End of campaign in Moroc-
           co; 1930 Resignation of Primo de Rivera; 1931 Restora-
           tion of the constitution leads to municipal elections and
           an overwhelming victory for the Republicans led by Nice-
           to Alcalá Zamora. Alfonso XIII leaves Spain. Royal prop-
           erty is confiscated and Zamora elected first president, im-
           mediately succeeded by Manuel Azaña

1932   Conservative revolt under General José Sanjurjo suppressed.
           Catalan charter of autonomy approved in principle by the
           Republican government

1933   Two radical uprisings of anarchists and syndicalists; both
           suppressed by the government. The Associations Law
           strips the Church of its property and traditional rights.
           Regular elections show a swing to the Right. Foundation
           of the Falange—a nationalist anti-Marxist youth move-
           ment—by José Antonio Primo de Rivera, son of the for-
           mer dictator

1934   Victory for the moderate Left in Catalonia. Strike in Barcelo-
           na. Formation of a cabinet under Alejandro Lerroux,
           broadly aligned with the Right. President Luis Companys
           of Catalonia declares independence but is suppressed by
           government troops, as is the Communist uprising in Astu-
           rias

1936   Popular Front (Republicans, Socialists, Syndicalists and
           Communists) wins a decisive electoral victory over the
           Right. Revolt of military garrison led by Generals Francis-
           co Franco and Emilio Mola at Melilla in Spanish Morocco
           spreads to mainland garrisons at Cádiz, Seville, Zaragoza
           and Burgos. The government retains control in Madrid
           and Barcelona and declares the confiscation of all clerical
           property. Military leaders declare a state of war. Rebels
           capture Badajoz, Toledo, (later relieved), Irún and San Se-
           bastián, establishing themselves in the north, west and
           south. General Franco is declared Chief of State by the

rebels. Popular Front government grants the Basques home rule. Siege of Madrid begins

1937   The rebels capture Málaga, but fail to encircle Madrid. Loyalists win battle at Brihuega. New socialist government formed (excluding the Anarchists and Syndicalists). German warships bombard Almería. Rebels capture Bilbao and, as Basque resistance collapses, Santander. Gijón and the whole of Asturias falls to the rebels. Government moves from Valencia to Barcelona. Franco establishes complete naval blockade of the Spanish coast

1938   The rebels capture Teruel and begin drive to the sea, taking Viñaroz on the coast, dividing the Loyalist centers in Castile and Catalonia. Pitched battles along the Ebro

1939   Barcelona taken by rebels. Over 200,000 loyalist refugees escape to France. Franco's government is recognized by Britain and France. Radical government replaced by a new National Defence Council under General José Miaja. Republican fleet flees Cartagena for French North Africa. Madrid government crushes Communist insurgency and sues for peace with honor, but Franco insists on unconditional surrender, the end of the Civil War coming with the surrender of Madrid. Franco institutes a massive purge of the Left wing at home, and joins the German-Italian-Japanese anti-Communist pact. German and Italian troops withdraw from Spain. Spain declares her neutrality in World War II

1942   The Cortes, the national representative body, is reestablished along Fascist lines

1945   Don Juan, the Bourbon claimant to the throne, calls for Franco's resignation. Despite the severing of diplomatic relations with Germany, Spain gives refuge to many Germans. Spain excluded from membership of the United Nations. Franco introduces nominal royalists to the cabinet and promises the restoration of the monarchy

1946   U.S.A., U.K. and France urge the removal of Franco and the restoration of democratic elections

1950   Spain joins the United Nations

1953   Spain agrees to the establishment of N.A.T.O. naval and air bases on its territory in return for economic and military aid

1956   Moroccan protectorate terminated

1968   Spain closes the frontier with Gibraltar

1969   Prince Juan Carlos de Bourbon named by Franco as his successor. President Nixon visits Spain, reaffirming U.S. defence interests there and continuing economic aid

1970   Eruption of the Basque problem. The court martial of 15 Basque nationalists for the assassination of a police official leads to widespread protest: state of emergency declared. Death and gaol sentences passed by the court martial are commuted and reduced in response to great unrest

1973   Franco's first prime minister, Admiral Carrero Blanco, as-
sassinated by Basque terrorists

1975   Spanish Sahara crisis. Under pressure Spain cedes the miner-
al-rich province to Morocco. Franco dies and is succeeded
by Prince Juan Carlos

The events of 1898 led to an increase in Liberal power and a decrease in the ability of the monarchy to control internal affairs. Waiting in the wings, as always, was the extreme Right, represented principally by the army. They were balanced by the increasingly politicized separatists, who devolved by degrees to the Left.

Spain's decline and loss of empire gave rise to a great deal of soul-searching which found an outlet in the literature of the day. The best known member of the literary "Generation of '98" was the novelist, essayist, philosopher and poet Miguel de Unamuno (1864–1937) whose many works include *The Tragic Sense of Life*. Other influential members included the philosopher and essayist José Ortega y Gasset (1883–1955), the novelist Pío Baroja (1872–1956) and the eccentric modernist writer and dramatist Ramón del Valle-Inclán (1866–1936).

For some it was time to leave Spain for better climes, not least for Spain's greatest modern painter, Pablo Picasso (1881–1973) who lived and worked largely in Paris. An innovator and stylist, his contribution to the development of Cubism and modern art in general was due to a profound knowledge of classical and primitive art and great technical facility. The modernist painter Juan Gris (1887–1927) was only one of a number who followed Picasso to Paris.

But such cultural dissatisfaction was only the tip of the iceberg. During the 19th century the economy had failed to keep up with either the rest of Europe or with a rapidly growing population. By the beginning of this century it was clear to both the monarchy and the Right that popular support was the key to power. The Left already knew this, but was plagued by factionalism; however, it made its presence felt in the industrial north and in Catalonia through widespread strikes, attacks on the clergy, repeated demands for autonomy, and resistance to conscription.

The government of General Primo de Rivera violently suppressed all dissidence in Spain and Morocco, and increasingly modeled itself on Italian Fascism, most notably in the creation of the right-wing youth movement, the Falange. Meanwhile, the Left rallied to present a popular united front, won a general election in 1936 and established the Second Republic. An ambitious program of social and political reforms was placed in hand—not least Catalonian autonomy—but the government was seen to be aligned with vociferous extremists—Communists, Anarchists and Syndicalists. The Church and the landowners were dangerously alienated, and it only needed a spark to unleash a vortex of destruction. This came with the arrest of Primo de Rivera's son and the murder of an Opposition politician, José Calvo Sotelo, apparently connived at by the government.

The army was secretly briefed, and on July 17, 1936, a military mutiny erupted in Spanish-occupied Morocco. It spread rapidly, coalescing into a Nationalist Front backed by the Church and the landowners, and General Franco swiftly emerged as its leader. Within the first few months Spain became a battleground for European ideologies, the Fascist regimes in

Germany and Italy sending arms, supplies, advisers and finally over 85,000 troops to support Franco. The U.S.S.R. sent food and arms to the beleaguered government, and radical sympathizers from all over Europe and North America—among them George Orwell—rallied to form the International Brigades. The struggle was particularly vicious; atrocities were perpetrated by both sides—the massacre of the clergy by Republicans in Catalonia and the saturation bombing of Guernica by the Right (using German planes) were only two examples which provoked international protest. As usual it was the common people who bore the brunt of the casualties which totalled over a million by 1939. The military discipline and experience of the Nationalist rebels, their single-mindedness and superior hardware, gave them the upper hand, finally overwhelming the last Republican outposts in Catalonia and Valencia in a crucible of blood and fire. The Republicans, where possible, fled to avoid the inevitable repression and recriminations which would follow. Those who remained faced trial and execution or internment in concentration camps.

The neutrality of Franco's government during World War II placed it in an ambiguous situation—then and in the post-war years. The economy was in ruins and fear of complete collapse forced the Western powers to provide economic support for Franco's regime, while quietly condemning it. Consciences were soothed by Franco's promise of a restoration of a constitutional monarchy. Franco himself, always afraid of loosening his steel grip on the country, lived long enough to see Spain becoming increasingly anachronistic in the democratic and industrial framework of modern Europe.

Culturally Spain contributed to many of the outstanding European movements between the wars. The work of Spanish artists—even when living abroad as many did during the Civil War—reflects the violence and paradox of their country's contemporary history. The most famous monument to the catastrophe of the Civil War remains Picasso's *Guernica* (1937). Joan Miró (1893–1983) and Salvador Dalí (b.1904) both developed unique and instantly identifiable Surrealist styles and became the old masters of the movement. The sculptor Julio González (1876–1942) developed plastic cubism (he taught Picasso to weld) and his work remains a seminal influence on modern sculpture. Non-representational painting and collage dominates the work of Antonio Tàpies (b.1923).

Another member of the Surrealist movement, Luis Buñuel (1900–83), became Spain's foremost filmmaker. Produced mainly abroad, his many works, from the early Surrealist essay *Un Chien Andalou* (made with Dalí, 1928) to the ferocious absurdity of *The Discreet Charm of the Bourgeoisie* (1972), consistently attacked the clergy and the obsessive hypocrisy of the rich middle classes.

The most significant Spanish composer of this period was Manuel de Falla (1876–1946), whose work, including the Ritual Fire Dance from *El Amor Brujo,* was inspired by native folkloric melody and rhythms.

Literary accounts of the Civil War were produced by foreign Republican sympathizers—notably Orwell, Hemingway and Eric Mottram—but the most famous figure of the time was the poet Federico García Lorca (1898–1936) who was himself a victim of the Nationalist partisans. He was shot early on in the Civil War, but not before he had completed stunning dramatic and poetic masterpieces. His best known plays are *Bodas de Sangre* (Blood Wedding), *La Casa de Bernarda Alba* and *Yerma,* whilst his *Romancero Gitano* (Gypsy Ballads) and *Poeta en Nueva York* (A Poet in New York) are his most outstanding collections of poetry. Other poets of the Civil War period include Miguel Hernández (1910–42), who died in gaol, and Rafael Alberti (b.1902) who was elected to the Spanish Parliament in 1977—both of them Republicans. Other outstanding poets of the period were the brothers Antonio (1875–1939) and Manuel Machado (1874–1936), and the 1956 Nobel Prize-winner Juan Ramón Jiménez.

The years immediately following the Civil War were grim—censorship was severe and arbitrary and there was a sharp break in literary continuity; Unamuno, Valle-Inclán, Antonio Machado and Lorca were dead and the great majority of the best writers had disappeared. The '40s were lean years for Spanish literature, and although the '50s saw a slight relaxation and change of mood as Spain's links with Europe were re-established, total freedom of expression was still not available to writers. Nevertheless, certain writers did contribute to a minor renaissance of the Spanish novel, notably Camilo José Cela (b.1916), one of the few truly experimentalist novelists in post-war Spain, and Miguel Delibes (b.1920), as well as the excellent novelists Sánchez Ferlosio, Juan Goytisolo and Daniel Sueiro.

After Franco

1977	First General Election for 40 years, won by the Center Democratic Union under Adolfo Suárez. The Movimiento Nacional, the only political organization permitted under Franco, is disbanded. The Communist Party, trade unions and the right to strike are all legalized
1978	Relaxation of censorship. New constitution promulgated restoring civil liberties
1979	Suárez government returned, but the Socialist Party makes major gains, especially in urban areas. Statutes of Autonomy for Catalonia and the Basque country successfully introduced. Resurgence of Basque terrorist (E.T.A.) activity
1981	Suárez resigns. Attempted military coup led by Colonel Antonio Tejero fails. Leopoldo Calvo Sotelo becomes Prime Minister. New anti-terrorist measures introduced
1982	Spain becomes a full member of N.A.T.O. Sotelo dissolves his parliament and loses the election to a Socialist landslide victory led by Felipe González
1985	Frontier with Gibraltar opened
1986	Spain becomes a full member of the E.E.C. Nationwide referendum votes for Spain to stay in N.A.T.O. Felipe Gonzalez's Socialist Party wins General Election with overall majority for second time.

King Juan Carlos' commitment to the restoration and protection of democracy has proved successful, and the reconstruction of Spain has proceeded apace. But old divisions still linger, especially in the Basque country where armed separatist activity by E.T.A., the minority Basque terrorist organization, is directed against the police and army, who are still regarded by many Basques as bastions or right-wing reaction. The fragility of Spain's fledgling democracy was demonstrated in Tejero's attempted coup of February 1981, but the government nevertheless went ahead with the granting of autonomy to Catalonia and the Basque country, followed in the mid-1980s by the division of the entire country into 16 autonomous regions. The establishment of these self-governing communities, albeit an often arbitrary and very costly process, has played a major part in furthering the cause of democracy in Spain. The considerable authority conceded by the government to the various autonomous communities has generally satisfied the desire of most Spaniards to be rid of the overcentralized power of Madrid that was the hallmark of the old Franco regime. Though guerrilla activity in the name of separatism continues today, only a tiny minority of Spaniards now sympathizes with such extremism.

The devaluation of the peseta boosted the economy immensely, increasing exports and providing a huge source of foreign income from tourism, which in turn has meant that many people have had first-hand experience of Spanish life and culture. For many, music and its performance has provided the most immediate experience of this. Andrés Segovia remained, until his death in 1987, the grand master of the guitar, and flamenco guitarists such as Carlos Montoya, Narciso Yepes, Paco Peña and Paco de Lucía are internationally famous, as is dancer and choreographer Antonio Gades. Virtuoso singers on the international circuit include Victoria de los Angeles, Montserrat Caballé, Teresa Berganza, Pilar Lorengar, José Carreras and, of course, Plácido Domingo. Popular music remains derivative of mainstream developments, although Rock Andaluz is an interesting variation, and there are thriving annual jazz festivals at Barcelona, Sitges and San Sebastián.

With the lifting of censorship the Spanish film industry has enjoyed a period of intense activity and creativity, with directors such as Carlos Saura *(Raise Ravens, Blood Wedding, Carmen, A Love Bewitched),* Victor Erice *(Spirit of the Beehive, The South),* and Manuel Gutierrez Aragón *(La Mitad del Cielo)* winning major prizes at international festivals and gaining substantial audiences overseas. However, the wave of excessive enthusiasm which greeted the abolition of censorship has now abated somewhat, though Spain still shares with other liberal countries the problem of controlling pornography and drug abuse.

The present Socialist government, faced with the unenviable task of alienating neither right nor left, has been forced to institute a tough line to deal with terrorism. But it at the same time has undertaken a thorough reform and modernization of the armed forces and police in an attempt to purge Spain once and for all of the vestiges of Francoism. The control of drug abuse, youth delinquency, and ever-increasing street crime—all arguably the result of Spain's horrendously high levels of unemployment—are, together with the Basque terrorist situation, the greatest problems facing the moderate Socialist government of Felipe González today.

However, the eventual fulfillment in 1986 of Spain's quest to join the European Economic Community, coupled with her decision to remain in N.A.T.O, has signified the end of her alienation from the rest of Europe and of her long 50-year struggle for recovery from the devastation and isolation caused by the Civil War. Now Spain is looking to the future with a new sense of vigor and European identity. In 1992 Barcelona will host the Olympic Games; Seville a world fair to commemorate Columbus' discovery of America—most probably the last great international gathering of the 20th century; and Salamanca and Madrid have both put in bids for nominations as European City of Culture.

EATING IN SPAIN

Gazpacho and Garlic, Shellfish and Squid

Eating in Spain can be a delightful adventure or a sad disappointment. The traveler who has the good sense to hunt out local specialties and to choose carefully the restaurants where he eats can enjoy his trip to Spain for the food alone. But many hotels, particularly in the popular coastal areas, put on their version of an Anglo-Saxon meal, which is usually disastrous.

Spanish cuisine is neither so dainty nor so varied as the French or, perhaps, the Italian, but it has virtues of its own. It is substantial and plentifully served and still has its light and delicate dishes for hot weather. One virtue for the traveler is that restaurant prices are still very reasonable, though for how much longer remains to be seen.

The Spanish, as a nation, eat out a lot, hence the huge number of restaurants, many of them colorful and full of local atmosphere. Service, for the most part, is courteous and highly professional but don't expect it to be swift; that is not the Spanish way.

Spaniards do not like their food very hot. They say it has no taste that way. Those who like their food piping hot should insist with the waiter that it be served *muy caliente*. Nor is Spanish food highly seasoned, as many visitors expect it to be. In fact, cooking with chilli is almost unknown in Spain, and pepper pots are not commonly placed on tables. Olive oil is the basis of all cooking, and when well used you will hardly notice it. The same cannot be said, however, for the liberal use of garlic which dominates many Spanish dishes. If you really don't like garlic, avoid any dishes that are served *al ajillo*.

Meat is generally good though not outstanding. Pork *(cerdo)* and veal *(ternera)* predominate along with the ubiquitous *biftec,* generally a thin piece of beef rather than the steak you might expect. In fact, ordering steak is not usually the wisest choice. Roasts tend to be good in Castile and game, particularly pheasant *(faisán),* partridge *(perdiz),* and quail *(cordonices)* are quite common when in season.

Vegetables and salads are plentiful. It is customary to order vegetables as a first course, usually lightly fried *(salteados)* and mixed with oil, tomato or diced ham making a very tasty starter. Examples are *judías verdes con tomate* (green beans in tomato sauce), *champiñones al ajillo* (mushrooms sautéed in garlic), and *alcachofas con jamon* (artichoke hearts and ham). Cold vegetable starters include *espárragos con mahonesa,* canned asparagus tips which in Spain are traditionally eaten with mayonnaise rather than butter, endives and palm hearts. Spaniards usually order a mixed salad to accompany their main course and this is served on a communal dish into which everyone dips at will. The salad is rarely served with dressing already on it; instead you mix your own dressing with the oil and vinegar on the table.

Where Spain scores best on the gastronomic front is in the sheer variety and abundance of fresh fish and seafood *(mariscos)* on offer in almost every region of the country. The rapid and efficient transportation of freshly caught fish to all but the farthest flung reaches of the nation is one of the country's better organized features.

Merluza (hake) is found all over Spain, and when served well can be quite tasty though it is not the most interesting of fish. *Rape* (angler or monkfish) is another popular whitefish and with its slightly chewy texture makes good fish kebabs. Other commonly found fish are swordfish *(pez espada)* with its delicate taste and close texture rather like meat, and sole *(lenguado)* which is especially delicious served in an orange sauce. Tuna fish *(bonito* or *atún)* is served fresh in the north, cut into steaks and cooked in a rich tomato and onion sauce. It is even more plentiful on the Atlantic coast between Gibraltar and Cádiz. Fresh trout and salmon can also be had in season though be careful not to confuse *salmón* (salmon) with *salmonete* (mullet). *Trucha a la navarra* is a popular way of serving trout, when it is fried and stuffed with a salt cured ham similar to bacon. In San Sebastián, Bilbao, Málaga and other fishing ports, fresh sardines, grilled or fried, are popular. A dish likely to be strange to Anglo-Saxon visitors is squid, or cuttlefish, and it is well worth sampling. Known as *calamares,* or if small, *pulpitos* or *chipirones,* it is at its best in the Basque country and Catalonia. It is served either in its own ink, in a dark sauce, or cut up and deep fried in batter rings *(calamares fritos)* and in this case should be served piping hot and with lemon wedges. Another popular shellfish dish is *almejas a la marinera,* small clams steamed in their shells and served in a delicious sauce of garlic, olive oil and finely chopped parsley. Lobster *(langosta),* crayfish *(langostinas)* and shrimp *(gambas)* are plentiful and very good. *Sopa de pescado* is a fish soup not inferior to French *bouillabaisse,* though less complicated. Traditionally the staple food of fishermen, it is made with shrimps, clams and chunks of *merluza* and other dainties, and is to be recommended in most restaurants. *Zarzuela de mariscos* is another Spanish delicacy, if this is the right word for such a robust dish. Here a great variety of shellfish and white fish are first fried, then cooked in a sauce made up of onions, garlic, tomatoes, wine and laurel. It is served in many of the better restaurants.

One of the basic elements of Spanish diet is pulses—dried beans, lentils and chick peas. They are cooked in all sorts of ways and the dishes have different names in each part of the country. The Basques like white or red beans stewed with *chorizo*—a peppery red sausage—and blood sausage. Farther west, Asturias is famous for *fabada,* a sort of simplified cassoulet of white beans with salt pork and sausage. Each region has its bean dish. Madrid's specialty is *cocido,* made with big yellow chick peas. Boiled beef, boiled chicken, boiled bacon and other choice bits are served with a great dish of peas, preceded by a broth made with the water they have been cooked in. It is a meal all by itself. *Garbanzos* are chick peas served in an earthenware casserole with olive oil, tomatoes and chorizo. These pulse dishes tend to be filling and are best ordered only when you feel like something warm and very satisfying.

Spanish desserts *(postres)* are something of a let-down. The patisserie is a far cry from what Central Europe has to offer. The Moorish-inspired dry cakes, like *polvorones* (*polvo* means "dust" to give you an idea), *manoletes, yemas* or *roscas* are far too sweet for most Anglo-American palates. More often than not you will be forced to fall back on the ubiquitous *flan* (creme caramel). There is no need to despair however: Valencia oranges, melons, strawberries, Almería grapes, Alicante dates and wonderful peaches from Aragón can usually make up for this gap in Spanish gastronomy. But don't be tempted to choose fruit dishes served *en almibar* as this is the Spanish way of saying "canned."

Finally we come to cheese. The best known one is *manchego,* from La Mancha. It comes in various shapes, sizes and tastes but the best should be slightly moist and with a taste that stops just short of being sharp. Roquefort is also becoming popular, but by far and away the best blue cheese is a delicacy usually found in the north, where it is made in the Picos de Europa mountains. This is the famous *queso cabrales* made from a blend of sheep, goat and cows' milk and left to mature wrapped in a large leaf. It is also on sale in Madrid and Barcelona and if you have an opportunity to try it, is a real treat.

Regional Specialties

Most of the dishes mentioned above can be found throughout Spain, but in addition, each region has numerous local specialties. The parador hotels are good places to sample these, as they have a special brief to concentrate on their regional cooking. Here are just a few of the things to look out for.

Galicia. Galicia in the far northwest of Spain offers an outstanding variety of fish and shellfish caught fresh from its shores. Especially typical are *centollas,* a large crab stuffed with its own minced meat. *Empanadas* are a kind of pie, half way between a pizza and a Cornish pasty and may be filled with either meat or fish mixtures. *Caldo gallego* is a typical Galician broth and *lacón con grelos* a regional meat dish consisting of ham and turnip tops and generally much better than it sounds. Make sure you sample some of the rich Ribeiro wines traditionally drunk out of white china bowls rather than glasses, and a *queimada* or two, a glass of the local *aguadiente* set alight (its name means "burning").

Asturias and Cantabria. The verdant provinces of Oviedo and Santander are famous throughout Spain for their dairy cattle and milk products. Here is your chance to sample the superb *cabrales* cheese, or maybe a creamy *cuajada*, a thick set yogurt flavored with honey. Recommended in Santander is the dessert of "fried milk," *leche frita,* a delicious caramelized custard. Asturias is known for its bean stew, *fabada asturiana,* and for its cider *(sidra).* Besides being the only region in Spain where cider is produced and drunk, the Asturians have an amazing manner of pouring their local drink. Holding the pitcher above one shoulder, they pour it over the other shoulder into a glass held almost at ground level, all of which is no doubt intended to improve the sparkle. Good in Santander are *percebes* (barnacles) and some tiny prawns said to be unique to this city. *Cocido montañés* is a bean, cabbage and pork stew.

Basque Country. The Basques have the reputation of being great eaters, and the food of the Basque country is among the best in Spain. It is one of the few regions where good beef can usually be found, though the traveler who insists on steaks may be disappointed as veal is the Basques' own preference. They like hearty dishes and usually eat several at a meal. One of their specialties that has spread all through Spain is salt codfish cooked with fresh tomatoes—*bacalao a la Vizcaina*—and another is the same fish cooked slowly *(pil-pil)* in olive oil. *Merluza a la vasca* too is best served on its home ground. This consists of baked hake served in a casserole in a sauce of clams and shrimps, and garnished with hard boiled egg, asparagus shoots and peas. *Xangurro* a crab shell stuffed with its own meat and baked with rum and coñac is sometimes a little over-rated but is delicious when well done.

In winter their great luxury is *anguilas,* baby eels, cooked whole and served in sizzling hot olive oil with garlic and pieces of red-hot peppers. It takes nerve to try them the first time and it remains an acquired taste.

Following the vogue for *nouvelle cuisine* in France, *Basque nouvelle cuisine* has taken off in a big way and can be sampled not only in the Basque region but in many top restaurants in other parts of Spain.

Aragón. Aragonese cooking tends to be reliable and basic and notable mainly for the quality of its fruit and vegetables.

Catalonia. Catalan cooking is notable for its liberal use of garlic, and tomatoes and peppers are also used lavishly. Spaniards, or rather Catalans, say that many of the dishes served in France *à la Provençal* are Catalan dishes introduced by the Spanish-born Empress Eugénie and baptized with French names to avoid offending national susceptibility. For real garlic lovers, they have a relish made principally of garlic, on the style of the French *aioli,* but it is a little powerful for many foreigners. *Pan tomate* is something you will see in many typical restaurants. This is slices of bread spread with olive oil and puréed tomatoes and eaten as an accompaniment to many dishes, especially seafood.

Pasta dishes tend to be more popular in Catalonia than elsewhere in Spain, and cannelloni and maccaroni appear on many menus as starters.

Snails too, are typical of this region, though you won't find them much anywhere else in Spain.

One of Catalonia's boasts is that its meat is usually better than other parts of Spain, because, in the foothills of the Pyrenees, there is good grazing. A local meat specialty is *butifarra,* a Catalan sausage.

Valencia and Alicante. Paella is now so universally popular that it is often thought of as Spain's national dish, but originally it came from Valencia and many of the best paellas are still to be found there and in the neighboring province of Alicante. Paella is based on rice, flavored with saffron, and embellished with many tidbits of seafood: shrimps, calamares, clams, mussels and anything else that takes the chef's fancy. Small pieces of meat and chicken are also included and the top is decorated with strips of sweet red pimento, green peas and succulent crayfish. It should be served in the shallow iron pan in which it has been cooked. Paella is made to order and will take at least 20 minutes to prepare so it is not a dish for those in a hurry. Traditionally it is eaten at lunchtime and not in the evening.

Valencia is also the orange growing area of Spain and its large succulent fruits are at their best around March. Alicante and Jijona are famous for their *turrones,* a kind of nougat made with almonds and other nuts and flavored with honey. The palm groves of Alicante province are also well known for their dates.

Castile. Castile is associated above all with roast meats *(asados).* Segovia is one of its prime culinary centers and all its restaurants serve the specialties *cochinillo* (suckling pig) and *cordero asado* (roast lamb). *Sopa castellana* is also much served and is a clear broth with chunks of ham, hard boiled eggs and a liberal scattering of vegetables. The dessert *ponche segoviano* will appeal to those with a sweet tooth.

Toledo is known for its game dishes, especially partridge *(perdiz).* Further south the region of La Mancha has a peasant cuisine of its own. *Migas,* a mixture of croutons, ham and chorizo, and *pisto manchego,* a strong tasting casserole of vegetables based on green peppers and olive oil, may not appeal to every palate, but you should not miss sampling the famous cheese *queso manchego,* here on its home ground, nor the delicate *flores manchegas,* a petal-shaped cookie.

Extremadura. This region, together perhaps with La Mancha, is one of the few in Spain where you are better off sticking to meat rather than fish. Sausages, hams and *chorizos* (a highly spiced and fatty salami-like sausage) have long been the livelihood of the region.

Andalusia. Seafood here is excellent especially in and around Málaga. One thing that deserves special mention is *gazpacho andaluz* whose popularity throughout Spain has ranked it second only to *paella* as the national dish. *Gazpacho* is a chilled warm-weather soup. Made with olive oil, vinegar and strained tomatoes, its predominant taste is of garlic. Diced cucumber, green pepper, egg, tomatoes and croutons are served as garnishes.

Almería is famous for its grapes and Málaga for its sweet muscatel raisins which are used in the making of *Málaga Virgen,* a sweet muscatel wine. In Granada the *tortilla sacromonte* is typical, a potato omelet filled with diced ham and mixed vegetables. *Tortillas,* by the way, are omelets in Spain and not unleavened bread as in Mexico. *Tortilla española* is a thick, chunky potato omelet and *tortilla francesa,* a regular thin omelet. Loja is known for its *sopa sevillana,* a fish soup flavored with mayonnaise and containing *merluza,* clams and sometimes shrimp, and garnished with hard boiled egg. Trout is also common here due to the nearby trout farms. Avocados are farmed around Almuñecar, and strawberries are grown around Huelva.

Breakfast and Other Snacks

No matter how well you have prepared yourself for continental breakfasts, the meager Spanish breakfast will almost certainly be a disappointment. A few of the better hotels now make an effort to serve something like an English breakfast, otherwise you had better brace yourself to be confronted by a plate of stodgy buns, known as *croissants, ensaimadas, suizos* or *madalenas,* usually dry and tasteless. The accompanying orange juice is often a disgrace to a country which grows good oranges. There will be a choice of tea or coffee, and hot chocolate may also be on offer. Many Spaniards skip breakfast altogether, making do with a coffee till they stop work for a mid-morning snack.

Chocolate and Churros. Churros are a kind of fritter deep fried usually in rings. They are eaten sprinkled with sugar, and are very popular at fiesta time. Some cafes serve them for breakfast but they are best when eaten piping hot from a *churrería* or a roadside stall, though the latter can cause digestive upsets if the oil is not too fresh. Churros are traditionally eaten with cups or tall glasses of hot chocolate.

Tea and Coffee. Tea is usually made with tea bags and served weak and on its own in the American style. If you want it with milk or lemon, ask for *un té con leche* or un *té con limón.* Coffee is served either black and very strong in a small cup *(café solo)* or with milk *(café con leche)* in a larger cup cappuccino style. If you want your coffee black but longer and weaker, ask for *un café americano.*

Ice Cream and Iced Drinks. Spanish ice cream is varied and delicious. A few particularly Spanish flavors are *almendra* (almond), *avellana* (hazlenut), *turrón* (nougat), *Málaga* (rum and raisin), *nata* (cream) and *mantecado* which is extra rich and creamy, similar to Cornish ice cream. Well worth trying in summer are the refreshing *granizado de limón* and *granizado de café.* Served only in ice cream parlors, these are lemon juice or cold coffee poured over crushed ice. *Blanco y negro* is cold black coffee with vanilla ice cream. *Horchata* is a delicious and exclusively Spanish drink. Served ice cold it looks but doesn't taste like milk. Instead it has a sweet and distinctive nutty taste for it is made from nuts. Look out for shops displaying the *Hay horchata* signs but beware the bottled variety.

Tapas and Raciones. Finally that most fascinating of all Spanish customs, tapas, those savory tidbits that you will see piled high on the counters of any bar or cafeteria. The variety of tapas on offer is immense: chunks of *tortilla, patatas bravas* (potato chunks in a spicy sauce), salamis, *chorizo,* cubes of marinated beef, squid, clams, mussels, shrimp, octopus, whitebait, fish roes, all served either plain or concocted into an elaborate salad. Ham is a delicacy—and often an expensive one. You can choose from either *jamón de York,* cooked ham, or the delicious and extremely rich *jamón serrano,* mountain ham, that has been laid out in the sun on the snow of the mountains, for the sun to cure it, while the snow keeps it from spoiling. It is a fine dark red in color, and when sliced thin, is translucent. Tapas are also served in larger portions called *raciones* and if you share three or four of these, they make a very adequate supper.

Worth observing is the "tapas and pastries ritual." Cafes and bars begin the day with their counters heaped with pastries. Around midday these are removed and replaced by the tapas for pre-lunch snackers. After lunch, at around 3 P.M., off go the tapas and back come the pastries which prove popular from 6–7 P.M. with afternoon shoppers. Finally, at about 8 P.M. out go the pastries for the last time and back come the tapas as the evening paseo and aperitif hour approaches. So, whichever of the two you wish to sample, make sure you get the timing right!

Bull fight in a Village by Goya

BULLFIGHTING FOR BEGINNERS

Art, Not Sport

Mention Spain to any non-Spaniard and one of the first things that springs to mind is the bullfight. However, although bullfighting may seem to be the national spectacle, you would be wrong to assume that every Spaniard regularly attends a bullfight or is even knowledgeable on the subject.

Far and away more popular is the national game of soccer (football to British readers) which the Spanish call *fútbol*. Spaniards pack the soccer stadiums of large cities during the season and are regularly to be found glued to their T.V. sets for a mid-week game. Soccer matches and bullfights both take place on Sunday afternoons but don't make the mistake of considering them rival sports, for the Spanish do not consider bullfighting to be a sport, rather it is an art form.

For the last 20 years the general popularity of bullfighting has waned considerably, at least among Spain's native population. But the spectacle continues to flourish, boosted largely by the ever-increasing number of tourists for whom a *corrida* is an obligatory outing. In many cases the quality of the bullfights has waned too, for many of the regular Sunday afternoon fights are now little more than performances put on for the benefit of tourists. However, that is not to say that there are not still some excellent bullfights, most of which are held at times of major fiestas such as

129

Valencia's fallas in March, Seville's April Fair, Jerez de la Frontera's May Fair, and the San Fermines bull runnings in Pamplona in July. In Madrid around May 15 the festivities for San Isidro see some of the best bullfights in the country. At all of these times the fights are televised on nationwide T.V. and it is not unusual to see Spaniards all over the country crowding into bars or hotel lounges to watch the coverage. Good toreros are still held in great esteem and frequently make news headlines.

The ritual slaughter in the ring may no longer be every Spaniard's idea of a Sunday afternoon's fun but it is still big business, employing some 158,000 workers and grossing around $275 million on ticket sales. A top matador can earn up to $18,000 for one fight alone, spectators will pay up to $180 for a ticket for one of the top fights, and each year the Spanish government earns some $35 million in revenue from bullfights. In 1985 "toro pools" were introduced, whereby competitors bet on the outcome of fights by guessing how many ears will be awarded. Half of the takings are returned in prize money, the other half, after deductions for expenses, are reinvested in bullfighting. As Spanish *fútbol* pools bring in some 2,000 million ptas. a year, the boost to the bullring was calculated to be spectacular. In the same year a record 31.6 million spectators attended a bullfight. Another proof that the popularity of the bullfight is far from dead came with Spain's negotiations to enter the Common Market, for no matter how hard the E.E.C. officials in Brussels insisted there should be an end to it, the Spanish were adamant: the bullfight would remain.

If you are dead set against bullfighting, there is no pressure to attend and you may be encouraged to know that there are anti-bullfight movements within Spain as well as outside the country; it is a debate which is given free rein these days. And Spain's anti-bullfight movement, the *Comite Antitaurina,* formed in 1986, is becoming ever more adept at making its protest heard. If you do decide to attend, you are quite frankly more likely to be bored during your first fight than you are to be revolted or deeply shocked, for appreciating a bullfight is a skill that can only be acquired with practice. The untrained eye will take in little at first and may quickly tire of the spectacle. So to help you understand something of what you will see, we offer the following pointers.

How to Watch a Bullfight

Anglo-Saxons, on their first introduction to bullfighting customarily voice an objection to it that indicates their lack of understanding of its basic nature. They consider that it is unfair. It is a contest between a man and a bull, in which the bull always dies. There is something wrong, they feel, in a sport in which the identity of the winner is fixed in advance.

So there would be, if bullfighting were a sport. But bullfighting is not a sport. Bullfighting is a spectacle. In a sense it is a play, with a plot. The plot calls for the bull to die. To object to that is as pointless as to object that the plot of *Julius Caesar* calls for Caesar to die. In another sense, it is a ballet. One of its essential features is the performance of stylized traditional movements, and a byproduct of their accurate performance is grace. In still another sense, it is an exhibition of physical dexterity, with the risk of injury or death accepted as the penalty for clumsiness, like the art of a trapeze performer. But in its essence, it is a demonstration of the mastery of a human over two living organisms—over the bull, for the point of the torero's art is to maneuver a thousand pounds of recalcitrant, malevolent armed muscle according to his will—and over himself, for perhaps the basic meaning of the bullfight is that it is an ordeal of the quality most prized by Spaniards, courage. The bullfighter must master his own fear before he can master the bull.

The brave man is not the one who does not feel fear; he is the man who feels fear and still faces the danger that frightens him. Bullfighters are invariably afraid when they enter the ring. Make no mistake about that. They are afraid, and they are right to be afraid. They know that their chance of dying in the ring is one in ten. They know that their chance of being crippled is about one in four. They know, usually, what the horn ripping through the flesh feels like; no bullfighters finish their careers completely unscathed.

The bull may always die (he can avoid that fate by refusing to fight, but this is rare), but he does not always lose. In that sense, bullfighting *is* a sport. But you will understand it better if you cease to regard it as a sport and look upon it instead as a spectacle—a spectacle to which death does not put an end, but is itself an intrinsic element.

The Plot

Bullfighting is a highly ritualized affair. All its details have been developed over a long period into a pattern that now never varies, each one ticketed with its own label in the extensive vocabulary of bullfighting. To begin with, the bullfight is not a fight—it is a *corrida,* a "running" of the bull. It is divided, like most plays, into three acts, the *tercios*—the act of the picadors, the act of the banderillas, and the act of death. There is also a curtain-raiser, the parade across the ring, in which all the participants in the coming spectacle take part, even to the men who will drag the dead bulls out of the arena.

The act of the picadors has scenes—the *doblando,* the first luring of the bull with the capes; the matador's first playing of the bull; the arrival of the mounted picadors to attack the bull with their lances; and the *quites*—which is the work of the matadors in luring the bull away from the picador. The fine points of these maneuvers will be explained in a moment.

The act of the banderillas also usually has three scenes, in the sense that three pairs of gaily decorated darts are ordinarily thrust into the bull's shoulders, but each of these scenes is the same.

The act of death, the *faena,* has two scenes—first, the playing of the bull with the small red flannel *muleta,* which replaces the billowing capes at this stage of the fight—and the killing with the sword—the moment of truth.

All of this you will see in every bullfight, good, bad or indifferent. How is a novice to know whether the manner in which it is performed is skillful or clumsy?

You may be surprised, at your first bullfight, to hear the crowd roar its approval for a maneuver that, to you, looks no different from those that preceded it, and were allowed to pass in silence. You may be baffled when seat cushions start flying into the ring, hurled by an angry crowd whose method of showing its ire is to attempt to trip up the matador and give the bull a chance at him. The fine points that arouse the admiration or the contempt of the crowd (and the crowd, at a Spanish bullfight, pro-

vides a spectacle second only to what is going on in the ring) cannot be
expected to be obvious to a newcomer. You will undoubtedly know whether the performance you are watching is, in general, skillful or clumsy, for
deft movements are graceful and awkward ones are not and it takes no
expert to appreciate the difference between the single clean thrust of the
sword that sends the bull down as though he had been struck by lightning
and the blundering butchery marked by thrust after thrust, with the sword
spinning into the air as it strikes the shoulder-blade of the bull instead
of piercing through the opening that leads to the heart. But in order to
know why a performance is good or bad, you will need some coaching.

What to Look For

The three elements by which the critics judge bullfighters (and the bullfight critic, in Spain, is a highly respected individual, whose verdicts can
make or break a matador's career) are *parar, mandar* and *templar.* Parar
is style, and consists in standing straight firmly planted, unyielding, bringing the bull past in a thundering rush with a gracefulness that gives no
ground. Mandar is mastery of the bull, controlling his every move and
spinning him about like a puppet. Templar is timing, and the acme of skill
in this respect is to perform the maneuvers of the fight in slow motion.
The more slowly the bull is moving as he passes the matador, the longer
the time of dangerous propinquity lasts, and the more opportunity is
granted to the animal to change tactics and go for the man instead of the
cape.
Watch the matador's feet. He should not move them as the bull thun-
ders past. If he really has control of the animal, he will make it avoid him;
he will not have to move to avoid it. Watch how closely he works to the
bull. Obviously his mastery of the beast must be more exact if he lets the
horn graze his chest than if he pulls it by a foot away. Closeness can be
faked. If the torero holds his arms with the cape far out from his body,
if he leans well forward so that, without moving his feet, he can still bring
the upper part of his body back when the bull reaches him, then he is not
showing the same skill as the man who stands ramrod straight and maneuvers the bull without budging himself.
Some grandstand plays are really dangerous. Some aren't. Kneeling really is, because it reduces the mobility of the bullfighter. Passes in which
the cape swings over the head of the torero are dangerous because it makes
him lose sight of the bull at a critical moment. Passes in which the cape
is held behind the bullfighter's body are also dangerous, obviously. Passes
in which the bull, charging towards one side of the torero, is drawn across
his body to pass on the other side are dangerous.

Psychology of the Bull

On the other hand, standing with one's back against the fence, which
looks dangerous, often isn't. It depends on the bull. Most bulls have no
desire to bang their heads against a hard wooden wall. It is often more
dangerous, close to the fence, to allow the bull to pass between it and the
bullfighter; bulls have a tendency to swerve outward from the fence. If
you notice that the bull returns habitually to a certain spot in the arena
after his various charges, it is more dangerous to fight him in that part

of the ring than elsewhere; he has elected it, by some mysterious instinct, as his home ground, and he is fiercer on it. It is more dangerous for the matador to taunt him into charging outward from this territory than into it. When he is returning to his base, he is intent upon getting back "home." He is paying no attention to the man who may happen to be standing on the edge of the path he is following. Bullfighters know that and sometimes take advantage of the bull's rush past to draw applause from spectators who haven't grasped the situation.

Paradoxically, the bull who looks most dangerous to you is the one who looks least dangerous to the torero—the one who comes charging into the ring full of fight and makes a vicious dash for the first bullfighter he sees. The type of bull that is out to kill is the type of bull the torero can handle. He has a one-track mind; and a bull with a one-track mind is predictable. You can tell what he will do. Therefore you can control him. Bullfighters like a fighting animal, one that is going to charge hard—and straight.

The Opening Scene

First of all you will need to identify the matadors. They will be the men walking in front of the opening procession into the arena, just behind the mounted escort. The senior will be on the right and he will kill the first and fourth bulls. The youngest will be in the center and he will kill the third and sixth bulls.

As each of the six bulls makes its entrance, its weight in kilos is posted at the edge of the ring.

When the bull first charges into the arena, one of the bullfighters will wave his cape at him and very probably, at the bull's rush, will dart behind one of the bulwarks that guard the openings into the corridor behind the barrier. Don't mark him down as a coward for that. It is all part of the ritual. The bull is not yet actually being played. He is being studied. Perhaps the first cape will be waved by the man closest to him, to find out if his near vision is good. Then a man on the other side of the ring will try, to test his vision at a distance. The matador is watching how he charges, and whether he has a tendency to hook to the left or the right. Upon his correct interpretation of the bull's reaction to these preliminary flaggings will depend his success in the rest of the fight.

After these opening evolutions, the matador comes out to demonstrate his skill with the cape. This is your first real chance to witness the art of the bullfighter. If, in reading bullfight stories, you have come across the term *verónica,* and wondered what it meant, it is probably what you are watching now. The verónica is the simplest and most basic of the various passes *(pases),* and it is almost always the one with which the matador begins. Its name, by the way, derives from the way St. Veronica is said to have held the cloth with which she wiped Christ's face. The torero holds the cape before him, more or less gathered into folds, his profile towards the bull, and as the animal charges, he spreads the cloth before the animal's snout, swings it by his body, and the bull follows it past. Ordinarily, as the bewildered bull turns, he swings him by again, then perhaps a third time, each time a little closer, as he becomes acquainted with the animal's reactions and acquires *mandar,* and perhaps finishes by gathering the cape in against his body in a half verónica as the bull passes. This usually stops the bull short, and the matador can turn his back disdainfully on the horns and walk away, a display of mastery over the bull that always brings a roar of *"Olé."*

The Picador

With the end of this scene, the picadors appear—the mounted bullfighters with lances. The object of this part of the fight is to launch an offensive against that tremendous hump of flesh on the top of the bull's neck, the tossing muscle. Until that has been tired, so that the bull will drop his head, he cannot be killed with the sword. The way to the animal's heart is opened only when the front feet are together and the head dropped.

The picador attacks the tossing muscle by meeting the bull's charge with his lance, which he digs into it. The role of the horse is to be tossed—not to be gored. He wears a mattress to protect him from goring and the management, which has to pay for the horses, sincerely hopes that it will succeed. But the bullfighters want the horse to be tossed. A bull whose tossing muscle has hoisted three heavy horses into the air is a bull beginning to be tired. There is also a second motive, to maintain the bull's combativity. He will not go on indefinitely charging into yielding cloth and empty air. He has to be allowed to hit something solid or he won't play.

There is perhaps one exception to the statement that the bullfighters want the horse to be tossed. The picador, though it is part of his job, isn't happy about it. When his horse is tossed, he goes down. The picador, unlike the horse, has no mattress. He does have a heavy piece of armor on the leg which is going to be on the side from which the bull will charge, and it is so heavy that when he goes down he can't easily get up unaided. He depends on his colleagues to draw the bull away.

Years ago, of course, the picador was even more vulnerable, because his horse had no protection at all against the bull. Everything depended on the picador's skill at holding off the bull with his lance. So many horses were gored, however, that the *peto* or mattress was prescribed. This last grew longer and longer until finally it began to scrape the ground. Picadors grew careless and sometimes jabbed away at a bull until he was half-dead from lance wounds alone. For this reason the size of the *peto* is now limited to about 60 pounds (instead of 90 or more), thus making the horse somewhat vulnerable and restoring a certain degree of skill to the picador's task. Horses are sometimes gored and this is often one of the nastier aspects of the fight.

Watch closely now, for here it is probable that you will have an opportunity to see some dexterous capework. The usual bullfight program calls for the killing of six bulls by three matadors. Although each matador has two bulls definitely assigned to him for the kill, at this stage of the fight all three will probably intervene. It is usual for the picadors to appear three times. The three matadors take turns in drawing the bull off, and in demonstrating their mastery of the animal. Thus this portion of the fight takes on the aspect of a competition among the three, and you may see exceptional brilliance displayed at this juncture.

Now you are likely to see some of the most intricate passes—though the chances are that at your first fight they will all look much alike. One pretty effect is to end a series of verónicas by holding the cloth of the cape to the waist and twirling as the bull passes, so that it stands up like the skirt of a pirouetting dancer. This is called a *rebolera*. In the *chicuelina*, a rather dangerous pass, the matador gathers in the cloth just as the bull is passing, wrapping it around his own body. He hopes the bull's rush will carry him past, in spite of the sudden removal of his target. Usually it does. This pass is named for the bullfighter who first used it. So is the *gaenera,* which starts like a verónica, but in which the cape is thrown up over the head as the bull is passing. So is the *manoletina,* in which the cape or muleta is held behind the matador's back while the bull is invited to charge only an arm's length away.

The Banderillas

The planting of the banderillas—the pairs of decorated darts that are thrust into the bull's shoulders—comes next. This is a spectacular feat to the uninitiated, but it is in fact one of the least dangerous parts of the fight. Watch closely, however, if you see the matador himself preparing to perform this maneuver, instead of entrusting it to the banderilleros, which is the normal course. That means he is particularly expert with the darts, and you may see an extra twist added.

The Climax

The last stage of the fight, the *faena,* is the final playing of the bull and his killing. This is when the matador, at least if he feels he had a good bull, a responsive animal, bold and aggressive, will put on his best show. If, before advancing into the ring, he holds his hat aloft and turns slowly round, to salute the whole audience, it is your cue to miss nothing. It means that he is dedicating the bull to everyone, and that is done only when the torero believes he has an opportunity to give a particularly fine performance with all the extra, spectacular flourishes.

This is also the most dangerous part of the fight. For the large cape, the muleta is now substituted, a small piece of red cloth that offers a much less conspicuous target for the bull's attention than the matador's body. It is now that his skill will be exerted to its utmost and now that you will want to follow more closely every movement of the torero until at last the great black bulk of the bull goes crashing down onto the sand.

You may think that the quality of the bullfighting has suddenly decreased at the beginning of the faena, for there may not be much grace in the opening passes. That is because their object is to attain complete mastery over the bull. His will to fight is being broken, and it is done by violence rather than by grace. It is at this stage that you will see the faena's counterpart of the opening act's verónica, that is to say the most simple pass of this part of the fight, the *natural.* This consists in presenting the muleta, held out in one hand to the left side of the matador, and swinging it before the bull's muzzle as he charges. This is more dangerous when done with the right hand *(un natural con derechazo).*

Once the bull has been shown again who is master, however, you may see some of the most daring and elegant passes of the whole corrida. Passes in which the matador stands erect holding the muleta with both hands, as though flagging the animal by, are called 'statues'—*estatuarios.* It is at this stage that you may see the *manoletina,* mentioned above, and some overhead passes *(pases por alto).* The most dangerous pass you are likely to see now is the *arrucina,* in which the muleta is held behind the body.

Also risky is the *pendulo,* in which the cloth is swung back and forth behind the matador's legs.

At the end of this demonstration, the time comes for the kill. First, it is necessary to square *(cuadrar)* the bull—that is, to maneuver him into a head-on position with the two front feet together. To judge this perfectly is an essential part of the matador's skill. For if he attempts to strike when the bull's feet are not perfectly together, or if its head is not lowered at just the right angle, or even if the bull moves his feet as the matador lunges forward with his sword, he will not make a clean kill. Instead the blade may strike bone and be sent flying high into the air leaving the bull writhing in agony and the matador needing to make another attempt. Such a misjudgement invariably elicits the wrath of the crowd who will start booing and jeering and possibly throwing cushions into the ring.

The Kill

With the bull fixed, the matador drives the sword in over the horns with his right hand, while his left, with the muleta, sweeps under his eyes and pulls his head down. It is a moment as dangerous for the man as for the bull; if the swing of the muleta fails to hold that head down, instead of sword into bull it will be horn into man. But if the matador has judged correctly, the bull crumples to the ground after a few moments' agony.

What the president of the fight, whose judgment is usually much influenced by the reaction of the crowd, thinks of the bullfighter's performance will be indicated now. If the matador did well, he is awarded an ear; exceptionally well, both ears; and for a really superlative performance, the ears and the tail. This is ordinarily as far as recognition goes, but there have been occasions on which a hoof or two has been added, and the all-time record is probably held by Carlos Arruza, who in Málaga was awarded the whole animal, at the end of a fight in which he had once been tossed. The dead bull may be dragged around the ring and cheered in tribute to his courage. This in no way reflects upon the performance of the matador—indeed, quite the contrary.

A few final points to bear in mind. A bullfighter is a *torero* (never, except in *Carmen,* a *toreador*) and only the star who kills the bull is a *matador (matar* meaning "to kill"). *Novilladas* are fights with young bulls and aspirant matadors, and for this reason, tickets are usually cheaper than for regular *corridas.* Should you come across a *rejoneador,* this is the revival of the old and spectacular style of bullfighting in which each phase of the contest is performed by the rejoneador mounted on a beautiful Arab horse which, needless to say, is kept out of contact with the bull's horns. It is closer to the Portuguese style of bullfighting than to the traditional Spanish style.

For information on purchasing tickets and tips on which seats to choose, see under *Bullfights* in *Facts at your Fingertips.*

ENGLISH–SPANISH TOURIST VOCABULARY

Pronunciation. The important thing to remember with Spanish pronunciation is that the vowels are emphasized much more than the consonants.

Spanish pronunciation is always regular—once you have mastered the basic rules there are no exceptions to them. It is a very easy language to read and speak.

The Spanish alphabet has 27 letters; most are the same as the English ones, except there is no "k" and no "w." The Spanish alphabet has three letters that do not exist in English—"ch," "ll," and "ñ." When looking anything up in a Spanish sequence, "ch" comes after "c," "ll" follows "l," and "ñ" comes after "n."

Of the tricky sounds to pronounce the most difficult can be:

c Can be hard as in "cat" or "cut"—casa (house); color (color) or soft and lisped, like "th" in "thanks." This happens before an "e" or an "i"—cielo (thee-ay-lo), celoso (thay-lo-soh).

d Said as in English when it starts a word—data and delta; otherwise a hard "th" sound (like "this")—moda (mo-tha) meaning fashion or style; dado (dah-tho) meaning given.

j A hard gutteral sound, harsher than the English "h" and made in the throat. There is no equivalent. Examples are—jamón (ha-mon) ham; jabón (ha-bón) soap; Jijona (Hee-hon-a) a town name; juro (hoo-row) I swear. If you have trouble with this sound, say it like an English "h" and you won't be far wrong.

ll Almost the English "y." Llamar (ye-am-ar) to call; billete (beeyey-tay) ticket.

ñ Nasal twang to an "n." Same kind of sound as in English "gnu" or the Italian "gnocchi."

z The same as the lisped "c." "Z" is always lisped before *all* vowels. Zamora (Tha-mo-ra) a town name; zebra (thay-bra) zebra; zumo (thoo-mo) juice.

Basics

yes	sí
no	no
please	por favor
thank you	gracias
thank you very much	muchas gracias
excuse me	perdóneme, perdon
sorry	lo siento
good morning	buenos días
good afternoon	buenas tardes
good night	buenas noches
goodbye	adiós /hasta la vista
see you soon	hasta pronto
be seeing you	hasta luego
goodbye (literally "until tomorrow")	hasta mañana

Numbers

1	uno, una	16	dieciséis
2	dos	17	diecisiete
3	tres	18	dieciocho
4	cuatro	19	diecinueve
5	cinco	20	veinte
6	seis	21	veintiuno
7	siete	30	treinta
8	ocho	40	cuarenta
9	nueve	50	cincuenta
10	diez	60	sesenta
11	once	70	setenta
12	doce	80	ochenta
13	trece	90	noventa
14	catorce	100	ciento, cien
15	quince	1000	mil

Days of the Week

Monday	el lunes
Tuesday	el martes
Wednesday	el miércoles
Thursday	el jueves
Friday	el viernes
Saturday	el sábado
Sunday	el domingo

Months

January	enero	July	julio
February	febrero	August	agosto
March	marzo	September	setiembre
April	abril	October	octubre
May	mayo	November	noviembre
June	junio	December	diciembre

Useful Phrases

Do you speak English?	Habla Usted inglés?
What time is it?	Qué hora es?
Is this seat free?	Esta plaza está libre, por favor?
How much does it cost?	Cuanto vale?
Would you please direct me to. . . the bullring?	Por favor, para ir a. . . la plaza de toros?
Where is the station? the museum?	Donde está la estación? el museo?
I am American, British.	Soy americano/americana, inglés/inglesa.
It's very kind of you.	Es Usted muy amable.
I don't understand.	No entiendo.

I don't know.	No sé.
Please speak more slowly.	Hable más despacio, por favor.
Please sit down.	Siéntese, por favor.

Everyday Needs

cigar, cigarette	puro, cigarillo
matches	cerillas, fósforos
dictionary	diccionario
key	llave
razor blades	hojas de afeitar
shaving cream	crema de afeitar
soap	jabón
city plan	plano de la ciudad
road map	mapa de carreteras
country map	mapa del país
newspaper	periódico
magazine	revista
telephone	teléfono
telegram	telegrama
envelopes	sobres
writing paper	papel de escribir
airmail writing paper	papel de avión
postcard	tarjeta postal
stamp	sello

Services and Stores

bakery	panadería
bookshop	librería
butcher's	carnicería
dry cleaner's	tintorería
grocery	tienda de comestibles
hairdresser, barber	peluquería
laundry	lavandería
laundromat	lavandería automática
shoemaker	zapatero (man), zapatería (shop)
stationery store	papelería
supermarket	supermercado

Emergencies

ill, sick	enfermo, enferma
I am ill.	Estoy enfermo.
My wife/husband/child is ill.	Mi esposa/marido/hijo (hija) está enfermo./enferma.
doctor	médico
nurse	enfermera
prescription	receta
pharmacist/chemist	farmacia
Please fetch/call a doctor.	Llame al médico, por favor.

accident	accidente
road accident	accidente de carretera
hospital	hospital/clínica
dentist	dentista
X-ray	rayos X, radiografía

Pharmacist's

pain-killer	calmante, analgésico
bandage	venda
sticking plaster	tiritas
scissors	tijeras
hot-water bottle	bolsa de agua caliente
sanitary towels	compresas higiénicas
tampons	tampones
ointment for stings	pomada para picaduras
coughdrops	pastillas para la tos
laxative	laxante

Traveling

plane	avión
hovercraft	aero deslizador
hydrofoil	hidrofoil
train	tren
boat, small boat	barco, barca
ferry	ferry
taxi	taxi
car	coche
truck	camión
bus, long-distance bus	autobus, autocar
seat	asiento
reservation	reservación/reserva
smoking/non-smoking compartment	compartimiento de fumadores/ de non fumadores
rail station	estación de ferrocarril
subway station	estación de metro
bus station	estación de autobuses
airport	aeropuerto
harbor	puerto
town terminal	terminal
sleeper	coche cama
couchette	litera
porter	mozo
luggage	equipaje
luggage trolley	carretilla, carro
single ticket	billete de ida
return ticket	billete de ida y vuelta
first class	primera clase
second class	segunda clase

When does the train leave?	A qué hora sale el tren?
What time does the train arrive at. . . ?	A qué hora llega el tren a. . . ?
When does the first/last train leave?	A qué hora sale el primero/ último tren?

Hotels

room	habitación
bed	cama
bathroom	cuarto de baño
bathtub	bañera
shower	ducha
toilet	aseo, servicio, retrete; lavabo (in a train)
toilet paper	papel higiénico
pillow	almohada
blanket	manta
sheet	sábana
chambermaid	camarera
breakfast	desayuno
lunch	comida (de mediodia)
dinner	cena

Do you have a single/double/ twin-bedded room?	Tiene Usted una habitación individual/con cama de matrimonio/con dos camas?
I'd like a quiet room.	Quiero una habitación tranquila.
I'd like some pillows.	Quiero unas almohadas.
What time is breakfast?	A qué hora sirven el desayuno?
Come in!	Pase!
Are there any messages for me?	Hay recados para mi?
Would you please call me a taxi?	Me llama un taxi, por favor?
Please take our bags to our room.	Nos lleva las maletas a la habitación, por favor.

Restaurants

menu	lista (de platos), carta, menú
fixed-price menu	menú del dia, menú turístico
wine list	la lista de vinos
waiter	camarero
head waiter	maitre
bill/check	cuenta

ON THE MENU

Starters

aguacate con gambas	avocado and prawns
caldo	thick soup
champiñones al ajillo	mushrooms in garlic
consomé	clear soup
gazpacho	iced soup made with tomatoes, onions, peppers, cucumber and oil
huevos flamencos	eggs with spicy sausage and tomato
judías con tomate/jamón	green beans with tomato/ham
sopa	soup
sopa de ajo	garlic soup
sopa de garbanzos	chick-pea soup
sopa de lentejas	lentil soup
sopa de mariscos	shellfish soup
sopa sevillana	soup made with mayonnaise, shellfish, asparagus and peas

Omelets (Tortillas)

tortilla de champiñones	mushroom omelet
tortilla de gambas	prawn omelet
tortilla de mariscos	seafood omelet
tortilla de patatas, tortilla española	Spanish potato omelet
tortilla francesa	plain omelet
tortilla sacromonte (in Granada)	omelet with ham, sausage and peas

Meats (Carnes)

cerdo	pork	cordero	lamb
chorizo	seasoned sausage	filete	beef steak
chuleta	chop, cutlet	jamón	ham
cochinillo	suckling pig	salchichón	salami
		ternera	veal

Poultry (Aves) and Game (Caza)

cordonices	quail	pato	duck
conejo	rabbit	pato salvaje	wild duck
faisán	pheasant	pavo	turkey
jabalí	wild boar	perdiz	partridge
oca, ganso	goose	pollo	chicken

Variety Meats, Offal

callos	tripe	hígado	liver
criadillas	literally,	lengua	tongue
	bull's testicles	mollejas	sweetbreads
	(shown on Spanish	riñones	kidneys
	menus as	sesos	brains
	"unmentionables")		

Fish (Pescados)

ahumados	smoked fish	besugo	sea bream
	(i.e. trout,	lenguado	sole
	eel, salmon)	lubina	sea bass
anchoa	anchovy	merluza	hake, white
anguila	eel		fish
angulas	elver (baby	mero	grouper fish
	eel)	pez espada,	
atún, bonito	tuna	emperador	sword fish
bacalao	cod	rape	angler fish
salmén	salmon	sardina	sardine
salmonete	red mullet	trucha	trout

Shellfish and Seafood (Mariscos)

almeja	clam	ostra	oyster
boquerones	whitebait	percebes	barnacles
calamares	squid	pulpo	octopus
cangrejo	crab	sepia	cattlefish
centolla	spider crab	vieiras	scallop (in
gambas	prawns, shrimp		Galicia)
langosta	lobster	zarzuela de	shellfish
langostino	crayfish	mariscos	casserole
mejillones	mussels		

Vegetables (Verduras)

aceituna	olive	espárragos	asparagus
aguacate	avocado	espinacas	spinach
ajo	garlic	espinacas	spinach with
alcachofa	artichoke	a la catalana	garlic, raisins,
apio	celery		and pine ker-
berenjena	egg plant		nels
cebolla	onion	guisantes	peas
calabaza	pumpkin	haba	broad bean
champiñon	mushroom	judía verde	green bean
col	cabbage	lechuga	lettuce
coliflor	cauliflower	lenteja	lentil
endivia	endive,	palmitos	palm hearts
escarola	chicory	pepino	cucumber
ensalada	salad	pepinos	zucchine
ensaladilla	potato	pimiento	green pepper
rusa	salad	patata	potato

| puerro | leak | tomate | tomato |
| seta | chanterelle mushroom | zanahoria | carrot |

Fruit (Frutas)

albaricoque	apricot	limón	lemon
ananás	pineapple	manzana	apple
cereza	cherry	melocotón	peach
ciruela	plum	melón	melon
frambuesa	raspberry	naranja	orange
fresa	strawberry	pera	pear
fresón	large strawberry	plátano	banana
		sandía	water melon
grosella negra	blackcurrant	uvas	grapes
		zarzamora	blackberry

Desserts (Postres)

cuajada	thick yogurt with honey	pastel	cake
		flan	caramel custard
ensalada de frutas, macedonia	fruit salad	fresas con nata	strawberries and cream
helado de vainilla, fresa, café, chocolate	vanilla, strawberry, coffee, chocolate ice cream	pera en almibar	canned pear
		piña en almibar	canned pineapple
		tarta helada	ice-cream cake
melocotón en almibar	canned peach	yogur	yogurt

Miscellaneous

a la brasa	barbecued	guisado	stewed
a la parrilla	grilled	mahonesa	mayonnaise
al horno	roast/baked	mostaza	mustard
arroz	rice	pan	bread
asado	roasted	pasta	pasta
carbonade	pot-roasted	pimienta	pepper
espaguettis	spaghetti	sal	salt
fideos	noodles	salsa de tomate	catsup, ketchup
frito	fried		

Drinks (Bebidas)

| agua | water | agua sin gas | still mineral water |
| agua con gas | carbonated mineral water | | |

blanco y negro	cold black coffee with vanilla ice cream	jerez	sherry
		leche	milk
		limonada	lemon-flavored lemonade
café con leche	coffee with cream	manzanilla	very dry sherry/ camomile tea
café solo	black coffee (expresso)		
		té	tea
caliente	hot	con limón	with lemon
caña	small draught beer	con leche	with milk
		vaso	glass
cava, champán	champagne	un vaso de agua	a glass of water
cerveza	beer	vermut	vermouth
chocolate	hot chocolate		
cuba libre	rum and coke	vino	wine
fino	very dry sherry	vino añejo	vintage wine
frío/fría	cold	vino blanco	white wine
gaseosa	English lemonade	vino dulce	sweet wine
granizado de limón (de café)	lemon (or coffee) on crushed ice	vino espumoso	sparkling wine
		vino rosado	rosé wine
		vino seco	dry wine
horchata	cold summer drink made from ground nuts	vino tinto	red wine
		zumo de naranja	orange juice

INDEX

Index

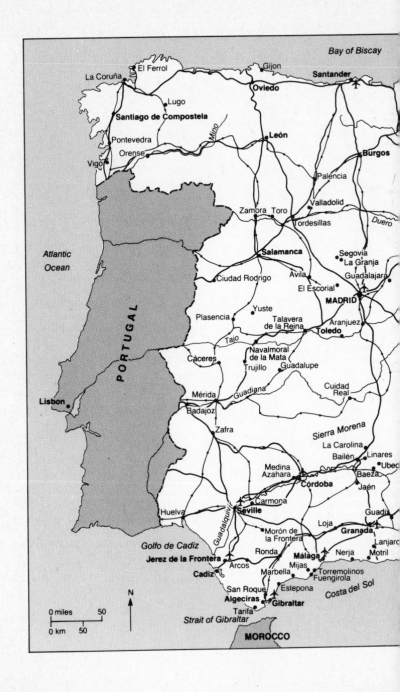

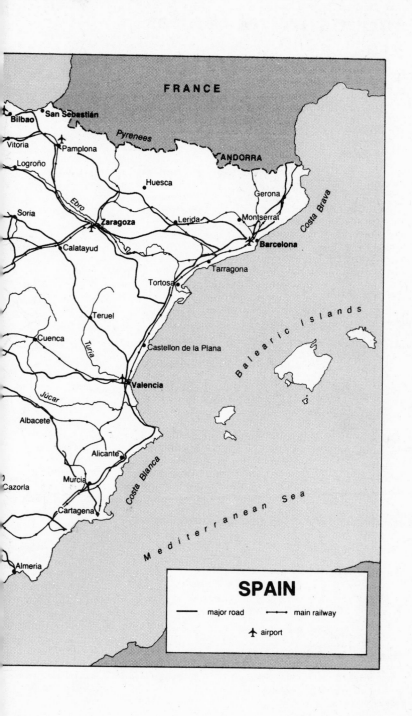

FRANCE

Bilbao
San Sebastián
Vitoria
Pamplona
Logroño
Pyrenees
ANDORRA
Huesca
Gerona
Ebro
Soria
Lerida
Montserrat
Costa Brava
Zaragoza
Calatayud
Barcelona
Tarragona
Tortosa
Teruel
Cuenca
Turia
Castellon de la Plana
Balearic Islands
Júcar
Valencia
Albacete
Alicante
Costa Blanca
Cazorla
Murcia
Cartagena
Mediterranean Sea
Almeria

SPAIN

— major road   •—•— main railway

✈ airport

Fodor's Travel Guides

U.S. Guides

Alaska
Arizona
Atlantic City & the
  New Jersey Shore
Boston
California
Cape Cod
Carolinas & the
  Georgia Coast
The Chesapeake Region
Chicago
Colorado
Disney World & the
  Orlando Area

Florida
Hawaii
Las Vegas
Los Angeles, Orange
  County, Palm Springs
Maui
Miami,
  Fort Lauderdale,
  Palm Beach
Michigan, Wisconsin,
  Minnesota
New England
New Mexico
New Orleans

New Orleans (Pocket
  Guide)
New York City
New York City (Pocket
  Guide)
New York State
Pacific North Coast
Philadelphia
The Rockies
San Diego
San Francisco
San Francisco (Pocket
  Guide)
The South

Texas
USA
Virgin Islands
Virginia
Waikiki
Washington, DC

Foreign Guides

Acapulco
Amsterdam
Australia, New Zealand,
  The South Pacific
Austria
Bahamas
Bahamas (Pocket
  Guide)
Baja & the Pacific
  Coast Resorts
Barbados
Beijing, Guangzhou &
  Shanghai
Belgium &
  Luxembourg
Bermuda
Brazil
Britain (Great Travel
  Values)
Budget Europe
Canada
Canada (Great Travel
  Values)
Canada's Atlantic
  Provinces
Cancun, Cozumel,
  Yucatan Peninsula

Caribbean
Caribbean (Great
  Travel Values)
Central America
Eastern Europe
Egypt
Europe
Europe's Great
  Cities
France
France (Great Travel
  Values)
Germany
Germany (Great Travel
  Values)
Great Britain
Greece
The Himalayan
  Countries
Holland
Hong Kong
Hungary
India,
  including Nepal
Ireland
Israel
Italy

Italy (Great Travel
  Values)
Jamaica
Japan
Japan (Great Travel
  Values)
Kenya, Tanzania,
  the Seychelles
Korea
Lisbon
Loire Valley
London
London (Great
  Travel Values)
London (Pocket Guide)
Madrid & Barcelona
Mexico
Mexico City
Montreal &
  Quebec City
Munich
New Zealand
North Africa
Paris
Paris (Pocket Guide)
People's Republic of
  China

Portugal
Rio de Janeiro
The Riviera (Fun on)
Rome
Saint Martin &
  Sint Maarten
Scandinavia
Scandinavian Cities
Scotland
Singapore
South America
South Pacific
Southeast Asia
Soviet Union
Spain
Spain (Great Travel
  Values)
Sweden
Switzerland
Sydney
Tokyo
Toronto
Turkey
Vienna
Yugoslavia

Special-Interest Guides

Health & Fitness
  Vacations
Royalty Watching

Selected Hotels of
  Europe

Selected Resorts and
  Hotels of the U.S.
Shopping in Europe

Skiing in North America
Sunday in New York